HARPERCOLLINS COLLEGE OUTLINE

Introduction to Psychology

Ann L. Weber, Ph.D.
University of North Carolina at Asheville

HarperPerennial

A Division of HarperCollinsPublishers

This book is for my first psychology teachers: Giles E. Maurey; James Statman; Richard Wunderlich and John Kinnane.

An American BookWorks Corporation Production

Project Manager: Judith A. V. Harlan
Editor: Thomas H. Quinn

Library of Congress Cataloging-in-Publication Data

Weber, Ann L.
  Introduction to psychology / Ann L. Weber.
    p.   cm. — (HarperCollins college outline)
  Includes bibliographical references and index.
  ISBN 0-06-467103-8 (pbk.) :
  1. Psychology.   I. Title.   II. Series.
BF121.W43   1991
150—dc20   90-56019

95 ABW/RRD 10 9 8 7 6

Contents

Preface

Psychology, the science of behavior and thought, is not so much a single discipline as it is a spirit common to many different fields of study. It bonds together the other social sciences: sociology, anthropology, economics, and political science. There are psychological aspects to history, art, music, and how they are experienced. Psychology emerges from the natural sciences, and illuminates how they are understood. Psychology is a central concern of much of philosophy and theology. It crosses cultures and spans millennia. The first humans undoubtedly wondered about one another's behavior, and may well have wondered about the very process of wondering.

I first decided to pursue the profession of psychology because, when I was young and interested in so many different subjects, I resisted narrowing my focus. Within psychology, I believed, I could retain my interests in so many other endeavors—art, archaeology, mathematics—without having to be undecided. I wanted to learn so much! Psychology seemed to be one common avenue leading through all the terrain I still wished to explore.

I have never changed my belief that psychology affords this liberal reach. It is my hope that new students will find psychology to be an invitation to explore and learn, as well, to begin here and go off in other directions—yet always encounter the familiar territory, the useful ideas, and the encouraging intrigue of psychology.

As an outline text, this book was based on the work of other scholars whose introductory psychology texts deserve careful appreciation. This book was not written to stand alone, although it should serve as a useful and concise review for an experienced psychology student. It will be a helpful supplement to any recent introductory text, especially in an "active" studying program that involves writing and talking with others. Finally, this book may provide, in its succinct but friendly presentation, a readable perspective on the huge, dynamic discipline of psychology. History, world view, method, and character—all come together in every field and level of analysis. The reader is invited to make connections, recognize familiar names and concepts, and consider practical applications. The best teachers empower students to learn; the best texts equip the student to ask questions, to look for more. This review text is a step in that direction.

Many people make this book possible. I acknowledge with gratitude the contributions of my colleagues in the Department of Psychology at UNC–Asheville who consulted with me and wrote material in their areas of expertise: Allan Combs, in research, methodology, biopsychology, perception, and consciousness; Gary Nallan, in learning; and Lisa Friedenberg, in developmental psychology and psychological assessment. Additionally, Theodore L. Seitz has been the most supportive chair that a teacher and writer could wish for. And my students provided invaluable "quality control" on all the good ideas in this text.

Two of my students contributed substantially to the pedagogy of this book: Kathleen Beasley compiled the Glossary, and René Wester researched the Bibliography. They did good work, fast!

My long-time friend and mentor, John Harvey, has always encouraged me to think I can when I feared I couldn't—I'm grateful as always. My partner, John Quigley, offered inspiration when I had writer's block and held my hand when I had typist's cramp. He is even happier than I to see this project completed.

Thanks, finally, to a great team of editors and publishers: to Harper-Collins for revitalizing the College Outline series; to Fred Grayson of American BookWorks Corporation, who asked me to write the book, and—amazingly—believed I could actually do it; to Judy Harlan, my simpatico managing editor, and to Tom Quinn, a copy editor who (apparently) only speaks constructive criticism.

To all of you, thanks.

To the psychology student, welcome!

Ann L. Weber
Asheville, NC
April 1991

1

The Origins and Scope of Psychology

The term "psychology" was first coined in 16th century Germany as a combination of two Greek root words: "psyche" (soul or mind) and "logos" (study). Its original use suggested "the study of the mind," something as old as the human race itself. In recent centuries this interest in human nature has been honed into a systematic discipline. Today psychology is defined as the science of behavior and mental processes.

The scope of psychology includes many different fields, distinguished by interest in different psychological processes, different populations, and different levels of analysis. Professional psychologists may be interested in basic research or applied techniques like therapy, or they may study humans or animals. They may focus on either internal or external processes, on changes among individuals or over time, and on the influence of either human nature or specific situations.

Because psychology is a science, all fields of psychology rely on the scientific method. The scientific method is a way of acquiring knowledge. This particular method emphasizes the study of how real events are experienced through one's senses, a perspective known as empiricism. Empirical research is research based on the evidence of sensory experience. A scientist conducts empirical observations, records measurements (data) of these events, and makes guesses (hypotheses) about their causes and connections. Many hypotheses about similar sets of events are summarized in theories, which are models or broad explanations of cause-and-effect connections.

In conducting scientific research on behavior and mental processes, psychologists may study either human or nonhuman subjects. Research can be conducted in the natural settings where the events occur (referred to as the field) or in the laboratory, which is any controlled environment. In laboratory research, psychologists control who the subjects are as well as the conditions they encounter. In all research, whether human or nonhuman, field or laboratory, psychologists record their observations and formulate hypotheses in order to explain behavior and mental processes. The goal of psychology is to understand, predict, and control behavior and mental processes.

THE HISTORY OF PSYCHOLOGY

Psychology has long been a common human interest, but it has been considered a formal scientific discipline only since the late nineteenth century. Several perspectives and disciplines contributed to the shaping of psychology as a science: philosophical perspectives; experimental methods and discoveries; therapeutic applications; and theoretical developments.

Philosophical Roots of Psychology

EARLY MEDICINE

Before 500 B.C. in the Western world, medical practices were largely controlled by priests, who explained both mental and physical illnesses in terms of divine causes.

Hippocrates (460-377 B.C.) rejected mystical and superstitious explanations for bodily processes. He argued that physical well-being, illness, and healing were natural processes. In *The Art of Healing,* Hippocrates described behavior patterns recognizable to modern psychologists as behavioral disorders. *The Nature of Man* contains his theory that the natural elements—earth, air, fire and water—combine to form bodily *humors* or natural fluids like blood, black bile, yellow bile, and phlegm. Any imbalances among these four humors would result in illness or disease.

Galen (A.D. 130-200), a physician in Imperial Rome, extended Hippocrates's ideas by suggesting a better understanding of human nature and emotions. Galen emphasized the usefulness and effectiveness of the parts and processes of human anatomy. He further argued that imbalances among the bodily humors would result in extremes or disorders of temperament. Too much blood would make a person "sanguine" or cheerful, excessive yellow bile would make one "bilious" or angry, too much black bile led to "melancholia" or sadness, and too much phlegm of course made one "phlegmatic" or lethargic and sluggish.

These early ideas of influences on behavior, while obviously crude and simplistic by today's standards, have persisted in our language (e.g., a "sense of humor") and our ongoing interest in how bodily processes affect thought, emotions, and action.

MONISM VERSUS DUALISM

Psychology has also been influenced by basic arguments about the very nature of reality. Ancient notions that all which exists is of one nature are collectively referred to as monism. Later, religiously-popularized notions that there are two kinds of reality in existence are referred to as forms of dualism. Both monism and dualism have left undeniable marks on the modern science of psychology.

Dualism. Dualist ideas about human nature were first detailed by the Greek philosopher Aristotle (384-322 B.C.), who conceived of the soul as the animator of all beings, including humans. According to Aristotle, humans have rational (reasoning) souls. Humans' ability to reason makes human thought abstract, separate from the material world. Thus a human being has a material body but a rational (reasoning) mind, and is governed by two systems of nature. Aristotle's dualism explains human thought and action as unique in all existence.

Thomas Aquinas (A.D. 1227-1274) extended Aristotle's dualistic view of human nature with the argument that, because human thought is rational, human action is freely decided instead of compelled by natural forces. This is the essential argument in favor of free will. Whether human will is free or not is an important consideration in determining the morality of human action.

The most articulate proponent of the dualism of human nature was French philosopher Rene Descartes (1596-1650). Famous for the dictum *Cogito ergo sum* ("I think, therefore I am"), Descartes distinguished between the free will that governs the rational human soul and the physical "passions" (appetites) and "emotions" (excitements) that govern the material body. Further, Descartes saw the relationship between body and soul as a conflict, an ongoing struggle for control of one's actions.

Modern psychologists continue to debate the nature of human behavior, with strong arguments both for forms of "free will" and for a more mechanical understanding of psychological processes.

Monism. Some of the earliest systems of philosophy were monistic philosophies, advocating that all of reality has but a single nature. One form of monism, idealism, argues that all of reality exists only in the mind, as ideas, and thus things are "real" only to the person who is presently experiencing them. One extension of this idealism is that, for things to continue when no one is thinking about them, they (and we) must all be figments of a supreme being's imagination—ideas of God, for example.

Another form of monism is materialism, arguing that the single nature of reality is matter. If all of reality is matter, then all that exists must be governed by the laws of matter, or the laws of mechanics. This view, known as mechanism, can be applied to human nature if one accepts that human beings, like all else in reality, are purely material beings, and thus human action is governed by the physical laws of mechanics. Mechanism has had an enduring influence on the science of psychology, especially in early theories about the relationship between bodily (physical) events and mental experiences.

Determinism. One implication of mechanism is that, according to the laws of mechanics, physical forces cause specific changes in other physical objects. Causes determine effects in the physical world. If one wishes to understand the present condition of an object or event, one must examine the events (causes) which led up to (determined) it. This understanding—that present conditions can be understood if one examines past influences—is known as determinism. It is a critical assumption in any science.

Empiricism. Another essential tenet of science is the reliance on observable events as evidence of reality. Instead of imagining how things "must" be, a scientist observes how they are, or rather how they look, sound, feel, taste, or smell. This reliance on the evidence of one's sensory experiences is known as empiricism.

Empiricism is such a familiar and common-sensical part of the scientific method that it is difficult to remember that the scientific way of knowing was once a new concept. Ancient and medieval scholars often argued that one could "reason" one's way to the truth, or be informed through revelation, prophecy, or inspiration.

The English scholar Roger Bacon (1214-1292) argued that empirical observation was essential to the scientific method. Later, John Locke (1632-1704) asserted that empirical (sensory) experience was the basis for all knowledge. Locke maintained that the human mind at birth is a *tabula rasa* ("blank slate") on which experience alone can inscribe knowledge.

Locke's influence continues with modern psychologists who argue that the way an individual is educated and nurtured vastly outweighs the power of any inborn talents or inherited nature. This "nature versus nurture" controversy has influenced many fields and topics in psychological research.

POPULAR CONCEPTS OF PSYCHOLOGY

Religious, political, and economic influences kept popular the idea that human nature is built-in and even inherited. With all our similar experiences and needs, critics observed, no two human beings are exactly alike. Many popular, nonscientific systems were developed in an effort to explain and even predict human behavior on the basis of such built-in factors as physical appearance and physical size.

Physiognomy. Physiognomic explanations for human behavior argued that it was possible to "read" one's character in his or her physical features. An early system of this was popularized by Johann Kaspar Lavater (1741-1801), and its effects can still be read in nineteenth- and early twentieth-century literature where physical descriptions are supposed to indicate certain personality traits, e.g., a "noble" brow, a "weak" chin, or a "generous" mouth. Lavater's ideas were later extended by an Italian criminologist who described the shifty-eyed, sneering "criminal type."

Phrenology. Franz Joseph Gall (1758-1828) popularized phrenology (literally from the Greek for "study of the personality"), a technique for inferring character from the shape and form of the skull. Phrenologists assumed that certain personality traits and mental faculties were revealed in the bumps and dents they could feel through patients' scalps. Though ultimately discredited, phrenology enjoyed immense popularity and success, and offered a simple (though invalid) way to predict behavior on the basis of a few observations.

Experimental Roots of Psychology

EXPERIMENTAL METHODOLOGY

Philosophical ideas about human nature inevitably influenced the shape of the science of psychology. Because psychology is a science, however, much of the shape of the discipline has been determined by experimental explorations and discoveries.

The scientific method relies on empirical observation, hypothesis formulation, and hypothesis testing. An important method of empirical observation is the experiment. In an experiment, a researcher manipulates changes in environmental conditions and treatments that subjects receive. By comparing the behavior of subjects who received one treatment with those who received others, the researcher is able to specify cause-and-effect relationships among changes (variables) in conditions and consequences.

Psychophysiology. Physicians and philosophers have long speculated on the relationship between body and mind. In the nineteenth century researchers began systematic experiments on how physical events are psychologically experienced. The first experiments in the relationship between physiological processes and psychological experience (psychophysiology) focused on the functioning of the senses, especially sight, sound, and touch.

Johannes Mueller (1801-1858) established the first institute for the study of physiology in Berlin. Although favoring a mechanistic view of human nature, he also believed in vitalism, a conviction that all living beings were animated by a "life force" that was ultimately impossible to analyze.

One of Mueller's students was Hermann L. von Helmholtz (1821- 1894). Helmholtz rejected Mueller's belief in vitalism and instead refined a mechanistic explanation of behavior in terms of the physical and chemical processes of the nervous system. In Helmholtz's experimental approach to the nervous system, he charted distances between stimulation and response points along the nerve fibers of frogs, demonstrating that behaviors could be evaluated by measuring reaction time, the interval between a stimulus and a response.

Psychophysics.   Another approach to understanding the body-mind connection was taken by the psychophysicists. Psychophysics as a discipline focused on the relationship between the physical and environmental changes (stimuli) and the sensory processes that they trigger. Gustave Feodor Fechner (1801-1889) had been a confirmed mechanist who later in life softened his mechanism in a quest for a more spiritual understanding of experience. In his 1860 work *Elements of Psychophysics*, Fechner argued that since matter and mind must be related, research must focus on how physical stimuli are related to the mental experiences they produce.

Ernst Heinrich von Weber (pronounced VAY-ber) (1795-1878) was a colleague of Fechner's who in 1834 had published a study of the sensory processes involved in touch. Weber's experimentation with people's judgements about the heaviness of hand-held weights led him to develop Weber's Law, a mathematical summary of how changes in sensory qualities are perceived. In brief, according to Weber's Law, the noticeability of a change in a stimulus depends on the magnitude of that stimulus. For example, if a person has lost five pounds, will weight loss be noticeable? Yes, if the person previously weighed only 90 pounds. No, if the person previously weighed 300 pounds. One pound less than 90 is more noticeable than one pound less than 300.

LABORATORY PSYCHOLOGY

Is psychophysics part of psychology or part of physics? Until the late nineteenth century, most "psychological" research was really focused on medicine, physiology, or physics rather than on psychological processes. This changed, however, as a body of work emerged that was distinctive of psychology—behavior and mental processes—rather than the domain of other disciplines. The "birthdate" usually assigned to this demarcation of psychological research is 1879, because it was in that year that the first scientific laboratory for psychological research was established.

Structuralism. In 1879 Wilhelm Wundt (1832-1920), a German professor of philosophy, founded the first laboratory for the scientific study of psychology at the University of Leipzig. Unlike his predecessors in psychophysics, Wundt was interested in decidedly psychological processes like consciousness, thought, and emotions. The "laboratory" Wundt established consisted of a group of people interested in these same phenomena, all of whom intended to study these processes scientifically.

The "scientific" technique Wundt employed was introspection, literally a "looking within," the common practice of considering one's own actions and reactions, and self-consciously trying to analyze their sequence and components. For example, in order to understand the tactile sensation of "wetness," Wundt would ask a subject to immerse his hands in water, and describe his various sensations separately. "Wetness" might equal a combination of the tactile sensations of "coolness" plus "smoothness." Wundt hoped thus to identify the basic components of more complex conscious experiences.

Wundt's work was extended in the United States by his student Edward Bradford Titchener (1867-1927), who emphasized the study of sensations as the building blocks of the content of consciousness, without concern for the processes of goals of consciousness. Because Titchener's and Wundt's perspective emphasized analysis of the structure of consciousness, this school of thought came to be known as structuralism. Structuralist assumptions are very common. They can be seen in action when a child tries to understand a new toy by taking it apart, or when an adult enjoys a meal and inquires about the ingredients. The structuralist perspective assumes that psychological experience is better understood only when the content of that experience has been analyzed and identified.

Functionalism. A very different point of view was espoused by William James (1842-1910), whose 1890 book *Principles of Psychology* is considered the first text in psychology. James himself is usually referred to as the father or founder of American psychology. Trained as a physician, James was a professor of physiology, psychology, and philosophy at Harvard. His interests in psychology were broad and his influence on the new discipline enormous.

James favored a school of psychology termed functionalism. A functionalist perspective assumes that the products of psychological processes—behaviors, emotions, and thoughts—must serve some function, or they would be changed or lost. The way to understand psychological processes, therefore, is not to analyze their structure, but rather to identify their goals. Whereas a structuralist looks at a behavior and asks, "What are the components of that behavior?" a functionalist asks, "What purpose does that behavior serve?"

Functionalist assumptions emerge whenever researchers question the usefulness or origins of a cross-cultural behavior pattern. For example, why do people in all parts of the world smile when they are happy? Because smiling is universal, it is probably built-in rather than acquired through learning. The functionalist question is: What purpose does smiling serve? Smiling must be useful, it must increase the chances of the smilers' survival. It must have at least one important survival function.

Gestalt Psychology. *Gestalt* is a German word which translates roughly to mean "form," "shape," or "pattern" in English. (The word Gestalt is capitalized because in German all nouns are capitalized). In the early twentieth century Gestalt psychologists in Germany studied perceptual phenomena that caused them to doubt the usefulness of structuralist assumptions. Max Wertheimer (1880-1943), Kurt Koffka (1886-1941) and Wolfgang Köehler (1887-1967) found that arrangements of perceptual stimuli close together in time or space created illusions of connections between the stimuli. For example, if blinking lights were positioned closely beside each other, a subject viewing them experienced the sensation that a single glowing light seemed to be "moving" from one light fixture to the next and the next. As another example, consider the powerful illusion of "motion" pictures: when a series of still photograph frames are projected in quick succession, one sees not separate frames but continuous motion of the characters and action on the screen.

Wertheimer, Koffka and Köehler dubbed such "apparent movement" the phi phenomenon. They observed that human perception seemed particularly prone to such illusions, and speculated that it is more meaningful to connect close-together events than to keep them artificially separate.

Gestalt psychologists focused on identifying the principles of perception and the conditions under which these principles apply. They concluded that the human mind imposes an order or "meaning" of its own, rather than passively absorbing the content of sensory experiences.

More recently Gestalt psychology has influenced both approaches to psychotherapy and the modern development of cognitive psychology. With its emphasis on the importance of meaning in human perception and behavior, Gestalt psychology contributes distinctively to psychological theories of human nature.

Behaviorism. Structuralism, functionalism, and Gestalt psychology all seek to understand human experience by "looking" at mental processes. However, mental processes—like sensation, perception, and cognition—are internal and cannot be directly observed. They are all examples of the perspective known as mentalism, the study of mental events and processes. Mentalism has long been criticized as a contradiction of the empirical basis of the scientific method. Recall that science relies on empirical (sense-experienced) observations of real events. If a researcher cannot see or hear or feel another's thoughts or hidden emotions, these processes cannot be studied scientifically.

Behaviorism is the alternative to mentalism. Behaviorism is a perspective in psychology that emphasizes the need to study only what is observable. Mental events are not observable; behaviors are observable. Thus behavior alone can be the foundation for scientific psychology.

The "father of behaviorism" was John B. Watson (1878- 1958). Watson originally trained in physiology but turned to a stronger interest in comparative psychology, the study of the behavior of nonhumans. Watson observed that while the rats he studied could not introspect or offer self-reports of their behavior, they could still behave, and their behavior could be objectively observed and measured.

Watson's heir apparent as champion of behaviorism was undeniably the late B. F. Skinner (1904-1990), who became best known for his studies of animal learning and what it can teach humans about better ways to live and function.

Therapeutic Roots of Psychology

For centuries, the need for scientific psychology has been expressed as a need for help as well as a form of intellectual curiosity. While philosophers speculated on human nature and researchers examined human sensory processes, educators and physicians struggled to find new answers to problems of helping people to learn and adjust. Much of modern psychology has been influenced by these early efforts to help others.

PSYCHOANALYSIS

The Viennese physician Sigmund Freud (1856-1939) developed an early interest in neurology into a system of treatment for psychological disorders. His system of therapy was known as psychoanalysis because it emphasized the importance of analyzing the "psyche" in order to gain insight into psychological conflicts. Psychoanalysis has also come to be known as a "theory" of personality and a perspective on human nature.

Psychoanalysis, a form of mentalism like structuralism and functionalism, assumes that psychological experiences are caused by biological drives and instincts. Living in civilized society inevitably frustrates many biological drives, but most of the resultant conflict is kept hidden from one's conscious mind. Conflicts and anxiety in one's unconscious can sometimes manifest themselves in disguised forms, safely in dreams, or more dangerously in physical symptoms. Such symptoms can be crippling unless the sufferer, through psychoanalytic therapy, achieves insight into the original conflict, and the symptoms become unnecessary.

Although the principles of psychoanalysis have captured the public imagination, they defy empirical testing. Scientific theories are formed, tested, modified, and sometimes rejected on the basis of empirical (experience-based) observations. Yet psychoanalytic concepts like that of the unconscious mind cannot be tested, confirmed, or rejected through observation. Thus psychoanalysis cannot acurately be called a "theory." Nonetheless the concepts of psychoanalysis are well known world-wide, and the application of psychology in the treatment of mental and physical illness has been shaped by many psychoanalytic ideas.

HUMANISTIC PSYCHOLOGY

Psychoanalysis assumes that human behavior is naturally selfish and uncivilized, and that people must be guided and coerced into being productive and helpful.

Humanistic psychology begins with a very different assumption. Humanistic psychologists assume that people are essentially motivated to be productive and healthy, and only need guidance when circumstances have impeded their natural progress.

Abraham Maslow (1908-1970) explained that while much of human behavior is devoted to gratifying needs, there are many different levels of human needs. Human motivation can be ranked in a hierarchy of needs. In this hierarchy, needs for physiological survival are most basic, followed by needs for safety and belongingness. Beyond these are "higher" needs for esteem and, highest of all, for self-actualization. Self-actualization is a process of becoming all one can be, of realizing one's individual human potential. Although Maslow asserted that self-actualization is the least basic of the needs in the hierarchy, his placement of such a motivation as a "need" distinguishes his perspective as humanistic.

Carl Rogers (b. 1902) developed a client-centered or person-centered approach to therapy based on a humanistic theory of personality. In Rogers' system, the client who seeks therapy is the "expert" on his or her own needs, goals, and how to meet them. This contrasts sharply with psychoanalysis, in which a patient seeks the expert assistance of an analyst. Rogers emphasizes the power of providing acceptance and feedback to the client in helping the client to discover his or her own best strategy for growth and adjustment.

Theory Development in Psychology

The development of psychology in the late nineteenth and twentieth centuries has taken place in the offices of therapists, the laboratories of researchers, and the classrooms of teachers. An important part of psychology's emergence as a scientific discipline has been its growth as an academic specialty.

PSYCHOLOGY AS AN ACADEMIC DISCIPLINE

G. Stanley Hall. The first professor of psychology at an American university was G. Stanley Hall (1844-1924). While on the faculty at The Johns Hopkins University, Hall founded a psychological laboratory in 1883, and established the *American Journal of Psychology*, the first American professional journal in psychology, in 1887. In 1888 Hall moved on to become president of Clark University, where he emphasized graduate training, especially in psychology. In 1892 Hall founded the American Psychological Association, still the preeminent professional organization for psychologists.

Later in his career Hall turned to an interest in developmental and child psychology, producing the seminal works *Adolescence* in 1904 and *Senescence* in 1922.

Mary Whiton Calkins. Although the history of psychology seems disproportionately to be a chronicle of the endeavors of men, women were as present in the early development of scientific psychology as they have been in other disciplines. An important example is the work of Mary Whiton Calkins (1863-1930), who studied with Wundt in Leipzig and William James at Harvard and went on to a distinguished career on the faculty at Wellesley

College. Although she had completed all requirements for her doctorate, Harvard refused to grant a Ph.D. to a woman. Because of this experience, she likewise refused Radcliffe's later offer to award her the doctorate.

Calkins became one of the early presidents of the American Psychological Association and authored two textbooks. Her work continued a lifelong interest in the interconnections between philosophy and psychology. Despite criticism from structuralists, she also maintained a particular focus on self-psychology, insisting that one's self is observed throughout introspective experience.

MODERN THEORY DEVELOPMENT

Academic environments and the networks they comprise have always provided important avenues of communication among researchers and theorists. Researchers seldom work alone, and the very act of publishing one's findings or theories invites others' comments and contributions. Two important influences on modern psychology that have stimulated such exchange are neobehaviorism and cognitive psychology.

Neobehaviorism. Behaviorism in its most extreme form rejects the examination of any unobservable process. For example, one sequence of psychological experience can be summarized as follows:

$$S \longrightarrow O \longrightarrow R$$

In this sequence, a stimulus (**S**) excites the sensory processes of an organism (**O**), which consequently makes a response (**R**).

In strict behaviorist terms, one might observe the S and the R, but not the processes occurring within the O. A behaviorist rejects as impossible and irrelevant questions such as "Did the O feel pain?" and "Did the O make the R deliberately?" Ultimately, since only the S and the R can be safely and objectively studied, the behaviorist approach is said to favor "S-R" ("stimulus-response") psychology.

Neobehaviorists ("new behaviorists") introduced the concept of intervening variables, changes in processes within the organism which cannot be observed but can be used to explain S-R patterns.

One such neobehaviorist was Clark L. Hull (1884-1952), whose 1943 work *Principles of Behavior* listed a series of postulates or rules regarding the effects on behavior of such intervening variables as drive and habit strength.

Another neobehaviorist, Edward Chace Tolman (1886-1959), found it necessary to hypothesize that learning can take place even when it is not observable. Tolman allowed rats to explore mazes without offering them any rewards for being fast or accurate. The rats showed no signs of having learned the maze—until a later time when they were rewarded for their maze running efforts. At that time the rats learned the maze faster than rats who had not explored the maze before. Obviously the experienced rats had learned something, although their learning had remained latent (hidden) until it was useful. Tolman developed the somewhat "mentalist" concept of latent learning while he conducted traditional behaviorist research on rats' performance times.

Cognitive Psychology. After World War II, problem-solving machinery and information technology combined to produce artificial intelligence, the software and hardware we take for granted as computers. Because to some extent computers simulate many human-like cognitive processes (like thinking, remembering, and problem-solving), the study of artificial intelligence can yield some answers about the dynamics of human cognition.

Ulric Neisser (b. 1928–) has been influential in developing a model of human cognitive processes as actively involved in seeking information and meaning. Cognitive psychology—the study of the psychological processes involved in cognitive functions—combines time-honored Gestalt principles of perception with an interest in information processing, the sequence of cognitive operations whereby sensory experiences are meaningfully interpreted and acted upon.

PROFESSIONAL PSYCHOLOGY

Fields of Psychology

EXPERIMENTAL PSYCHOLOGY

"Experimental" techniques refer to a particular method of collecting information, rather than to a specific subject matter. Almost any subject matter in psychology—development, group behavior, or personality, for example—could be studied experimentally. However, over the decades the description "experimental psychology" has come to connote primarily the subject matter of basic psychological processes: learning, memory, sensation, perception, cognition, motivation, and emotion.

Physiological psychology. Physiological psychologists study the biological bases of behavior, usually concentrating on the nervous system (the brain and other nervous tissue) and the biochemical processes underlying behavior.

Comparative psychology. Comparative psychologists study physiological effects on behavior by specifically studying nonhumans, in an effort to make comparisons between nonhumans and humans.

Cognitive psychology. Cognitive psychologists study the so-called "higher" mental processes—thinking, feeling, learning, remembering, and problem-solving—as distinguished from the somewhat "lower" mental processes involved in awareness, sensation, and perception. Cognitive psychology is not only a field of study, it is a perspective on what "belongs" in psychology. Cognitive psychologists maintain that although internal psychological processes are not directly observable like behaviors, they are indirectly accessible to study, and so are a proper focus for scientific psychology. In this they are in opposition to behaviorists.

Developmental psychology. Developmental psychologists study the changes in psychological function as an organism grows and ages. Developmental psychology adopts a life span perspective, focusing on the influences on behavior and mental processes of changes that occur from conception and birth, through infancy and childhood, to adolescence, adulthood, old age and death.

Personality psychology. Personality psychologists specialize in the study of individual differences, how and why individuals differ from one another. Personality psychologists also work to develop techniques for assessing personality characteristics among different individuals.

Social psychology. Social psychology is the study of how the individual interacts with the social environment. Social psychologists examine social cognition or thinking (including attitudes and impression formation), social influence (such as persuasion and peer pressure), and social relationships (including aggression, helping, intimate relationships, and group dynamics). In contrast to personality psychologists, who look at the power of individual personality or disposition, social psychologists study the effects of situational influences on individuals in certain places, conditions, and times.

APPLIED PSYCHOLOGY

Experimental psychologists are strongly motivated by their interest or curiosity in psychological processes. In contrast, applied psychologists use psychological knowledge and techniques to solve problems, such as finding better ways to teach or learn, correct disordered behavior, or improve people's health and productivity.

Educational psychology. Educational psychologists are experts in the processes of teaching and learning, and conduct applied (practical) research to identify questions and answers in these processes.

School psychology. School psychologists provide advice and guidance within schools and school systems, concentrating on the needs of the student within the educational environment.

Counseling psychology. Counseling psychologists provide guidance and therapy to normal individuals with adjustment problems.

Clinical psychology. Clinical psychologists diagnose and treat the more severe problems of "clinical" populations, individuals who need in-patient care in institutions like hospitals or regular out-patient therapy through mental health clinics.

Industrial and organizational psychology. Industrial psychologists work within industrial or employment settings to study and improve the relationship between workers and their jobs and workplace. Organizational psychologists more specifically study the relationship between the employee and his or her employing organization, focusing on group dynamics, leadership, management, and communication. Many professional psychologists have developed expertise in both these fields, and are known as industrial-organizational or "I-O" psychologists.

Engineering psychology. After World War II, engineering psychology developed as a special application of psychology to the relationship between human workers or equipment operators—like airplane pilots—and the machines and equipment they operate. Engineering psychology is also called human factors psychology because it focuses on the human factor in the person-machine relationship, and is sometimes called ergonomics (from the Greek *ergo* for "work") because of its applications to work environments. Engineering psychologists' contributions range from training programs so that people can operate equipment more effectively to designing easy-to-read, mistake-proof control panels and signs.

Health psychology. In recent years the distinct field of health psychology has emerged as a special focus on the psychological processes involved in wellness and illness, both physical and psychogenic (originating in the mind).

Allied Professions

Other disciplines besides psychology employ professionals who work on similar problems.

PSYCHIATRY

Psychiatry is a medical specialty focusing on the diagnosis and treatment of disordered behavior. Psychiatrists do very similar work to clinical psychologists, but while psychologists have degrees (a master's [M.A. or M.S.] or doctorate [a Ph.D. or Ed.D.]) in psychology, psychiatrists have a degree in medicine (an M.D.). Psychiatrists, as licensed physicians, also have the legal power to prescribe drugs or surgery as treatments for behavior disorders.

PSYCHOTHERAPY

Psychotherapy involves a wide range of therapies or treatments for behavior disorders. Psychotherapists employ psychological techniques like talking, instead of medical techniques like drugs or surgery, to change behavior.

One particular kind of psychotherapy is psychoanalysis, a system of diagnosis and treatment based on the principles originally developed by Sigmund Freud. Some psychoanalysts are physicians like Freud himself, but non-M.D.'s can also be trained as so-called "lay psychoanalysts."

COUNSELING

Counseling refers to the broad profession of helping and guiding normal individuals with behavioral or emotional problems. Many counselors are trained and certified by schools or departments of education rather than psychology. Others obtain master's degrees in social work (M.S.W.) and practice as psychiatric social workers. Social workers' training emphasizes treatment as part of a general provision of social services to members of a community.

POPULAR PSYCHOLOGY

Most people who know "something" about psychology are not professional psychologists. "Amateur" psychologists range from people who are interested in learning about psychology to professionals in fields like sales, education, or health care who use principles of psychology in their work.

Psychology and Other Disciplines

The interests of psychology frequently overlap with related disciplines, including philosophy, medicine, and sociology. Much is gained in both research and application when the expertise and perspectives of these different disciplines work together.

PHILOSOPHY

Because psychologists study human behavior and mental processes, they study themselves. This self-interest has its roots in philosophy, the study of knowledge. Psychology differs from philosophy mainly because psychology encompasses other phenomena—including emotions and behaviors, nonhumans as well as humans—than does philosophy. Another important distinction is psychology's emphasis on the scientific method as its standard approach to knowledge.

MEDICINE

Medicine examines illness, including disturbances of mental processes and behavior as well as physical disease. In contrast, psychology encompasses normal as well as abnormal behavior and mental processes.

SOCIOLOGY

Sociology is the study of group structure and behavior. Whereas sociology's focus is the group—including social class, institutions, cultures and subcultures—psychology focuses on the behavior and dynamics of the individual.

Popular Psychology

Psychological issues and discoveries are popular topics in the news and everyday life. An interest in psychology, however, does not guarantee a good understanding of psychological ideas and methods.

PROFESSIONAL VERSUS AMATEUR PSYCHOLOGY

It is important to distinguish between the amateur psychologist and the professional psychologist. Professional psychologists adhere to strict codes of ethics (standards for morally correct practice) and professional conduct in the course of their training and membership in professional organizations. Amateur psychologists, individuals who have not had specialized training or certification, are not equipped to conduct valid research or apply research findings safely and effectively.

One goal for the introductory psychology student can be to become a more critical consumer of psychological information. A knowledge of psychology will equip a student to make sound judgments about identifying and applying psychological principles in real-life problems and decisions. Psychology is an enormously practical science. Its findings can be applied usefully in all human enterprises.

PSYCHOLOGICAL SELF-HELP

In recent years the concepts of humanistic psychology have been popularized in the human potential movement and in many self-help programs for behavior change. Popular literature offers many easy-to-read sources for practical applications of psychology. While many such sources are sound interpretations of psychological research, others are based more on author opinion and preference. A basic education in psychology can assist the interested reader in distinguishing between worthwhile and worthless popular literature and behavior-change programs.

*P*sychology *is the science of behavior and mental processes. It has philosophical roots in dualistic concepts of rational thought and free will as well as monistic concepts of determinism and empiricism. The experimental* *roots of modern psychology include the development of experimental methods, research on psychophysiology and on psychophysics.*

The first laboratory for the scientific study of psychology was founded by the structuralist Wilhelm Wundt in 1879. Wundt employed introspective techniques to understand the structure of consciousness. Functionalists like William James favored a goal-analysis of behavior, while Gestalt psychologists focused on the importance of meaning in human perception.

Behaviorist John B. Watson rejected the mentalism of the schools of structuralism, functionalism, and Gestalt psychology. Behaviorism concentrates on observable stimuli and reponses and connections between them.

The therapeutic roots of psychology include early medicine's attempts to identify the body-mind connection. Sigmund Freud's psychoanalysis explained disordered behavior as a function of biological instincts and unconscious conflicts, which could be identified and relieved through analysis. More recently the humanistic movement in psychology has argued that, contrary to psychoanalytic characterizations of humans as selfish and anxious, people are essentially motivated toward growth and productivity.

Much of psychology's modern structure as a profession has derived from its development as an academic discipline. Psychology has grown through undergraduate major programs and programs of graduate training, as well as through increasing professional organization and research publication. This academic and professional structure has also made possible important theory development and refinement, including neobehaviorism and cognitive psychology.

Professional psychologists work in a broad range of fields, both in conducting experimental research and in applying research findings to the solution of practical problems. Especially in their therapeutic work, psychologists frequently work beside allied professionals trained in medicine, education, and social work.

Although psychology's focus on individual behavior and mental processes is unique, its interests overlap broadly with the disciplines of philosophy, sociology, and medicine. Professional psychologists are formally trained and accredited, but many non-professionals retain an avid interest in psychological news and principles. Psychology is an enormously useful and practical science, with applications in daily life as well as in programs of self-help and behavior change. A good grasp of introductory psychology is essential for the critical consumer of psychological information.

Selected Readings

Colman, A. M. *Facts, Fallacies, and Frauds in Psychology*. London: Hutchinson. 1987

Fancher, R. E. *Pioneers of Psychology*. New York: W. W. Norton and Company. 1979

Gay, P. *Freud: A Life for Our Time*. New York: W. W. Norton and Company. 1988

Hilgard, E. R. *Psychology in America: A Historical Survey*. New York: Harcourt Brace Jovanovich, Publishers. 1987

Hothersall, D. *History of Psychology*. New York: Random House. (1984)

Schultz, D. P. and Schultz, S. E. *A History of Modern Psychology, 4th Edition*. New York: Harcourt Brace Jovanovich. 1987

Woods, P. J. *The Psychology Major*. Washington, D.C.: American Psychological Association. 1979

2

Research Methods and Statistics

This chapter presents an overview of the basic methods of research that characterize psychology. It also introduces key statistical concepts that are used to assess research findings. As a science, psychology depends on a variety of research methods for its accumulated knowledge. To appreciate the findings of psychology, to evaluate their strengths and weaknesses, it is necessary to understand these methods.

BASIC AND APPLIED RESEARCH

Basic research addresses fundamental questions about the nature of things, while applied research attempts to solve immediate practical problems.

Examples of basic research in psychology include investigations of the nature of learning and memory, of how the ear analyzes sound and the eye light, how deeply our opinions are influenced by those of others, what needs are met by sleep, and many more.

Examples of applied research include investigations of the most effective ways to teach particular topics such as geography, how to effectively select applicants for a particular type of job, and how to design an airplane instrument panel to be used easily and without mistakes.

Although much research that is well funded is applied, advances in fundamental knowledge and major leaps in technology usually come from basic research. In addition, most applied research relies strongly on the information already yielded by basic research.

THE EXPERIMENTAL METHOD

While psychologists utilize many research methods, the experiment is considered the most desirable. This is true because the experiment allows a greater degree of control over the research situation than any other method. Second, under ideal conditions such control lets the researcher establish clear causal relationships. No other method offers the researcher the possibility of being able to specify without question the cause of a psychological event, though some methods provide very helpful suggestions.

The basic idea of an experiment is to perform a manipulation upon some system of interest and observe the results. For example, a physicist might subject a bar of iron (a very simple "system") to a magnetic field and observe the results (the bar becomes magnetized). Unlike the bar of iron, organisms and particularly human beings are very complex systems, ones that are not passive but constantly interacting with their environments. Humans are complex, individually different, and constantly interacting with their environments. As a result, the simple method of choosing a natural environment and introducing a manipulation (or treatment) and observing the results is unsatisfactory in the behavioral sciences. The solution usually involves the use of groups of organisms (subjects or participants).

Experimental and Control Groups

A typical experiment in the behavioral sciences utilizes at least two groups of subjects, termed the experimental group (experimental condition) and one or more control groups (or control conditions). The subjects are treated exactly the same in all of the groups, except that those in the experimental group receive the treatment, or manipulation, while the others do not.

EXAMPLE: SUBJECTS AND VARIABLES

Suppose, for example, that we wanted to study the effect of sugar on the activity level of children in school. The subjects are school-age children, and the variables of interest (see Independent and Dependent Variables, below) are respectively sugar and activity level. We might start out with two groups of children, by providing those in one group (the experimental group) with candy, and those in the other group (the control group) with none. Otherwise, we would treat them exactly the same. We would then compare the activity levels in the two groups after giving candy to the experimental group alone.

We would need an objective way to measure activity levels. That is, the behavioral measurements should be ones that any researcher could use, such as the amount of time each child spends out of his or her seat without permission, speaking without being called on, or wrestling with other children.

In contrast, a subjective measure, like using one's own impressions to rate one child as "more active" than others because one "just can tell," depends too much on the insights and biases of a particular rater. This contamination of data with personal bias is unacceptable in scientific research. Considerable attention is therefore given to identifying and devising objective ways to measure the phenomena under study.

CONTROL

Ideally, the two groups in the sugar-activity experiment could be observed at the same time. This could be done by assigning the children at random to the two treatment conditions (getting candy versus not getting candy) and allowing them to interact as usual. In this typical experiment we are attempting to expose both groups equally to any unknown influences (e.g., rainy weather, noisy construction nearby), so that the only difference between them is the candy.

The process of ensuring that all other influences on the two groups are the same, with the only difference between them being the treatment, is known as control. Control is essential to guarantee that any results are due to the power of the treatment, and not merely to chance differences between the groups or their situations. The most common way experimenters maintain control is to conduct the experiment in the laboratory (a controlled environment) rather than in the field (the behavior's natural setting).

RANDOM ASSIGNMENT

It is very important that subjects be assigned at random to the experimental and control groups. This means that in choosing subjects for the two treatment conditions, the researcher assures that each subject will have an equal chance of being assigned to either condition. (This could be done by having subjects draw straws, or by drawing their names out of a hat).

With systems as complex as human beings it is virtually impossible to create "matching" groups by assigning them on the basis of equal abilities or qualities. For this reason, people are assigned at random, so that each group will contain some subjects of high ability, some of low ability, and so on. If we have reasonably large numbers of subjects in each group, individual subject differences will average out equally between the groups.

Thus, random assignment minimizes any influence of important subject differences in skill, background, or motivation prior to the experimental treatment.

Independent and Dependent Variables

Every experiment utilizes one or more dependent and independent variables. The broad term variable refers to any aspect of the experiment that can be quantified or measured.

THE INDEPENDENT VARIABLE

The independent variable is the manipulation or treatment itself. In the above example, it is the amount of candy given to the participants in the experimental group.

The dependent variable is the measurement of interest, in the above case the activity level of the participants. In psychological research, the dependent variable is usually a measure of behavior, mood, or cognitive function.

THE DEPENDENT VARIABLE

The dependent variable derives its name from the fact that it is dependent upon the independent variable. For example, it might turn out that the activity level is dependent upon the presence of candy. It is precisely this dependence of the dependent variable on the independent variable that gives the experimental method the power to identify causal relationships. The independent variable, on the other hand, is independent in the sense that the experimenter can set its value as desired.

Other Aspects of the Experiment

PLACEBOS

It probably comes as no surprise that passing out candy to children could effect their behavior, even if it contains no sugar at all. Aside from the excitement of receiving the candy, some of the children may have been told by their parents that candy makes them hyperactive. For these children, the candy may have a placebo effect due to such expectations. "Placebo" is Latin for "I will please," and represents the first line in a Medieval healing prayer. The term placebo was originally used to refer to medicines, such as pills, that actually have no active or effective substance. Such a "medicine" can render dramatic effects if the user has strong expectations for it. The disappearance of a headache, for example, after taking such a pill is referred to as the placebo effect.

The placebo effect can have serious implications for experiments involving drugs, or any other treatment for which participants already have well developed expectations. In the above experiment with candy, it would be wise to have a second (placebo) control group made up of children who receive candy with no sugar. For this to be effective, the placebo candy must be indistinguishable from the regular candy, so that the children themselves do not know which they have received. (Indeed, it is best not to mention the presence of the placebo at all). Now we have three groups: an experimental group with candy, a control group with no candy, and a second control group with placebo candy. Differences in activity levels due to sugar alone should appear in the experimental group alone, but differences due simply to receiving candy, sugar or not, will appear between the first control group and the two candy groups.

BIAS VERSUS OBJECTIVITY

Experiments in psychology can become very complex, in part because experimenters themselves are not perfectly objective observers. In experiments such as the above, ambiguities are often present, even in the best observational situations. The researcher may then be forced to make subjective judgments during the experiment.

For example, a researcher may see a child with his or her arms around another child in such a way that it is not clear whether they are wrestling (which is included in our activity count) or hugging (which is not included) or simply reaching around for drawing materials. If the experimenter knows that the child has had candy with sugar he may be inclined to add the behavior to the activity count. On the other hand, if the child did not receive real candy the experimenter may look more closely at the situation before forming a conclusion, discovering that the child actually was only reaching for a crayon.

Because it is so natural to have expectations affect our perceptions, even the best-intentioned investigator can exhibit such experimenter bias in making judgments during an experiment. The only solution is to be sure that the person who collects the data, that is, who actually observes the activity of the children, does not know to which group each child belongs.

BLINDS

For reasons of control, reducing unexpected placebo effects, and reducing experimenter bias, it is desirable to keep participants blind to the exact conditions and assignments of an experiment. Subjects who do not know which conditions they are in—control versus experimental group—are said to be blind to their assignments. A researcher may have someone other than himself or herself collect the data in order to keep measurement more objective. If the data-collector does not know which treatments are real and how subjects are assigned, he or she is said to be blind as well. A study where neither the subjects nor the observers know the subjects' group assignments is called a double-blind experiment. While difficult to set up, such devices as "blinds" are necessary to obtain unbiased results in many areas of psychology.

LIMITATIONS OF EXPERIMENTATION

While the experimental method is the most powerful research tool available to psychologists, it has limitations. Many questions cannot realistically be put into an experimental framework. Even among questions that can be addressed experimentally, there are ethical limitations on what manipulations psychologists can do. For instance, questions regarding the effects of malnutrition on the development of the human infant brain, or the impact of alcohol on the unborn human fetus, cannot be answered by imposing these afflictions in controlled experimental situations.

It has been common in both psychological and medical research to study nonhumans when human subjects would be inappropriate. However, the use of animals as subjects is strictly constrained by guidelines for their ethical treatment in experiments. Abiding by these guidelines can add to the expense and complexity of experimental research.

For reasons such as the above, psychologists often turn to other, non-experimental research methods to obtain information.

OTHER RESEARCH METHODS

A variety of research methods is available to the psychologist. They often are referred to broadly as correlational methods, meaning that they seek to find consistent relationships, or correlations, between variables of interest. They frequently make use of statistical correlation coefficients (see Descriptive Statistics, below), as well.

Correlational methods do not fall into distinctly separate categories, but the most common ones are discussed separately below.

Naturalistic Observation

The method of naturalistic observation is the opposite of the experimental method. This is because it focuses on behavior in its natural setting rather than in the controlled environment of the laboratory. Such studies can involve animal populations as well.

If the study requires that the researcher travel to the natural setting—whether a mundane environment like a shopping mall or an exotic location like a jungle—the investigation is called a field study. An example of the latter is an investigation of the behavior of gorillas in the wild.

Case Studies or Case Histories

Case studies are intensive investigations of single situations, incidences, or people. For example, a case history focuses intensively on the life of a single individual. Clinical psychologists often use this method to deepen their understanding of unique or instructive cases. All of Freud's early clinical investigations, for example, were case histories that he published along with his observations. The case study method, based on single instances, often leaves many questions unanswered but is a rich source of ideas for future research.

Surveys

In a survey, also called a poll, one or more questions are asked of a relatively large number of people. Political polls ask people, for example, about their preferences toward particular candidates or governmental policies, while consumer polls ask about shoppers' needs and preferences.

Surveys may utilize questionnaires (lists of questions) to allow respondents to answer sets of questions that can cover a range of topics, or they may use interviews to obtain detailed information in a more flexible format.

SAMPLING

It is rarely practical to question everyone of interest—for instance, all Americans of voting age. For this reason, the survey usually must select a smaller number of individuals whose answers can be taken to represent the larger group. This smaller group is termed the sample, and the larger group they represent is termed the population.

Random Sampling. The population, in fact, can be fairly small. A marketing study of an exclusively priced men's cologne, for instance, is directed only toward men with a high income, and perhaps only executives among these. The sample must be chosen carefully, therefore, to provide an unbiased representation of the target population, otherwise serious errors can occur in drawing any conclusions. This can usually be accomplished by drawing the sample at random from the population, so that each of its members is equally likely to be chosen.

Stratified Sampling. In reality, the goal of selecting at random from the entire population can be difficult to achieve, so researchers often use stratified sampling procedures. This requires that a preselected number of people be drawn from various sectors, or strata (the plural of *stratum*, "layer") of the population. To be useful, a political poll, for instance, may seek to include a number of professional people and a number of non-professional people, a number of uneducated and a number of highly educated people, a number of caucasians and a number of people of color, and so on.

GENERALIZATION

Sampling also plays an important part in the experimental method. An experimenter may want to understand the behavior of one population but have convenient access to only an unusual or specialized sample of people from which to select subjects.

For example, a social psychologist may want to study how "adult American women" react to sexism, but may have access to only "female college sophomores in the Midwest" for a campus psychology survey. This sample of Midwestern female college sophomores is more specific, and its members have more in common with each other, than the larger population, adult American women. Therefore, the results of an experiment involving this particular sample may not be useful in understanding the population.

The more representative the sample is of the larger population of interest, the better the study's results will generalize, or apply in general, to that population.

Surveys are particularly dependent upon sophisticated sampling procedures, because they seek to describe populations as they are without any tests or manipulations.

Longitudinal Studies

Longitudinal studies follow individuals for significant periods of time. Such studies are important in developmental psychology, where psychologists monitor developmental processes for substantial periods. Likewise, questions regarding the success of various types of psychotherapy, or the effectiveness of teaching methods, are often best approached through longitudinal studies.

METHODS OF ANALYSIS

The results of a psychological study can be qualitatively descriptive (e.g., verbal), as is often the case with naturalistic observations.

Where possible, however, psychologists prefer quantitative, or numerical, results. These allow a more objective analysis and lend themselves to a number of useful statistical procedures. Statistics are numbers, like sums or ratios, that represent information about samples of events or individuals.

Statistical procedures fall into two general categories: descriptive statistics and inferential statistics.

Descriptive Statistics

Descriptive statistics serve the important function of characterizing, or summarizing, large amounts of data so that they can be readily comprehended. There are two common types of descriptive statistics: measures of central tendency, and measures of dispersion.

MEASURES OF CENTRAL TENDENCY

The first type of descriptive statistic characterizes the central tendency of a set of data. The most common measures of central tendency are the mean, the median, and the mode of a distribution of data (e.g., scores on a test).

The Mean. The most frequently used statistic of this type is the mean or average, a single value that characterizes a potentially large number of cases or scores. For example, the mean (average) height of male students at a particular university might be five feet ten and one-half inches. This mean is a single value that represents the center of all the values representing the heights of each and every male student. The mean is a democratic statistic in that it is influenced by every value in the data set.

The Median. Another measure of central tendency is the median, the score that appears exactly in the middle of a rank-ordered distribution of scores. (For example, in the distribution 2, 3, 3, 4, 4, 4, 8, the median is 4).

The median is useful because it characterizes a "real" score rather than a numerical average that might not be one of the scores. It also helps to divide the distribution into an upper and lower half. For example, if the median height in the male student sample above is five feet eleven inches, then half the students are that height or higher, and half are that height or lower.

The Mode. A third measure of central tendency is the mode. The mode is simply the most frequently occurring single score. For instance, there may be more male students that are exactly five feet eleven and one-half inches than are any other single height. In that distribution the mode would be five feet eleven and one- half.

The median and the mode are relatively unaffected by the presence of a few scores that are extremely large or small, for instance the presence in the population of a small number of unusually tall or short males. The mean, on the other hand, can be markedly affected by such extreme values.

MEASURES OF DISPERSION

The second common type of descriptive statistic characterizes the spread or dispersion of a distribution of values. In other words, it characterizes the degree to which individual values differ from the mean value.

The Range. The most easily understood of these is the range, which simply gives the highest value minus the lowest value. For example, in a distribution of test scores wherein the highest score obtained was a 96 and the lowest a 54, the range = 96 - 54, or 42.

The Standard Deviation. In statistical analyses, a more common measure of dispersion is the standard deviation. The meaning and computation of the standard deviation are complex, but essentially the standard deviation is a single value calculated so that, for a normal population, about two-thirds of the population fall within one standard deviation on either side of the mean.

For instance, if the mean height of college males is five feet ten and one-half inches, and the standard deviation is one inch, then about two thirds of them have heights between five feet nine and one-half inches and five feet eleven and one-half inches (the mean of five feet ten and one-half inches, plus and minus one inch).

THE CORRELATION COEFFICIENT

One other common descriptive statistic is the correlation coefficient. This represents the degree to which two variables change together.

The correlation coefficient is usually expressed as a decimal form of a ratio (e.g., 0.45). A correlation coefficient is said to be "high" if it approaches (is near) the value of +1.00 or -1.00. A correlation coefficient is said to be weak if it approaches zero (0).

We might expect that height and weight in the above group of college males, for example, would yield a fairly positive correlation coefficient. In other words, the taller they are, the more they are likely to weigh. The two variables, height and weight, "go together," that is, they are correlated.

If two variables "go together" or seem to be correlated in a reverse fashion, they are said to have a negative correlation.

Finally, we might guess that a student's height is unrelated to his or her grade point average, so that correlating these two variables would yield a correlation coefficient near zero.

Inferential Statistics

Whereas descriptive statistics describe a sample in terms of the variables or scores of interest, inferential statistics provide measures of the comparison between groups. For example, we would use inferential statistics to measure the difference in the activity levels of the control versus experimental groups in the experiment studying the effects of sugar on school children's behavior.

SIGNIFICANCE

Inferential statistics help researchers make decisions as to whether or not their findings are reliable, or in statistical terms, significant.

Suppose, in the example described earlier, that the experimental group (which received candy with sugar in it) produced a higher mean activity level than the two control groups (which received either placebos or nothing). Before jumping to any conclusions about the relationship of sugar to activity in children, the experimenter must first ask if this difference is reliable—whether it could be repeated—or rather whether it is due to chance alone.

An inferential procedure such as the analysis of variance (commonly abbreviated ANOVA) would indicate whether or not the difference is reliable (significant), and the extent of the reliability.

For instance, it might indicate that the difference is significant "at the five-percent level," meaning that the observed difference would be expected by chance alone no more often than five times in a hundred.

The higher significance of the "one-percent level" would indicate the mere chances of the observed results are less than one in one hundred.

The lower the likelihood that the results are due to chance, the greater the likelihood that the results are due to the treatment, the independent variable, under consideration. Thus inferential statistics are a measure of the weight of the "evidence" in favor of a particular conclusion about the causal relationship between variables.

REPLICATION

Despite the assurance of statistical significance, replication is an invaluable part of the scientific process. By this is meant that the findings will not be considered established until they are shown to be repeatable (replicable).

*B*oth basic and applied psychological research rely on conclusive methods of conducting research and interpreting the data yielded by such research. Research methods may be either experimental or correlational.

Compared with correlational techniques, the experiment allows both greater control over the research situation and a clearer inference about causal relationships. Experiments basically manipulate a system to permit observation of the results. The manipulation or treatment is applied to one group of subjects, the experimental group, and withheld from a comparison group, the control group. Objective measures of the results indicate the relative effects of the treatment.

During the experiment, greater control is maintained when the treatment is the only distinction between the experimental and control groups. Other influences must be minimized, most effectively by conducting the experiment in a laboratory or controlled environment rather than in the field. In addition, subjects must be randomly assigned to the various groups, to minimize differences between subjects.

Every experiment utilizes dependent and independent variables, factors whose values change with time or conditions. The dependent variable (usually a behavior) is assumed to depend on changes in the independent variable (the treatment).

An experimenter can make a variety of decisions about experimental design. In experiments on the effects of drugs, for example, subjects could be given placebos to distinguish the effects of taking "something" from the effects of taking the experimental drug. Experimenters must develop effective ways of ensuring their objectivity and eliminating experimenter bias. One strategy is to keep subjects and/or experimenters blind to the conditions and/or subjects' specific assignments.

Despite its usefulness, experimentation has limitations, particularly in terms of ethics. Both human and nonhuman subjects must be treated humanely, and such constraints make it necessary to explore other research methods besides experimentation.

Non-experimental methods are usually correlational, in that they seek to identify relationships among variables without pinpointing causality. Naturalistic observation is set in the field rather than the laboratory. Case studies investigate only one subject at a time, and thus make no comparisons at all. The most popular correlational studies are surveys, in which many individuals are polled for their responses to questions of interest. To be effective, surveys must be administered to representative samples of the population of interest, whether the sample is random or stratified. The broader the sample, the more confidently the results can be generalized to the larger population. A final type of correlational research involves longitudinal studies, which follow individuals over long periods of time, as in developmental, educational, or therapeutic research.

Once data are collected, they can be analyzed either descriptively or inferentially. Descriptive statistics summarize large numbers of data, using both measures of central tendency, like the mean, median and mode, and measures of dispersion, like the range and standard deviation. Inferential statistics measure the results of comparisons between groups, and provide an index of the significance or reliability of research findings. An important quality of inferential research is replication, or repetition of findings in similar studies.

Selected Readings

Conrad, E. and Maul, T. *Introduction to Experimental Psychology*. New York: Wiley. 1981

Elmes, D. G., B. H. Kantowitz and H. L. Roediger. *Research Methods in Psychology, 3rd Edition*. St. Paul: West Publishing. 1989

Eysenck, H. J. Fact and Fiction in Psychology. Baltimore: Penguin Books. 1988

Haimson, B. R. and M. H. Elfenbein. *Experimental Methods in Psychology*. New York: McGraw-Hill. 1985

Kerlinger, F. N. *Foundations of Behavioral Research, 3rd Edition*. New York: Holt, Rinehart and Winston. 1986

Martin, D. W. *Doing Psychology Experiments, 2nd Edition*. Monterey, CA: Brooks/Cole. 1985

Mitchell, M. and J. Jolley. *Research Design Explained*. New York: Holt, Rinehart and Winston. 1988

Robinson, W. *Fundamentals of Experimental Psychology: Comparative Approach, 2nd edition*. Englewood Cliffs, NJ: Prentice-Hall. 1981

Stanovich, K. E. *How to Think Straight About Psychology, 2nd Edition*. Glenview, IL: Scott, Foresman and Company. 1989

3

The Physiological Basis of Behavior

The human body contains at least two major communication systems. One is the nervous system, which transmits by rapid traveling chemical-electrical signals, and processes information in exquisitely elaborate networks of nerve cells called neurons. The other is the system of endocrine glands that communicates by blood-borne chemical messengers called hormones.

THE NERVOUS SYSTEM

The nervous system is conceptually divided into two major parts, the central nervous system and the peripheral nervous system (see Figure 3-1). The central nervous system includes the brain and spinal cord enclosed in the bony protective sheaths of the skull and the spinal column. The peripheral nervous system extends throughout the body outside of the brain and spinal cord.

The nervous system is comprised of two basic types of cells. These are neurons, which are most important in the function of the nervous system, and glial cells (glia), which provide nutrition, support, and insulation to the neurons.

Neurons

The neurons are specialized cells which are the working units of the nervous system.

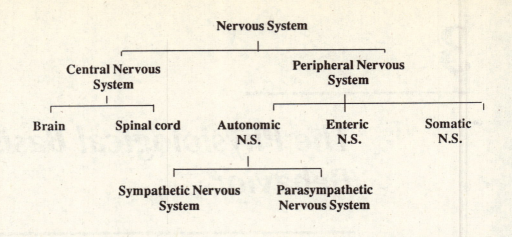

Fig. 3.1 The Organization of the Nervous System

PARTS OF THE NEURON

There are three parts or regions to each neuron, the dendrites, the cell body, and the axon (see Figure 3-2). Most neurons have many dendrites that radiate and branch, root-like, from the large central cell body. The cell body contains the cell nucleus where the genetic material for the cell is found. Also extending from the cell body is a single axon, a long thin tube or fiber-like extrusion that may be up to several centimeters or even a meter or more in length.

FUNCTIONS OF THE PARTS OF THE NEURON

The Dendrites. The dendrites carry chemical-electrical signals into the cell body, which in turn may send signals to other cells via the axon. The signals of the dendrites and cell bodies are termed graded potentials because they can range in size. They travel relatively slowly and get smaller the farther they go.

The Axon. The axon, on the other hand, carries action potentials, or impulses. They travel rapidly, have a fixed size (they are "all-or-none"), and do not get smaller with distance. When action potentials occur, the cell is said to discharge. The axons of certain neurons—e.g., those involved in some muscular function—are wrapped in specialized glial cells called myelin sheath cells.

Axons carry signals large distances through the body, allowing the brain to control the body's muscles. They also carry sensory signals from the senses to the brain for processing.

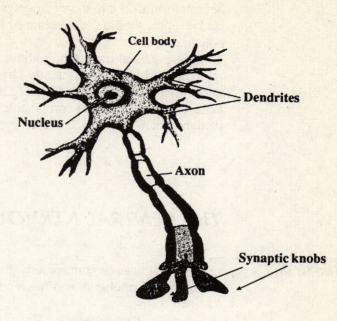

Fig. 3.2 Structures of a neuron

TYPES OF NEURONS

Nerve cells that send information outward to control the muscles are termed motor neurons (or "efferent" neurons, from the Latin for "carrying outward"). Those that bring signals in from the senses are termed sensory neurons (or "afferent" neurons, from the Latin for "carrying toward").

A third type of neuron is the class of associative neurons. These provide linkages among other neurons in the brain.

Outside the central nervous system axons typically form bundles, each surrounded by a sheath. These are termed nerves or nerve fibers. Each one contains several dozen to several thousand axons.

Neural Transmission

Neurons do not usually communicate with each other directly but across a small space (synaptic gap) between the two cells. The gap and the adjacent regions of the two cells form a synapse. Synapses are typically found at the ends of axons, where a small enlargement of the axon (the end button, or synaptic knob) is positioned very close to a dendrite or cell body of another cell.

Transmission of a signal is always from the axon of the first nerve cell to a dendrite or the cell body of another. It occurs when the arrival of an action potential in the region of the synaptic knob triggers the release of a small quantity of a transmitter chemical (transmitter substance or neurotransmitter) into the synaptic gap. The chemical is sensed by specialized receptor sites in the membrane of the adjacent cell, stimulating a graded potential in it.

This potential travels through the cell, and one or more action potentials are produced if it is sufficiently large when it arrives at the axon. Many transmitter substances have been found in the nervous system. Among the better studied to date are norepinephrine, serotonin, and acetylcholine. It is thought that as a rule each neuron produces only one transmitter substance.

THE CENTRAL NERVOUS SYSTEM

The Brain

The brain can be conceptually divided into three major components, the forebrain, the midbrain, and the hindbrain. The major brain structures are outlined below:

Forebrain

Cerebral cortex

Frontal lobe

Termporal lobe

Occipital lobe

Parietal lobe

Diencephalon

Thalamus

Hypothalamus

Limbic system

Basal Nuclei (Basal Ganglia)

Midbrain

Reticular formation

Hindbrain

Cerebellum

Pons

Medulla

Reticular formation (continuing)

THE FOREBRAIN

Most prominent in the forebrain is the cerebral cortex (see Figure 3.3). It is only a few millimeters thick but large in total area and infolded to form the wrinkled surface of the brain. Of all the brain structures, the cerebral cortex is thought to be most directly involved in higher intelligence and conscious experience.

Cerebral Hemispheres. The cerebral cortex is formed into two large cerebral hemispheres (half-spheres) that are connected by a large bundle of axons termed the corpus callosum. In most people the left hemisphere is important for language abilities and logical, analytic thinking. The right hemisphere is important for spatial thinking, and perhaps intuitive and creative thought as well as art and music.

Lobes of the Cerebral Cortex. The cerebral cortex is divided into four areas or "lobes" (see Figure 3.3). The frontal lobes, covering more than a third of the frontal-most region of the forebrain, are involved in planning future behavior and in initiating behavior. They also are involved in short-term memory and in the regulation of emotion. The back edge, or strip, of the frontal lobes is an important area for the motor control of the body.

The temporal lobes, beneath the temples, are important hearing (audition) and for memory. The left temporal lobe in most persons is vital to language ability.

The occipital lobes, at the back of the forebrain, are involved almost entirely in vision.

The parietal lobe, above the temporal lobe and in front of the occipital lobe, is important for body sense (touch).

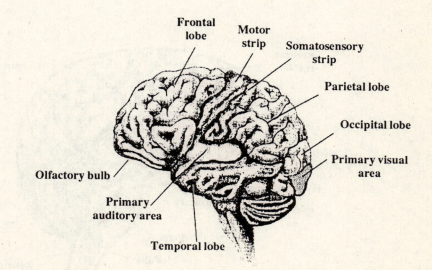

Fig. 3.3 The Cerebral Cortex

Gray Matter and White Matter. The cerebral cortex is gray in appearance (called gray matter) because it contains many cell bodies and synaptic connections. Beneath it is a thicker region formed mostly of the axons of cortical cells. This region is termed white matter because of the white appearance of the myelin sheaths around these axons. Beneath this region are found a variety of structures that form the core or the forebrain.

Thalamus and Hypothalamus. The diencephalon, deep in the core of the forebrain, is comprised of the thalamus and hypothalamus (see Figure 3-4). The thalamus is a round structure roughly an inch in diameter that is located very near the center of the brain. It is vital to many brain functions, including the processing of sensory information. Most of the senses, including seeing, hearing, and the skin senses, send axons to specific areas (nuclei) of the thalamus, where they synapse with other neurons that carry signals on to the cerebral cortex. Thus, the thalamus is sometimes referred to as a sensory relay station. The thalamus also plays a role in the motor control of the body.

The hypothalamus is a small structure near the lower surface of the brain, beneath the thalamus. It is important for drive states such as hunger, thirst, and sexual arousal. It also plays an important role in the expression of emotions. The hypothalamus is directly connected to the pituitary gland, which is embedded in bone beneath the brain. Through this connection the hypothalamus exerts a strong influence on the endocrine system.

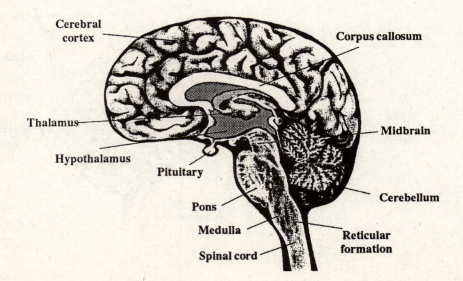

Fig. 3.4 Structure of the Brain (cross-section)

Basal Nuclei. The basal nuclei (or basal ganglia) are the major components of a system of structures near the thalamus that is important in motor control of the body, especially the regulation of slow movements. This system also plays a vital role in the initiation of rapid, whole-body movement, such as stepping-off to walk or run. Parkinson's disease is caused by the deficiency of a particular neurotransmitter, dopamine, in this area.

The Limbic System. The limbic system is a set of structures in the core of the forebrain that is involved with drive states, emotion, and memory. It includes the hippocampus, a structure important in certain kinds of environmental memory (e.g., remembering a recently-learned short cut between geographic locations).

THE MIDBRAIN

The midbrain is a small region between the forebrain above and the hindbrain below (see Figure 3-4). It includes part of the reticular formation (also known as the reticular activating system), important in the regulation of overall states of activity of the brain such as sleeping and waking. During sleep, it controls the occurrence of dream and non-dream sleep.

THE HINDBRAIN

The hindbrain, along with the midbrain, forms a stalk-like extension from the forebrain to the spinal cord.

The Pons and Medulla. The upper portion of the hindbrain is termed the pons (from the Latin for "bridge"), and its lower portion is termed the medulla ("core") (see Figure 3-4). These are the site of origin of several cranial nerves. They also control a number of involuntary functions such as respiration and the coordination of the two eyes. The reticular formation forms a cylindrical core through the mid- and hindbrain.

The Cerebellum. The cerebellum (or "little brain") is also part of the hindbrain, though located above its main axis. Connected to the pons, the cerebellum plays a vital role in the production of rapid and whole-body movement, such as walking and jumping, and in well-learned or automatic behavioral sequences.

THE SPINAL CORD

The spinal cord is actually a downward extension of the brain. In cross-section it is seen to contain a butterfly-shaped central gray region, comprised of cell bodies and many synapses. It also contains a surrounding white region of sensory axons carrying signals towards the brain and motor axons carrying signals out towards the muscles of the body.

The spinal cord also controls a variety of reflexes (responses that are automatic or "hard wired") that regulate posture when the body is stationary. Such reflexive adjustments are also continuously made when the body is in motion. The cord is the source of 31 pairs of spinal nerves that connect with it through openings between the vertebrae.

THE PERIPHERAL NERVOUS SYSTEM

The peripheral nervous system comprises all parts of the nervous system outside of the brain and spinal cord. It is divided into three functional units: the enteric nervous system, the somatic nervous system, and the autonomic nervous system.

The Enteric and Somatic Nervous Systems

The enteric nervous system is concerned with the control or the viscera, for example, in the digestion of food. The somatic nervous system consists simply of the motor (efferent) nerves that supply the muscles of the body and the sensory (afferent) nerves that carry signals to the central nervous system from the senses such as the eyes, the ears, the tongue, and the skin.

The autonomic nervous system is of special interest to psychology and is discussed separately below.

The Autonomic Nervous System

The autonomic nervous system is so named because it is "self-governing" and essential to maintaining the organism's survival. The autonomic nervous system is divided into two major "branches" termed the sympathetic nervous system and the parasympathetic nervous system. These operate in opposite but complementary ways in the regulation of many of the biological functions of the body. Since they have opposite effects on many organs, such as the heart, they are often said to be "antagonistic."

The Sympathetic Branch. The sympathetic nervous system is known as the "fight or flight" system, because when it dominates it tends to prepare the organism for high levels of activity. Its effects include increasing the blood pressure, accelerating the heart, stimulating the release of adrenaline into the bloodstream, and many others.

The Parasympathetic Branch. The parasympathetic nervous system, when dominant, tends to move the body toward relaxation and energy conservation by decreasing the blood pressure, lowering the heart rate, and so on.

In reality, the sympathetic and parasympathetic branches of the autonomic nervous system interact in an exquisitely complex and highly coordinated fashion in the regulation of actual physiological events, such as in the sexual response.

THE ENDOCRINE SYSTEM

Function of the Endocrine System

The endocrine system is a system of ductless glands that control many biological functions of the body by releasing small quantities of chemicals known as hormones directly into the blood where they influence target organs such as the heart. The endocrine glands include the pituitary gland, the thyroid gland, the adrenal glands, the pancreatic islets and intestinal mucosa, and the gonads (testes in men and ovaries in women).

Endocrine Glands

THE PITUITARY GLAND

Sometimes called the "master gland" because of its pervasive influence over the other endocrine glands, the pituitary gland is embedded in the bone of the skull under the hypothalamus (see Figure 3-4). Its close association with the hypothalamus forms a major connection between the rapid acting nervous system on the one hand, and the slower acting endocrine system on the other. The pituitary gland is also termed the hypophysis.

The pituitary gland is actually two glands. These are the posterior pituitary gland, in back, and the anterior pituitary gland, in front. The posterior pituitary gland is controlled directly from the hypothalamus by axons that pass through a small stalk from the hypothalamus, secreting specialized neurochemicals at their synapses. The anterior pituitary is controlled by very small quantities of chemicals carried through the stalk from the hypothalamus by a specialized group of blood vessels called the portal system.

Under control of the hypothalamus, the anterior and posterior pituitary glands secrete small quantities of a wide variety of hormones that stimulate the other endocrine glands into activity. The posterior pituitary, for example, produces ADH, which regulates the salt level of the blood and thus the retention of water in the body. It also produces oxytocin, important in childbirth. The anterior pituitary produces at least three hormones that regulate the sex glands. These are called gonadotrophic hormones. The anterior pituitary also produces thyrotropin, which regulates the thyroid gland, and ACTH (adrenocorticotropic hormone), which stimulates activity in the adrenal cortex (see below). A variety of other hormones are produced by the adrenal glands as well.

THE ADRENAL GLANDS

Each adrenal gland actually consists of two glands, a body of glandular tissue or medulla (the adrenal medulla), and a covering of glandular tissue surrounding the medulla, or cortex (the adrenal cortex).

The adrenal medulla produces epinephrine (adrenaline), which activates the body during states of alarm signaled by the sympathetic nervous system.

The adrenal cortex secretes corticosteroids, associated with long-term stress and muscle strength.

THE OTHER ENDOCRINE GLANDS

The thyroid gland, located in the neck in front of the windpipe and below the vocal cords, regulates the metabolic rate of the body.

The gonads—testes in men and ovaries in women—are responsible for the development and maintenance of secondary sexual characteristics as well as reproductive functions proper.

The two major communication systems in the human body are the nervous system and the endocrine system.

The nervous system is conceptually divided into the central nervous system, consisting of the brain and spinal cord, and the peripheral nervous system, extending throughout the body beyond the central nervous system.

The nervous system is comprised of neurons, nerve cells, and glial cells that nourish and support the neurons.

Each neuron consists of a cell body, dendrites which receive signals into the cell body, and an axon which carries rapid action potentials away from the neuron.

Neurons can be classified as motor (efferent), sensory (afferent), or associative. Bundles of axons are referred to as nerves or nerve fibers.

Neurons are separated from each other by a synaptic gap. Transmissions cross the synapse when the impulse from the sending neuron's axon stimulates the release of a transmitter substance into the synapse. The receptor site in the receiving neuron's dendrite senses this chemical release and experiences its own graded potential.

The central nervous system consists of the brain and spinal cord. The brain can be divided into regions known as the forebrain, midbrain and hindbrain.

The forebrain contains the cerebral cortex, divided into two cerebral hemispheres connected by the corpus callosum. Each cerebral hemisphere contains four lobes: frontal, temporal, occipital, and parietal. Each lobe is associated with different cognitive and sensory functions. Also located in the forebrain is the diencephalon with its two structures, the thalamus and hypothalamus. The hypothalamus is involved in motivation and emotion and interacts with the nearby pituitary gland. Near the thalamus are the basal nuclei which are important in the regulation of movement. The limbic system is a set of structures in the core of the forebrain that is involved with drive states. It includes the hippocampus.

The midbrain includes part of the reticular formation, a structure important in the regulation of brain activity states such as waking and sleeping.

The hindbrain extends to include the pons and medulla, the site of the origin of several cranial nerves. The posterior of the hindbrain is the cerebellum which controls whole-body movement and coordination.

The spinal cord, a downward extension of the brain, controls a variety of reflexes and is the source of spinal nerves.

The peripheral nervous system, comprised of all parts of the nervous system outside the brain and spinal cord, includes the enteric, somatic, and autonomic nervous systems.

The enteric nervous system controls visceral functions. The somatic nervous system consists of the motor and sensory nerves and their bodily counterparts.

The autonomic nervous system is important in maintaining survival, and is divided into two complementary and "antagonistic" branches. The sympathetic branch involves the "fight or flight" functions that prepare the organism for activity. The parasympathetic branch relaxes the body and conserves energy.

The endocrine system consists of the body's ductless glands which secrete hormones directly into the bloodstream. The pituitary gland is the master gland. It connects the slow action of the endocrine system to the rapid action of the nervous system. The adrenal glands—each consisting of a medulla and a cortex—produce hormones important in sympathetic nervous system function and long-term stress response. Other endocrine glands include the thyroid which regulates metabolism and the gonads (testes in men and ovaries in women) which influence sexual development and function.

Selected Readings

Carlson, N. R. *Physiology of Behavior, 3rd Edition*. Boston: Allyn and Bacon. 1986

Gazzaniga, M. *The Social Brain: Discovering the Networks of the Mind*. New York: Basic Books. 1985

Kolb, B. and I. Winshaw. *I. Q. Fundamentals of Human Neuropsychology, 2nd Edition*. New York: Freeman. 1985

Restak, R. *The Brain*. Toronto: Bantam. 1984

Thompson, R. F. *The Brain: An Introduction to Neuroscience*. New York: Freeman. 1985

4

States of Consciousness

Almost a hundred years ago William James observed that ordinary consciousness is but one of many potential types of consciousness which surround it, separated from it by the thinnest of veils. Some of these other types of consciousness, such as dream sleep, are relatively well-known, while others, such as mystical states, are not so well understood.

A state of consciousness is a stable configuration or pattern of psychological processes such as mood, memory, ability to reason, body sense, sense of self, and so on. Much of what is known by psychologists about consciousness is in fact the result of research focused on so-called altered states or alternative modes of consciousness, such as sleep, hypnosis, meditation, and the effects of psychoactive drugs. Research on these altered states allows us to infer what is "normal" in nonaltered states of consciousness.

SLEEP

Circadian Rhythms

Sleep is one of several types of daily rhythm, also known as circadian rhythm, seen in the human body (from Latin *circa*, "about," and dies, "a day"). Other rhythms involve the body temperature, which peaks for most people between about five and seven P.M. and is lowest between about four and six A.M.

Most of the endocrine glands operate according to circadian rhythms as well. When a person moves to a new activity cycle, as when going from a day shift to a night shift, or flying to a new time zone, it can take several days, even a week or two according to some studies, to completely readjust. During this time he or she is said to experience jet lag, a feeling of general fatigue accompanied by decreased efficiency, difficulty with sleeping, and even digestive disorders.

Methods of Study

Much of what is known about sleep has been learned through the study of the small continuous electrical signals recorded from the cortex. These are recorded by a device called an electroencephalogram (EEG) that depicts arousal patterns in a waveform graph. A number of distinct EEG patterns, or "rhythms," are commonly recognized (see discussion below).

Types of Sleep

Psychologists distinguish between two major categories of sleep: dream sleep and non-dream sleep. Subjects who are observed to experience rapid eye movement (REM) during sleep are most likely to report dreaming. Thus while REM and dreaming are not the same thing, REM is generally interpreted as a sign of dreaming, and non-REM (NREM) sleep is generally expected to be non-dream sleep.

NON-DREAM SLEEP

Upon first going to sleep we usually enter non-dream or NREM sleep.

There are four levels or stages of NREM sleep: Stage One, Stage Two, Stage Three, and Stage Four. Typically, we progress in order through these four stages—from Stage One through Stage Four—during the first 30 to 45 minutes of sleep. After that we move between them throughout the night, spending proportionately larger amounts of time in Stages Two and Three.

The EEG pattern that characterizes ordinary wakefulness is the beta rhythm, a low amplitude pattern of "fast" activity of twelve or more cycles per second. ("Cycles per second" is a unit of waveform energy speed, and is abbreviated cps or Hz [pronounced "hertz"], after Heinrich Hertz, the electromagnetic physicist who identified this unit of measurement).

With the onset and deepening of sleep, the EEG patterns change from fast rhythms of low amplitude (small voltage) to slow rhythms of high amplitude (relatively high voltage). (Amplitude, a waveform measure of voltage, indicates the power of the energy source, in this case the electrochemical activity of the brain in sleep).

Stage One. This most superficial stage of sleep is not actually sleep at all in the usual sense but simply the first stage of relaxing into sleep. It is characterized by a passive, restful, state of mind. The EEG is dominated by alpha rhythms in the range of eight to twelve Hz.

Stage Two. This stage carries a feeling of drifting off to sleep. There may be a pleasant sense of falling, or the presence of hypnogogic images: vivid but usually stationary images that drift before the mind's eye. These are not dreams, which are much more complex than hypnogogic images. The EEG in Stage Two sleep exhibits slower and larger theta rhythms, ranging from about four to seven Hz. The presence in the EEG record of brief bursts of high amplitude activity called sleep spindles indicate that the person is drifting into the deeper stages of sleep.

Stage Three. This is considered an intermediate level of sleep. It is during this stage that most large body movements occur during the night. The EEG pattern seen in this stage is termed delta rhythm. Delta rhythm can range from one to three Hz, but tends towards two or three Hz in Stage Three.

Stage Four. This is the deepest stage of NREM sleep. It is also the most restful stage, though we typically spend only about 20 percent of the night in it. In this stage the body is deeply relaxed and there is little movement. The EEG seen here is delta rhythm and is very large in amplitude and very slow—close to one Hz.

Periods of Stage Four sleep may be relatively long early in the sleep cycle but become shorter as the night goes on. Sleepwalking and sleep talking occur in this stage and are not associated with dreaming. Nightmares, different from ordinary bad dreams, can also occur in this stage. Nightmares or "night terrors" are characterized by unpleasant emotional arousal but are not necessarily accompanied by vivid visual or auditory images. Nightmares are not uncommon in children, who usually grow out of them.

DREAM SLEEP

About every 90 minutes during the course of the night the EEG pattern makes a rapid transition from the deeper stages (Three and Four) to a rhythm that resembles that of Stage One or Two. This new sleep pattern is associated with dreaming (dream sleep). It has also been called paradoxical sleep because according to the EEG the individual appears only lightly asleep, while in fact he or she is behaviorally harder to awaken than even from Stage Four, the deepest sleep.

Dream sleep is also termed REM (Rapid Eye Movement) sleep, because of the tendency of the eyes to move quickly under the closed eyelids—as if the dreamer's eyes were following dream activities.

During REM sleep, the large skeletal muscles of the body become completely flaccid, though movement may be seen in the extremities.

Unlike Stage Four sleep, periods of REM tend to be very short during the first hours of the night, growing in length as the night goes by. They may be as long as 30 to 45 minutes by the early hours of the morning.

THE MEANING OF DREAMS

Dreams have been interpreted in most cultures since ancient times. Modern theories of the meaning of dreams began with Sigmund Freud. In his great work *The Interpretation of Dreams* (published in 1900), he suggested that the manifest content of a dream (the dream events as experienced) conceal a hidden or latent content which expresses some form of wish fulfillment—often dealing with sex or violence—that is not acceptable to the conscious mind.

Other psychoanalytic dream theorists, such as Carl Jung (1875- 1961), believe that dreams are the symbolic language of the unconscious mind, communicating to the conscious mind.

At the opposite pole, some brain scientists suggest that dreams have no meaning at all, but represent random activity of the cortex during sleep. A variation on this view is offered by Nobel Prize-winning scientist Francis Crick, who argues that dreams are the accidental by-products of the fine-tuning and "review" that the brain undergoes while we sleep. One implication of this "fine-tuning" theory is that the meanings or stories we find in our dreams are actually interpretations we impose on the otherwise random bits and pieces of information and memory our brains are reviewing, all in a night's work.

Perhaps the most balanced view is to recognize that dreams are a basic biological event, but that their content reflects major psychological issues of the dreamer.

HYPNOSIS

Hypnosis is not well understood, though it has been known in one form or another for almost two hundred years. It appears to be a state of deep relaxation in which the subject is highly susceptible to suggestions made by the hypnotist.

*Explaining
Hypnosis*

PERSPECTIVES ON HYPNOSIS

Some researchers view hypnosis as a trance state while others have analyzed it in terms of classical or instrumental conditioning.

Social psychologists have discussed it in terms of modeling or role playing, suggesting that "hypnotized" individuals are simply acting out the behaviors expected of them. As evidence for this, they point out that most if not all of the feats performed under hypnosis can be performed just as well when the subject is not hypnotized. Some subjects may be simply pretending.

NEODISSOCIATION THEORY

Ernest Hilgard, a leading researcher of hypnosis, suggests in his neodissociation theory that consciousness itself is capable of division into distinct streams. The hypnotized individual experiences a passive state of deep relaxation, while a deeper or separate aspect of consciousness, called the hidden observer, witnesses all that transpires with the first part but is usually not accessible unless "called out" under hypnosis.

APPLICATIONS

Whatever its origins, hypnosis has long been effectively used for pain control in surgery and dental procedures, and it is found by many psychologists to be a useful adjunct to psychotherapy.

MEDITATION

Meditation is best defined as a self-induced process of relaxation providing heightened awareness and opportunities for internal reflection.

Background

Since its wide-scale introduction in the West during the 1960s, meditation has been the source of considerable research and controversy among psychologists, who have been interested in it primarily as a method of relaxation and stress management. Research suggests that, while useful in these ways, meditation is perhaps no better than other methods. The latter include techniques such as progressive relaxation (see chapter 6), exercise, and biofeedback, in which patients learn to monitor their own physical processes (such as heart rate or muscle tension) and to control them.

Forms of Meditation

Meditation has been practiced in a variety of forms in many cultures, both in the East and the West, for thousands of years. Its traditional contexts have been religious or spiritual, or having to do with personal growth.

There are many forms of meditation; some are active, such as dancing, but most are passive. The latter seem to fall into two general categories. One, termed concentrative meditation, includes forms of meditation that develop a concentrated attention focused, for example, on one's own breathing, as in Zen meditation, or on a mantra (a word or phrase selected for this purpose), as is common in Indian practices.

Another form of passive meditation, termed opening-up meditation, develops an unencumbered, objective observation of oneself. The latter is common in many Buddhist traditions.

Benefits of Meditation

Aside from controversial issues about the usefulness of meditation as a relaxation technique, research suggests the possibility that meditation, when practiced correctly and for a substantial periods of time, may lead to increased creativity and interpersonal sensitivity.

Table 4.1
Common Classes and Examples of Psychoactive Drugs

Drug	Effect	Tolerance	Physical Dependence
Stimulants caffeine amphetamines (Dexadrine*) (Benzedrine) cocaine nicotine	Stimulate activity in the nervous ststem short-term stimulant long-term depressant	Y	Y
Antidepressants Elavil	Overcome psychological depression	N	N
Sedatives barbiturates alcohol	Depress activity in the nervous system	Y	Y
Tranquilizers Miltown Equanil Valium	Reduce anxiety	N	N
Narcotics (Opiates) codeine morphine opium heroin Demerol	Produce feelings of euphoria, pain reduction	Y	Y
Psychedelics (Hallucinogens) LSD mescaline cannabis (marijuana)	Heighten sensory experience. Differ greatly with drug and setting.	N	N
Antipsychotics Thorazine Haldol	Reduction in psychotic symptoms, episodes	N	N

* *An initial capital letter indicates a trade name.*

DRUGS

Background

Drugs are chemicals that affect the body in deliberate ways. Psychoactive drugs in particular affect the nervous system, producing psychological changes in the persons who take them. Americans are the consumers of a remarkable number of both legal and illegal drugs (see Table 4.1). Perhaps the most common of these are alcohol and tobacco. Both have had very destructive consequences on individuals who use them immoderately, and to others as well (e.g., victims of the consequences of others' altered behavior).

Other highly addictive drugs have recently become widely available, with major negative social consequences. Ironically, the wide spread use of drugs other than alcohol and tobacco began in the 1950s with the development of powerful psychiatric drugs such as tranquilizers and antidepressants. Within a decade, "recreational" drug use came to be commonplace.

Characteristics of Drugs

Two important characteristics of drugs are whether they lead to increased tolerance and physiological dependence.

Increased tolerance is the tendency to need more and more of the drug to produce the same effect. Alcohol and tobacco both produce this effect, while tranquilizers and antidepressants, taken in moderate doses, do not.

Psychologists generally prefer the term "physiological dependence" to the term "addiction" in accurately describing certain effects of psychoactive drugs. Physiological dependence is the tendency to acquire a physical need for the drug so that withdrawal from it is uncomfortable, painful or even dangerous. Again, alcohol and tobacco produce this result, while tranquilizers and antidepressants, in moderate doses, do not.

Some psychologists also speak of psychological dependence, alternatively referred to as "habituation," the tendency to become psychologically dependent on a drug, even in the absence of physiological dependence. Some people, for example, might be said to be psychologically dependent on a particular soft drink. Evidence suggests that heavy marijuana users become psychologically dependent upon this drug.

Consciousness refers to a stable pattern of psychological processes. Much of what is known about consciousness is in fact a result of research focused on altered states of consciousness. The most thoroughly researched altered state of consciousness is sleep. Sleep is a type of circadian rhythm observable in human physiological function. Sleep has been categorized as either dream sleep or non-dream sleep, depending on whether or not rapid eye movements have been observed in these periods.

Most sleep research involves the use of electroencephalogram (EEG) records which indicate arousal or brain wave activity at various stages and times.

There are four stages of NREM sleep, designated Stages One, Two, Three, and Four. As sleepers progress through these stages, in order, in the course of the night, they spend more time in the intermediate stages (Two and Three) than in the fast, low- amplitude Stage One or the slow, high-amplitude Stage Four. The EEG waveforms are dubbed, in stage order, alpha, theta, and delta rhythm, with Stage Four delta being the strongest and slowest.

Dream sleep is characterized by rapid eye movements. It is considered paradoxical because it is "light" in terms of EEG measurement but very deep in terms of difficulty of rousing the sleeper.

Theories abound about whether dreams have meaning and what that meaning might be. Psychoanalytic theories favor interpretation of dreams in terms of unconscious processes like wish fulfillment or symbolic language. Modern biological theories argue that dreams are inherently meaningless, only appearing to have meaning because the dreamer imposes meaning on his or her own sleep-time mental experiences.

Hypnosis is a familiar but hard to explain altered state of consciousness. A deeply relaxed, suggestible state, it has been defined as a trance, a learned behavior pattern, and a social role. Hilgard's neodissociation theory argues that hypnosis is one of many separate, parallel streams of consciousness, all of which can be tracked by one's own "hidden observer." Hypnosis has been found to have useful applications in pain control and psychotherapy.

Meditation is a self-induced altered state thought to have benefits for the meditator in terms of relaxation, heightened awareness, and internal reflection. Meditation can be active or passive, with passive forms involving either concentration (e.g., focusing on breathing or on a mantra) or opening up (objective self-observation). Meditation may also increase one's creativity and interpersonal sensitivity.

Psychoactive drugs affect the nervous system and produce psychological changes in drug takers. Americans consume a wide variety of drugs, with tobacco and alcohol the most common. Recreational drug use can be traced to the popularization of therapeutic drugs like tranquilizers and antidepressants.

Psychoactive drugs can produce serious side effects in the form of increased tolerance, physiological dependence, and psychological dependence.

Selected Readings

Borbely, A. *Secrets of Sleep.* New York: Basic Books. 1986

Bowers, K. S. *Hypnosis for the Seriously Curious, 2nd Edition.* New York: Norton. 1983

Bratter, T. E. and G. G. Forrest, (Eds.). *Alcoholism and Substance Abuse: Strategies for Clinical Intervention.* New York: Free Press. 1985

Foulkes, D. *Dreaming: A Cognitive-Psychological Analysis.*   Hillsdale, NJ: Erlbaum. 1985

Hartman, E. *The Nightmare: The Psychology and Biology of Terrifying Dreams.* New York: Basic Books. 1984

Hobson, J. A. *The Dreaming Brain.* New York: Basic Books. 1988

Ornstein, R. E. *The Psychology of Consciousness, 3rd Edition.* New York: Viking Penguin. 1986

Zilberg, B., M. G. Edelstein, and D. C. Araoz (Eds.). *Hypnosis: Questions and Answers.* New York: Norton. 1986

5

Sensation and Perception

*M*uch *of what we know of the world we live in comes to us through our senses. These include vision, audition, the skin senses such as touch and sensitivity to heat and cold, the chemical senses of taste (gustation) and smell (olfaction), as well as internal senses dealing, for example, with nutrient and salt levels of the blood and the angles of the joints (proprioception).*

THE SENSES

Each sensory organ and system—like the eye or ear—is structured to receive a particular form of physical energy, translate it into the electrochemical energy of neural impulses, and transmit this information to the brain.

Vision

Sight depends upon information conveyed by light, a form of electromagnetic radiation related to radio waves and x-rays. Paradoxically, light can be understood as both waves, like surface waves on water, or as particles (photons). The fact that light travels in straight lines allows it to be formed into images by optical instruments that use lenses. The human eye can be understood as such an optical instrument.

VISUAL STRUCTURES

The eye itself is a spherical structure bounded by a tough covering of tissue termed the sclera layer (see Figure 5.1). Light enters the eye through the transparent cornea, an extension of the sclera layer. From there it passes through a variable- sized opening called the pupil, which is controlled by the iris. Then it passes through the optical (crystalline) lens and on through the

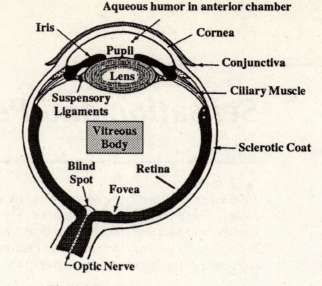

Fig. 5.1 The Eye

eye to the inner light-sensitive surface of the eye (termed the retina) where it forms an image of the object seen. The retina contains more than 120 million light sensitive cells called rods and cones, as well as many other nerve cells.

ACCOMMODATION AND ACUITY

Muscles in the eye adjust the thickness of the optical lens according to the distance of the object seen. When these eye muscles are relaxed the eye is naturally focused on objects in the distance. Accurate visual focus is termed visual acuity.

Nearby objects require the lens to become thicker (an adjustment termed accommodation). In some eyes the relaxed lens does not focus the image of a distant object onto the retina itself, but to a point somewhere in front of or behind it. In the first instance the eye is said to be myopic, or nearsighted, and in the more common latter case the eye is said to be hyperopic, or farsighted. Both can be corrected by appropriate corrective lenses.

VISUAL SENSITIVITY

The process of vision depends on the sensitivity (sensory detecting ability) of special neurons in the eye. Instead of dendrites, sensory neurons or receptors have special sensitivity to certain kinds of physical changes. Thus, visual receptors are sensitive to qualities of light, auditory receptors are sensitive to qualities of sound, and so on.

Of the light sensitive cells of the retina, the cones are primarily involved in day vision, while the rods are responsible for night vision. Cones are found in high concentrations near the center of the retina, in a region called the fovea, which corresponds to the center of the visual field. It provides high acuity vision. There are three types of cones, each sensitive to a different region of the color spectrum. One is primarily sensitive to red, one to green, and one to blue. The combined activity of these three yields color vision, which is all but absent at night.

THE EYE-BRAIN CONNECTION

The axons of other nerve cells of the retina form the optic nerve, which carries visual activity to the thalamus. There they connect with other neurons whose axons carry signals on to the visual cortex of the occipital lobe.

Audition

Audition is the experimental psychologist's term for hearing. Audition depends on sound, mechanical compression waves transmitted through the air at a speed of about 1100 feet (30 meters) per second.

PITCH AND LOUDNESS

The frequency (number of oscillations per second, expressed in hertz or Hz) of a sound determines its pitch; low frequencies produce low pitched tones, and high frequencies produce high pitched tones. The healthy young human ear hears an enormous range from about twenty to 20,000 Hz. Most types of hearing loss involve insensitivity to higher frequencies like violins rather than lower frequencies like drumbeats or bass.

Loudness is determined by the size of the waves, and is measured in decibels (dB). The decibel range increases exponentially. This means that as sound increases by ten dB over the previous level, the new sound is actually ten times louder than the first. For example, the sound of a single train roaring through a subway tunnel is about 90 dB; the sound of ten trains running by simultaneously is 100 dB; and the sound of one-hundred trains is 110 dB.

Normal conversational sounds range from about 40 to 60 dB, while prolonged exposure to sound levels of greater than about 100 dB can damage the ears.

THE OUTER EAR

The structures of the ear, depicted in Figure 5.2, can be seen to channel sound energy progressively from the outside world closer and closer to the human nervous system that detects it. The tasks of these auditory structures can be understood by examining the structure and function of three stages in this progression: the outer ear, the middle ear, and the inner ear.

Sound is slightly concentrated by the funnel-like, external auricle or pinna, and travels down the auditory canal to the eardrum (tympanic membrane).

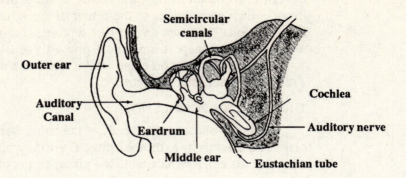

Fig. 5.2 The Ear

THE MIDDLE EAR

The fluctuations in air pressure that accompany sound waves cause the eardrum to move back and forth like a drumhead. Connected to the inner surface of the eardrum are three of the smallest bones of the human body, known by both their common names and the Latin equivalents: the hammer (*malleus*), anvil (*incus*), and stirrup (*stapes*). Together they form a set of levers that convey the vibrating motion of the eardrum to the inner ear.

The three middle ear bones are located in a small air-filled cavity behind the eardrum. This cavity, along with the three bones and the eardrum itself, is termed the middle ear. It is connected to the throat by a small air-filled canal, the Eustachian tube, allowing air pressure to equalize between the inner ear cavity and the outside air. The tube can become blocked during respiratory infections, causing pressure and discomfort.

The middle ear bones amplify the force of the air vibrations by about 3dB, thus providing some of the force necessary to convey air vibrations into the fluid of the inner ear. The rest of the necessary force, about 23dB (for a total of 26dB), is gained from the difference in size between the eardrum and the small membrane (oval window) upon which the stirrup acts to transfer the sound vibrations into the inner ear.

THE INNER EAR

The inner ear is contained in a fluid-filled, cartilage spiral termed the cochlea. It is imbedded in the bone of the skull.

The vibratory action of the middle ear bones is converted, in the inner ear, into traveling waves that flow the length of the cochlea. They set in motion two membranes, the tectorial and the basilar membrane, that extend the length of the cochlea, one stretching above the other. Resting on the basilar membrane are specialized receptor cells for hearing. Termed hair cells, these neurons have small cilia (hairs) which extend into the tectorial membrane above them. When traveling waves set the two membranes into motion, a "shearing stress" is created between the membranes, bending the hairs of these cells. This is the stimulus that activates the hair cells to produce neural activity in the auditory nerve, leading to the experience of hearing.

Viewing the basilar membrane from above, it is seen to be widest at the top (apex) of the cochlear spiral, and narrowest at the bottom (base). The physics of this membrane is such that high frequency sounds produce the greatest motion near its base and low frequency sounds produce the greatest motion near its apex, with intermediate frequencies falling between. This place principle allows the brain to analyze tones by a process (called frequency analysis) of detecting the location, or place, of maximum activity of the basilar membrane, the point at which the hair cells are most active.

Activity in the auditory nerve is carried through several synapses to the thalamus, where it is transmitted to nerve cells that carry it to the auditory cortex of the temporal lobe.

Other Senses

BALANCE

The vestibular organs, anatomically associated with the cochlea of the inner ear, provides the sense of balance, acceleration, and orientation as the head moves. Its connection with the ear explains why infections of the middle and inner ear can result in difficulties with balance.

SKIN SENSES AND PROPRIOCEPTION

Small specialized organs and "free" nerve endings (dendrites) located in the tissues beneath the skin are the source of the skin senses, which include sensitivity to touch, texture, deep pressure, heat, and cold, as well as pain. Deeper, specialized organs associated with the joints provide a sense of body position, or proprioception.

GUSTATION

Specialized organs termed taste buds are found in the mouth, especially on the tongue, providing the chemical sense of taste (gustation). Each taste bud is comprised of a packet or bud of many taste cells from which small extensions (microvilli) extend into the saliva of the mouth, responding to chemicals dissolved there. There seem to be four basic tastes—sour, salty, sweet, and bitter—distributed differently across the surface of the tongue. Other tastes derive from combinations of these along with a considerable influence from the sense of smell.

OLFACTION

The sense of smell is termed olfaction. Odors are sensed by specialized olfactory cells located in the roof of the nasal cavity (the olfactory epithelium). Like taste cells, they have small specialized extensions (cilia) that respond to chemicals dissolved in the mucus on the surface of the epithelium.

SENSORY THINKING

Sensory messages are relayed within the brain through the limbic system of the brain. Part of the limbic system's function is interpretation of messages about, for example, the current nutrient level of the blood and its salt level. Based on such sensory messages, therefore, we experience hunger and thirst, as well as more subtle states of drive and motivation. (See chapter 10 for a fuller discussion of how sensory information is involved in drive states).

PERCEPTION

Sensation versus Perception

Perception is usually taken to mean the final, organized, and meaningful experience of sensory information. The difference between sensation and perception is one of degree of understanding. Sensation (from a Latin word meaning "to feel") involves the neural stimulation of sensory systems by physical changes. Perception (from the Latin per or "thorough" and capio or "grasp") involves recognizing the meaning of what has been sensed. When one senses a stimulus, one is aware of it. But when one perceives that stimulus, one understands what it is.

Investigating Perception

INTROSPECTION

In the early years of psychology, perception was studied by analytic introspection. That is, investigators conducted a self- reflective analysis of raw experience into elements such as color, brightness, pitch, loudness, and so on. This can be recognized as a hallmark of the techniques employed by Wilhelm Wundt, the structuralist who established the first laboratory for psychological research in the late 19th century. Structuralists took for granted the validity of the senses and the accuracy with which they represented physical change in the environment. However, the structuralists were not the first to examine the relationship between stimuli and conscious experience.

PSYCHOPHYSICS

Perhaps the oldest area of experimentation in psychology examines the relationship between physical stimuli, such as light and sound, and conscious experience. This area is termed psychophysics (see Ch. 1 for a review of the historical influence of psychophysics on early psychology).

Threshold Theory. Classical psychophysical studies have examined absolute thresholds (the minimum energy needed to see or hear a stimulus) for light and sound as well as for other senses. Such studies have also examined difference thresholds (the minimal stimulus change that can be recognized). The difference threshold is also referred to as the just noticeable difference (jnd).

Research on thresholds has traditionally focused on identifying the minimal stimuli that a given sensory system (vision, audition, touch, smell or taste) can detect. Many of these threshold findings have been published in tables of norms (comparison standards) listing the minimal stimulus strengths that most people can detect.

Weber's Law. The earliest formulation of a psychophysical relationship is considered to be Weber's Ratio or Weber's Law, after E. H. von Weber, its formulator. According to Weber's Law, the noticeability of a change in stimulus strength depends on the level of magnitude (power) of the stimulus before the change. Expressed as a ratio, Weber's function says that

$$\Delta I/I = k$$

or the change in stimulus intensity (ΔI) divided by the background intensity (I) is equal to a constant value.

Loosely translated, this means that, for a given sensory system (vision, touch, etc.), a noticeable change in the intensity of a stimulus must be proportional to (depends on) the already-present stimulus intensity.

For example, the noticeability of an increase in the light in a room depends on how much light is available before the increase. If the room is dark, even a very faint increase in light will be noticeable; if the room is already well-lit, however, an increase in light—even a bright increase—may not be noticeable against the bright background. Another example of Weber's Law is the noticeability of a dieter's weight loss. The noticeability of, say, a five-pound weight loss depends on how much the individual weighed before the loss. A five-pound loss will be much more noticeable on a 100-pound person than on a 200-pound person.

Weber's Law provides a practical insight into human perception because it characterizes the relationship between psychological experience (e.g., vision) and physical stimulus (e.g., brightness of light) as one of proportion. In other words, we do not see exactly what is actually changing in light energy. Instead, we see a meaningful proportion or percentage of the change, always automatically comparing it to the background. This is an early identification of the enormous adaptability and flexibility of human perception.

Signal Detection Theory. The threshold theories formulated by early psychophysicists relied on the assumption that sensory systems like eyes and ears will be "activated" by any stimulus strong enough to enter the system. But a self- reflection exercise suggests that sensation and perception are not so simple: If someone in the same room with you whispers to you, will you hear it? Modern psychophysicists point out that the answer to this is, "It depends." Whether you hear the person's whisper can depend on several factors: how noisy the room already is; whether you are preoccupied with other matters; whether the person whispers your name—a salient stimulus— or some less meaningful word. In essence, modern theorists argue, perception depends not so much on the strength of the stimulus as on your ability to detect the stimulus amidst all the noise in the environment and in your own system, and your decision that what you heard was real—a signal—instead of your imagination.

This characterization of perception as a process of decision making is the essence of signal detection theory, the favored approach of modern psychophysicists. Signal detection theory, sometimes referred to as theory of signal detection and abbreviated TSD, was originally developed to explain the pattern of responses radar operators made when vigilantly monitoring wartime radar screens. When a blip (flash of light) appeared on the sweep screen, was it an enemy aircraft—or a cloud formation? If the operator saw no blip, was that because nothing was really "out there"—or because the operator was not paying close enough attention?

Signal detection theory focuses on the subject's ability to detect a signal in a background of noise. The signal includes "real" stimuli and stimulus changes. Noise refers to any non-signal event, whether internal (preoccupation, fatigue) or external (cloud formations, a flock of birds). Signal detection theory emphasizes the judgment criteria of the subject in the experimental setting—whether, for example, he or she is liberal or conservative in approaching the detection task.

The signal detection approach makes the following assumptions: (1) the judgement criteria of the subject must be taken into account; (2) there is actually no such thing as an exact absolute threshold; (3) signals always occur against a noise background; and (4) the determining variable is not the signal's intensity but the ratio of the signal to the noise.

The higher the signal to noise (signal:noise) ratio, the stronger the signal "stands out" against the noise background, and the easier the detection process will be. The lower the signal:noise ratio, conversely, the harder it is to detect the signal, even if one is there.

Instead of threshold values for various sensory systems, the signal detection approach measures d' (d-prime), an index of the ability of the subject to detect the signal.

Gestalt Principles

Early in this century the Gestalt school of psychology emphasized the holistic (patterning) nature of perception (see chapter 1 for a review of Gestalt influences in the history of psychology). Gestalt psychologists emphasized that perception is not a passive translation of sensation into ideas but rather an active process of seeking meaning. Meaning could be inferred in perceived stimuli by means of several Gestalt principles of perception: figure-ground relationships; closure; and grouping principles.

FIGURE-GROUND RELATIONSHIPS

The Gestalt psychologists stressed the dynamic aspect of perception, noting that a seen object always appears as a vital figure against a broader or open background (ground). Thus, they stressed the figure-ground relationship in perception.

CLOSURE

They also stressed the concept of closure, meaning that we tend to perceive complete figures, though in fact part of the figure may be hidden from view. For instance, we do not need to see the entire arc of a circle to perceive it as complete. Another example of closure is the Zeigarnik effect, named after an early researcher, Bluma Zeigarnik, who discovered that experimental subjects had better memory for interrupted tasks than for those they had been allowed to complete. Unfinished business prevents us from achieving closure. This violation of Gestalt principles may make an experience more distressing and thus more memorable.

GROUPING PRINCIPLES

Gestalt psychology provided a number of principles by which the eye "groups" things seen (grouping principles). These include proximity (objects that are positioned close to each other are seen together as groups or clusters), similarity (like-shaped objects tend to form groups), and common fate (objects in common motion like a flock of birds are seen as a unit)

APPARENT MOTION

Gestalt psychologists, as observed in chapter 1, also studied the nature of apparent motion, as seen when each of a row of lights flashes in sequence, a feature of some neon signs. This induced motion was termed the phi phenomenon. It is important in explaining illusions, such as perceiving "motion" pictures to be in "motion," when each frame is in fact a still photo.

Depth Perception

A well studied instance of perception involves the ability to recognize the distance or depth in the visual field of a seen object. Depth perception is evident very early in human development, as illustrated by research using the visual cliff. In these studies, infants are urged to crawl across a sturdy transparent bridge over a several-foot drop in a floor. The infants have little experience with substances like glass, but have also seldom fallen. Nonetheless, eager as they are to crawl across the glass bridge, the babies become distressed when they see the depth of the visual cliff, and are reluctant to take the risk of crossing it. Research like this has been used to support the contention that depth perception is to some extent innate, or inborn, rather than learned.

MONOCULAR VERSUS BINOCULAR CUES

In depth perception the visual system utilizes a variety of cues. Some are available to each eye (one-eyed or monocular cues), and some require both eyes (two-eyed or binocular cues). These are listed in Table 5.1.

The most important single depth perception cue is binocular disparity. You can demonstrate binocular disparity—the difference in images provided to each eye—by looking at a near object first with one, then the other eye, blinking each eye alternately. The image of the object will seem to hop from side to side because of the binocular disparity in the two images sent to your brain. At the level of the visual cortex, the part of the brain in the occipital lobe that interprets visual information, these two images are combined and the difference between them used as a sign of the object's nearness or distance from you. Because of the importance of binocular disparity, depth perception through a single eye is limited at best.

In Table 5.1, the cues of accommodation and convergence are considered to be physiological cues, while the others are visual cues. This is because accommodation (changes in lens shape) and convergence (meeting of the eyes to focus on a near object) are noticed in senses—such as the feeling of muscle tension when your eyes are almost crossed—other than vision.

The Constancies

The complex combination of cues available to the eye allows us to see an object as comprised of constant perceptual characteristics despite changes in the retinal image itself.

SIZE CONSTANCY

Size constancy refers to the fact that objects do not appear to change in size when they come nearer the eye (producing a larger retinal image) or farther from it (producing a smaller image).

Table 5.1 Depth Perception Cues	
Monocular Cues	
Interposition	Near objects partially overlap farther ones.
Relative Size	Near objects produce larger retinal images.
Linear perspective	Straight lines, such as railroad tracks, tend to converge to a point in the distance.
Texture gradient	The texture of the visual field is smoother in the distance.
Aerial perspective	Objects in the distance appear as through a bluish haze.
Motion parallax	When the viewer is moving, objects in the foreground appear to move by rapidly.
Shadows	Shadows can convey a sense of depth
Binocular Cues	
Accomodation	The adjustment of the optical lens reflects the distance of the seen object.
Retinal disparity	The images of an object on the two retina are slightly different in the two eyes because of the distance of the eyes from each other. From this the brain triangulates distance.

SHAPE CONSTANCY

Shape constancy refers to the fact that the apparent shape of an object does not change as it rotates or moves in space, though in fact it produces altered retinal images.

COLOR AND BRIGHTNESS CONSTANCY

Color constancy and brightness (or lightness) constancy refer to the steady appearance of an object's color and brightness despite changes in lighting conditions.

Illusions

Illusions, such as optical illusions, are erroneous perceptions. They are the result of complex interactions of visual cues and are not in all cases well understood. Often they seem to occur when there are few cues upon which to base a perceptual judgment, and one or more are supplying misinformation.

For example, looking with one eye through a small hole at a balloon in a box eliminates most of the cues for depth perception. In this situation, if the balloon is slowly inflated it gives the impression of actually remaining the same size but "moving toward" the viewer. This is because the size of the retinal image is ordinarily an important cue for distance. We judge relatively large things to be closer to us than relatively smaller objects. Young children who have learned this will sketch trees and people as tiny objects to indicate they are "far away" in the drawing they are producing.

Illusions may be learned and influenced by one's cultural context. Many popular textbook illusions, for example, feature straight-lined figures like arrows and lines. Research suggests that in primitive non-Western cultures, where buildings and natural surroundings offer few examples of straight lines, natives have developed no sets, or perceptual expectations, about straight-lined figures, and thus are not "fooled" by such illusions.

The Cognitive Approach

Cognitive psychologists have emphasized the information processing aspects especially of higher order processes in perception. For instance, the recognition of something seen can be a bottom-up or a top-down process.

BOTTOM-UP MODELS

In the bottom-up model, information travels up from the senses to the brain, where it is passively interpreted. In this instance, the perceptual system must run through all possibilities to locate the correct choice. This is like reviewing all of the faces that are stored in one's memory to locate a correct match with the one seen.

TOP-DOWN MODELS

In a top-down model, the brain "sends" down important information—like preliminary guesses about what is seen—to the sensory system as it collects information. A top-down approach identifies the important features of the object seen and narrows the search to these. For instance, one might limit the search to young men with red beards.

INTERACTIVE MODELS

Interactive models of perception argue that perception will use bottom-up and top-down processes for a variety of senses and stimuli. The interactive approach recognizes that, while sensory systems have limitations and can make mistakes, overall human information processing is meaning-oriented, as well as enormously flexible. The cognitive approach to perception assumes that perception is influenced by learning and experience. Thus certain stimuli—names, faces, melodies, fragrances—become noticeable and even expected as our experiences bring us new sensations and new meanings.

Much of our knowledge begins as sensation. Information about physical changes is received by sensory neurons, transmitted to the brain, and interpreted or perceived. Each sensory system is structured to receive a particular form of physical energy and convert it into neural impulses to the brain.

The visual system processes light information, which is focused by the cornea and lens, received by light sensitive neurons in the retina called rods and cones, and transmitted to the brain via the optic nerve.

The process of audition or hearing involves translating sound—a form of mechanical energy—into neural energy. The qualities of sound amplitude and frequency are translated into the experiences of loudness and pitch. Both qualities are funneled via vibrations through the outer ear, along the structures of the middle ear, and to the vibration-sensitive hair cells in the inner ear. These specialized neurons transmit impulses along the auditory nerve to the brain.

Other senses studied included the vestibular sense or sense of balance; the skin senses, including touch and proprioception; gustation or taste; and olfaction or smell.

Whereas sensation involves mere awareness that a sensory system has been activated, perception requires interpretation or recognition of sensory information. Early structuralists focused on sensory consciousness by means of introspection. Psychophysicists studied the relationships between physical stimili and psychological perceptions. Early psychophysics emphasized a threshold approach to understanding the detection of stimuli and stimulus changes. More recent psychophysical work favors signal detection theory, which characterizes perception as a decision-making process in which signals must be detected against a background of noise.

Gestalt principles of perception emphasize the importance of meaning in human perception. Gestalt psychologists have identified such principles as figure-ground relationships, closure, and grouping principles.

A well-studied phenomenon is depth perception, including both monocular and binocular cues. Research examines the contributions to depth perception made by innate abilities and cultural experiences.

The brain is able to identify constancies across perceptual impressions although images are constantly changing and varied. Illusions, or erroneous perceptions, involve interactions between visual cues, as well as some experience effects.

The cognitive approach characterizes human perception as information processing, involving the bottom-up sequence of interpreting sensations as well as the top-down process of narrowing the perceptual search according to expectations and meaningful experiences. An interactive model, combining features of both these processes, preserves an understanding of human perception as dynamic, flexible, and meaning-seeking.

Selected Readings

Coren, S. and L. M. Ward. *Sensation and Perception, 3rd Edition.* San Diego: Harcourt Brace Jovanovich. 1989

Engen, T. *The Perception of Odors.* New York: Academic Press. 1982

Goldstein, E. B. *Sensation and Perception.* Belmont, CA: Wadsworth. 1984

Hershenson, M. (Ed.). *The Moon Illusion: An Anomaly of Visual Perception*. Hillsdale, NJ: Erlbaum. 1989

Matlin, M. W. *Perception*. Boston: Allyn and Bacon. 1983

Rock, I. *The Logic of Perception*. Cambridge, MA: MIT Press. 1983

Sekuler, R. and R. Blake. *Perception, 2nd Edition*. New York: Alfred A. Knopf. 1990

Uttal, W. *Taxonomy of Visual Processes*. Hillsdale, NJ: Erlbaum. 1981

Warren, R. M. *Auditory Perception: A New Synthesis*. New York: Pergamon. 1982

6

Learning and Behavior

*P*sychologists have been interested in learning since the founding of the school of psychology called behaviorism by John B. Watson (1878-1958). The behaviorists thought that the proper subject matter for psychology was overt (observable) behavior. They emphasized the objective, scientific study of the effect of experience on behavior.

LEARNING

Definition of Learning

Learning is defined as a change in behavior due to experience , when the behavior change cannot be explained by instinct , maturation , or temporary states of the organism. The key word in the definition of learning is experience. Instinct is excluded from the definition of learning. Instinctual behaviors are those that occur because of the inherited nature of an organism. Maturation is excluded from the definition of learning. Maturational changes are those that develop from growth due to developmental processes. Temporary states are excluded from the definition of learning. Illness and drug-induced changes are examples of temporary states.

Learning Theory

The history of learning theory spans most of the twentieth century. The early learning theorists worked in the behaviorist tradition. Hence, their learning research emphasized the scientific analysis of behavior change as a result of experience. Much of the work was done in laboratories with non-human animals. In more recent times, learning theorists have applied their findings to human behavior, and especially to the therapeutic treatment of people with psychological disorders.

The two basic (fundamental) examples of behavior change as a result of experience are classical conditioning and operant conditioning. A third type of learning that explains human behavior is observational learning, also known as modeling.

CLASSICAL CONDITIONING

Pavlov's Discovery of Classical Conditioning

Ivan P. Pavlov (1849-1936) is generally credited with the discovery of classical conditioning (also called Pavlovian conditioning). This great Russian scientist was awarded the Nobel prize in 1904 for his work on the physiology of digestion. In his laboratory he used dogs as subjects. Pavlov developed a research program to investigate the parameters of the salivary reflex in dogs. He planned a number of experiments to try to understand the stimulus-response relationship between food and salivation.

Work with new dogs went as expected at first. The animal was confined in a harness. Food was presented, and the salivation response was measured. However, with experience, dogs salivated at the sight of the harness apparatus. Sometimes in their home cage they salivated at the sight of a laboratory assistant. Pavlov realized that these salivary responses had been learned. He proceeded to study this type of learning, and in 1927 reported his findings in a lengthy book entitled *Conditioned Reflexes*.

Salivary Conditioning in Dogs

SEQUENCE OF CONDITIONING

Pavlov presented the dogs with a series of learning trials. On each trial a neutral stimulus—for example, a tone—was paired with a biologically important stimulus, food. Pavlov accomplished the pairing in a number of ways. An especially effective way was to have a lengthy waiting period between trials. The waiting period was called the intertrial interval (ITI). An effective ITI was two to three minutes. The learning trial consisted of pairing the tone with food. The tone presentation was rather short—for example, 10 seconds. The food was presented at the end of the 10-second tone presentation. The tone was called the conditioned stimulus (CS) , and the food was called the unconditioned stimulus (US).

On early trials the dog salivated when the food was presented. This salivation response to the food was called the unconditioned response (UR). Later, the dog salivated when the tone was presented. This salivation response to the tone was called the conditioned response (CR).

DEFINITION OF TERMS

Pavlov chose the terms US, UR, CS, and CR carefully. The US and UR share the word unconditioned. This was a reminder that the animal does not need to be conditioned to respond to the stimulus in this way. That is, dogs naturally salivate to food. The CS and CR share the word conditioned. This is a reminder that dogs do have to be conditioned to respond to the stimulus in this way. Dogs do not naturally salivate to a tone.

Classical Conditioning Phenomena

ACQUISITION

The acquisition phase of classical conditioning consists of the development of the CR as trials proceed. On each trial the CS is paired with the US. For early trials the animal does not make CRs. Then the first CRs appear, but they are small. As the trials proceed, the CRs rapidly become stronger. Finally, the CRs reach their maximum strength, called the asymptote.

EXTINCTION

In the extinction phase of classical conditioning, the CS is presented on each trial as during acquisition, but the US is not presented. As the extinction trials proceed, the CRs weaken and eventually disappear.

REACQUISITION

In reacquisition the CS is again paired with the US. The CRs quickly return to asymptote. Thus, this phase is sometimes called rapid reacquisition.

GENERALIZATION

Once a CR is learned to a CS, the subject will generalize the CR to similar CSs. In Pavlov's work he found that if a particular tone was used as CS, the dog would make CRs to similar tones. Generalization is considered to be a fundamental behavioral process. That is, organisms have a tendency to generalize responses from situation to situation.

DISCRIMINATION

Although generalization is a fundamental process, organisms can learn to make a discrimination. Pavlov performed research with tones that differed in frequency. If one tone served as the CS paired with a US, whereas the other tone was presented without the US, the dog learned to make CRs only to the tone paired with the US. This is an example of the formation of a discrimination. (During the acquisition process, once CRs appeared they were made to both CSs, demonstrating generalization. The discrimination only appeared later in training).

SPONTANEOUS RECOVERY

Research demonstrating spontaneous recovery begins with pairing a CS with a US many times (acquisition). Next, the CS is presented without the US many times (extinction). The subject is then given a waiting period, perhaps as short as one day. When presented the CS (without the US) the subject will make a CR for a number of trials. This defines spontaneous recovery of the CR.

How to Analyze and Understand Classical Conditioning

Each new example of classical conditioning can be analyzed in three steps. This three step analysis is illustrated below with salivary conditioning in dogs.

BEFORE CONDITIONING

First, find a stimulus which reliably leads to a response before conditioning. Before salivary conditioning with a dog, food (a stimulus) leads to salivation (a response). When the stimulus and response have been found, they may be labeled the US (food) and UR (salivation).

DURING CONDITIONING TRIALS

Second, find a neutral stimulus that is paired with the US. During salivary conditioning with a dog, a tone (a neutral stimulus) may be paired with food (the US). When these two stimuli have been found, they may be labeled the CS (tone) and US (food).

WHEN CONDITIONING HAS OCCURRED

Third, find a response that is made to the CS. Once salivary conditioning has occurred, the dog makes a salivation response to the tone. Label this new response as the CR.

Other Examples of Classical Conditioning

HUMAN EYE-BLINK CONDITIONING

In this procedure the subject is fitted with a helmet that can measure the eye-blink reflex. During the conditioning trials a neutral stimulus, for example a dim yellow light presented on a panel, is paired with the presentation of a puff of air to the eye. Before conditioning, the puff of air (US) causes an eye-blink response (UR). During the conditioning trials, the dim yellow light (CS) is paired with the puff of air (US). Once conditioning has occurred, the dim yellow light (CS) leads to an eye-blink response (CR).

TASTE AVERSION CONDITIONING

In taste aversion conditioning a novel taste (e.g., saccharin) is paired with stomach illness. With rats, the illness is typically caused by injection of a small dose of poison. Before conditioning, the injection (US) leads to illness (UR). During conditioning, the saccharin (CS) is paired with the injection (US). The result of this procedure is that when saccharin (CS) is presented to the rat, the rat avoids it (CR).

People experience taste aversion if they consume a distinctively flavored food and later become ill from an unrelated virus like influenza (the flu). Although they "know" it was not the food that caused the illness, they still have an aversion to the taste of the food.

A Modern View of Classical Conditioning

Robert Rescorla is a modern scientist producing important research and theory regarding classical conditioning. He views classical conditioning from an information-processing perspective. According to Rescorla, a subject in classical conditioning attempts to learn patterns of stimuli. The goal is to learn about predictive relationships in the environment.

Rescorla has shown that pairing a CS with a US is necessary but not sufficient for classical conditioning to occur. In one of Rescorla's experiments a group of subjects experienced a CS paired with a US. The CS and the US always occurred in this paired predictive relationship and strong CRs occurred. Another group of subjects experienced as many CS-US pairings, but they also experienced presentations of the US alone. This group lacked the important predictive relationship between the CS and the US and did not develop strong CRs.

An Application Of Classical Conditioning: Systematic Desensitization

Systematic desensitization was developed by the therapist Joseph Wolpe as a treatment for phobia (irrational fear) in humans. Wolpe believed that such fears were learned through classical conditioning. Therefore, they could be treated with a classical conditioning method.

The treatment has three phases: (1) construction of the fear hierarchy; (2) relaxation training; (3) pairing of fearful thoughts with relaxation.

In step one, the client and the therapist develop a list of the client's fears. The list orders items from strongest fear to weakest fear. For example, a client with a fear of heights might create a list of 15 fearful situations, ranging from "strongest fear: falling down a mountain," to "weakest fear: walking down a slight incline."

In step two, the therapist instructs the client in techniques of deep relaxation. These techniques include muscle tension and relaxation, breathing exercises, and peaceful imagery.

Step three is the actual classical conditioning treatment. The client first uses the various techniques to become totally relaxed. Then the therapist asks the client, while relaxed, to imagine being in the situation at the bottom of the fear hierarchy. The idea is to pair the thought of the fear situation with relaxation. Since the item at the bottom of the fear hierarchy is used first, it is likely that the relaxation will overwhelm the fear. Once that item is conquered, the therapist and client proceed up the fear hierarchy, one item at a time. Research has demonstrated that systematic desensitization is an effective treatment for phobia.

OPERANT CONDITIONING

Operant conditioning (also called instrumental conditioning) is based on a contingency (causal connection) between a response and the consequence that follows the response. Contingencies can be expressed as if-then statements. In operant conditioning there is a contingency of this nature: if the response occurs, then this consequence follows.

The Work of Edward L. Thorndike

CATS IN PUZZLE BOXES

Edward L. Thorndike (1874-1949) was an early pioneer in conditioning research. He studied the behavior of cats in a chamber called the puzzle box. The cat was confined inside the chamber. A number of devices inside the chamber included rings, loops of wire, and panels. The cat's task was to learn to escape from the box. However, only by pulling a particular device could the cat escape. Since there were several devices, the task was difficult. The cat usually escaped after a number of minutes.

THE LAW OF EFFECT

As trials proceeded, the escape response occurred more quickly. The learning was gradual and orderly. Thorndike concluded that the cats did not use reasoning to solve this problem but rather slow trial-and-error learning. He stated this formally as the law of effect: responses followed by a satisfying state of affairs were gradually stamped in (developed) as habits; responses followed by an annoying state of affairs were gradually stamped out as habits (eliminated from the animal's behavioral repertoire).

The Work of B. F. Skinner

Before his recent death, B. F. Skinner (1904-1990) was considered the most influential living psychologist. In the second half of the twentieth century he was the leading advocate for behaviorism.

RATS IN SKINNER BOXES

Skinner developed an experimental chamber to study learning in laboratory rats. He always called this an operant conditioning chamber , but others refer to it as a Skinner box. (An operant is a voluntary behavior which a person or animal emits in response to its environment). The chamber included a lever, a metal bar attached to the front wall. Pressing the lever was the response studied in this chamber. Small pieces or pellets of food were presented in a food cup. The floor of the chamber consisted of metal rods through which electric shock could be applied to the feet of the animal.

Skinner performed many experiments with the operant conditioning chamber. He developed operational definitions of reinforcement, punishment, shaping, and schedules of reinforcement.

REINFORCEMENT

Positive Reinforcement. Skinner defined reinforcement as any operation that increases the rate of a response. An operant conditioning contingency that leads to reinforcement is: if the rat responds (presses the lever), then food is presented. The rate of response increases. This procedure is called positive reinforcement. The word "positive" is used because the consequence is the presentation of food. The word "reinforcement" is used since the effect of the contingency is to increase the rate of response. In most examples "positive reinforcement" is recognizable as a form of reward.

Negative Reinforcement. There is another and quite different way to increase the rate of response. Suppose the rat receives electric shock to the feet every second. Now, when the lever is pressed, the shock is removed for ten seconds. The rate of response increases. This procedure is called negative reinforcement. The word "negative" is used because the consequence is the removal of shock. The word "reinforcement" is used since the effect of the contingency is to increase the rate of response.

This kind of negative reinforcement is also called escape. A similar procedure called avoidance occurs when lever pressing allows the animal to totally avoid shock.

Shaping. One can train an animal by positive reinforcement by waiting for the desired response and immediately rewarding the animal. But this may involve a long period of waiting. Shaping is a process that speeds up the training process. To shape the animal's behavior, the experimenter reinforces the animal for more and more specific steps in the desired behavior. For example, a dog can be trained to roll over first by learning to lie down, then to lie down and roll onto one side, and ultimately to lie down, roll onto one side, and then over onto the other. Because of the step-by-step procedure, shaping is called the method of successive approximations.

Schedules of Reinforcement. The examples provided so far have all been cases of continuous reinforcement , because every response was reinforced. Alternatively, there are many ways to provide partial reinforcement, which involves less attention and expense because not every response is reinforced.

Reinforcement schedules may be timed according to either the ratio or the interval of the responses. Ratio schedules involve reinforcing every fixed number of responses. Interval schedules involve reinforcing every specific time period, no matter how many responses have occurred.

In addition, both ratio and interval schedules can be either fixed or variable. A fixed schedule reinforces for the same ratio or interval every time in the learning process. A variable schedule involves changing the ratio or interval between reinforcements from trial to trial.

According to research on schedules of partial reinforcement, the rates at which organisms learn and lose what they have learned depend both on the specific behavior involved and the nature of the reinforcement schedule adhered to.

EXTINCTION: CONTINUOUS VERSUS PARTIAL REINFORCEMENT

Extinction refers to the loss of an acquired response, or the failure to make a learned response. Extinction is brought about when, following a period of reinforcement for responding, reinforcement is no longer provided.

After continuous reinforcement, extinction is very fast. On the other hand, following partial reinforcement, extinction is typically very slow. This is called the partial-reinforcement extinction effect.

In human behavior, there are similar effects. Parents who reinforce a child's crying on a partial schedule have a very difficult time extinguishing the crying behavior.

PUNISHMENT

Positive Punishment. Skinner defined punishment as the opposite of reinforcement. Therefore, punishment is any operation that decreases the rate of response. For example, when the rat presses the lever, shock is presented. This leads to a decrease in lever pressing, hence punishment has occurred. When shock or other painful consquences are applied to decrease behavior, the consequence is referred to as positive punishment. It is called "positive" because the consequence involves presenting or applying a painful or shocking treatment. It is "punishment" because it is followed by a decrease in behavior.

Negative Punishment. An alternative to positive punishment is negative punishment. An example of negative punishment might be to follow an undesirable behavior with removal of a privilege. For example, a child who misbehaves has her favorite toy taken away for two days. As a result she does not misbehave as often. This procedure is "negative" because something is removed or taken away (a toy or privilege). It is still a form of punishment because it results in a decrease of the unwanted behavior.

Issues in the Use of Punishment. In child-rearing, punishment contingencies are often used. Parents identify a behavior they wish to decrease. The contingency might be: if the child engages in the behavior, the child will receive a spanking. Or, if the child engages in the behavior, the child must go to bed early.

Skinner was a strong advocate for the use of reinforcement rather than punishment. He thought that reinforcement led to stronger control of behavior than did punishment. Another reason was concern that, although punishment does eliminate unwanted behavior, it cannot in itself teach or encourage alternative behaviors. Finally, repeated use of punishment has been found to make subjects behave in hostile or helpless ways.

Operant Conditioning: Learned Helplessness

Operant conditioning has been applied in a number of ways to human behavior. One example is work by researcher Martin Seligman that has led to a theory of depression.

EXPERIMENTAL HELPLESSNESS

Seligman's work began with dogs in escape and avoidance conditioning procedures. He set up a chamber with a barrier in the center. Every few minutes a light came on for 10 seconds, followed by a painful electric shock. The dog could escape the shock by jumping over the barrier; the dog could avoid the shock altogether by jumping over the barrier during the light presentation.

Dogs learned to escape fairly quickly, and most learned to avoid the shock with extensive practice. However, Seligman was disappointed with the slow avoidance learning. He tried a different procedure with some new dogs. These animals were first restrained in a harness and given several light-shock pairings. Seligman thought that this might teach them the significance of the light as a signal for shock, and that this might encourage fast avoidance learning in the chamber. To the contrary, these dogs performed poorly in the chamber. When the light was presented they acted afraid. Although unrestrained, the animals lay on the floor and whimpered when the shock was presented.

DEPRESSION AS LEARNED HELPLESSNESS

After thinking about this result, Seligman realized that the training with light and shock in the harness had taught these animals that they could not do anything about the delivery of shock. He called this phenomenon learned helplessness. Seligman and colleagues have performed many additional studies, and learned helplessness has been demonstrated in cats, rats, and humans.

According to Seligman, the key factor in the development of learned helplessness is the experience of having a lack of control over the environment. Further, he has theorized that several such experiences of lack of control, and the accompanying feeling of helplessness, is the cause of human depression. He has pointed out that losses of a spouse, relative or loved one are cases where one may perceive a lack of control. These situations lead to helpless feelings and depression.

This view of depression has implications for therapy with depressed clients. Seligman has proposed that depressed clients should be encouraged to engage in activities that will lead to success and a perceived sense of control over the environment.

OBSERVATIONAL LEARNING

*Bandura's
Work on
Modeling*

LIVE MODELS

Albert Bandura studied learning by observation in nursery-school- aged boys and girls in the 1960s. The subjects were tested individually in the laboratory. While the child was playing alone, an adult entered the room and displayed verbal and physical aggression to a plastic punching-bag clown ("Bobo") doll. Later, the child was frustrated by being shown some highly attractive toys but being allowed to play with them only for a few minutes. Then the child was watched through a one-way mirror. Children displayed aggression toward the Bobo doll, in many cases mimicking the behavior of the adult model of aggression. (Children who were frustrated in the same way, but who had not seen the adult model of aggression did not act so aggressively toward the Bobo doll.)

MEDIA MODELS

In other research, Bandura and colleagues found that children could learn aggression by observing the behavior on a cartoon. These results have caused some psychologists to caution parents about television and movie violence that children observe.

*Social Learning
Theory*

Social learning theory explains behavior patterns as having been learned through a process of operant conditioning and observational learning. According to social learning theorists, the reinforcement, punishment, and models are provided by the social environment.

Social learning theories of human aggression, for example, have analyzed the many rewards (reinforcement), direct and indirect, for behaving aggressively in our society. Moreover, ironically, many authorities' and parents' attempts to discourage aggressive behavior by punishing aggressive offenders results in the provision of models for further aggressive behavior.

Social learning theories do argue in favor of the power of positive models as well as the obvious antisocial or aggressive examples. Some research has indicated that televised or publicized examples of prosocial (helpful) behavior are much more influential than comparable examples of antisocial or aggressive modeling.

Learning is defined as a change in behavior due to experience rather than instinct, maturation, or temporary states of the organism. Research on learning has been influenced by the behaviorism perspective with its emphasis on observable behaviors, stimuli and responses. Much of learning theory has been established in research with nonhuman subjects and extended to applications with humans. Three major types of learning have been identified: classical conditioning, operant conditioning, and observational learning.

Classical conditioning was originally discovered by the Russian physiologist Ivan Pavlov in his research on the digestive processes of dogs. Pavlov found that reflexes like salivation were made in response to other stimuli as a result of learning. In classical conditioning, repeated pairing of a conditioned stimulus (CS) with an unconditioned stimulus (US) results in a response to the CS alone. The natural response to the US is termed the unconditioned response (UR); when this response is made to the new CS, it is termed the conditioned response (CR).

Pavlov's research identified the conditions under which the CR (the response to the CS) is acquired, extinguished, reacquired, generalized, discriminated, and spontaneously recovered. The classical conditioning sequence has been applied to both human and nonhuman reflexive responses, and can explain such diverse phenomena as phobias and taste aversions.

A modern view of classical conditioning is offered by Robert Rescorla, who suggests that the power of the CS-US connection lies in its predictiveness of the onset of the US. The stronger the prediction connection, the greater the likelihood of the CR.

Useful human applications of classical conditioning include the development of systematic desensitization to overcome phobias.

Another important kind of learning is operant conditioning. An operant (voluntary environmental behavior) is increased or decreased as a function of the contingencies of those actions. Actions which result in reinforcement increase; those which result in punishment decrease or are eliminated.

Early research on operant conditioning was conducted by Edward L. Thorndike, who studied the law of effect in cats' trial-and-error attempts to escape puzzle boxes. Later research by B. F. Skinner identified conditions in which rats' level-pressing behaviors changed in Skinner boxes.

Reinforcement, including positive reinforcement like reward and negative reinforcement like escape opportunities, results in an increase in the affected behavior. Behavior can be shaped if successive approximations of the criterion behavior are reinforced. Reinforcement can also be either continuous (contingent on every response) or partial (contingent on only part of the responses displayed). Reinforcement can be applied according to either ratios or intervals of responses, on either a fixed or variable schedule. Extinction occurs much more quickly after continuous reinforcement than after partial reinforcement. Punishment, including positive punishment like infliction of pain and negative punishment like removal of privileges, results in a decrease or elimination of affected behavior. Skinner has criticized punishment, arguing that reinforcement results in stronger behavior change and fewer unpleasant side-effects.

One application of operant conditioning to human experience is research on learned helplessness. Seligman's original research indicated that when dogs were unable to learn escape successfully, they acted fearful and did not explore new escape options. This finding has been applied to the human experience of depression, and has led to the recommendation that depressed individuals need to learn to effectively control their lives and environment.

Observational learning occurs when behavior changes to imitate that of models. Work by Albert Bandura and colleagues has shown the power of both live and media models. Social learning theories have argued that behavior patterns in general are learned as a result of social reinforcements, punishments, and models.

Selected Readings

Bower, G. H. and E. R. Hilgard. *Theories of Learning, 5th Edition*. Englewood Cliffs, NJ: Prentice-Hall. 1981

Domjan, M. and B. Burkhard. *The Principles of Learning and Behavior*. Monterey, CA: Brooks/Cole. 1982

Flaherty, C. F. *Animal Learning and Cognition*. New York: Random House. (1985)

Garber, J. and M. Seligman, (Eds.). *Human Helplessness*. New York: Academic Press. 1980

Kalish, H. I. *From Behavioral Science to Behavior Modification*. New York: McGraw-Hill. 1981

Miller, L. K. *Principles of Everyday Behavior Analysis*. Monterey, CA: Brooks/Cole. 1980

Roitblat, H. L. *Introduction to Comparative Cognition*. New York: W. H. Freeman and Company. 1987

Shattuck, R. *The Forbidden Experiment*. New York: Farrar, Straus and Giroux. 1980

Skinner, B. F. and R. Epstein. *Skinner for the Classroom*. Champaign, IL: Research Press. 1982

7

Memory

*P*sychologists consider memory to be a different process from learning, although the two are closely related. Whereas learning refers to the acquisition of new behaviors, memory refers to the process of saving or storing information so that it might be available when needed.

Thus, for example, extinction, which refers to the loss of a stimulus-response connection, is not the same as forgetting, the loss of the ability, or potential, to recall information. Moreover, memory is discussed in the language of cognitive psychology (derived from computer studies and artificial intelligence engineering) rather than that of behavioral psychology. The use of cognitive language rather than behavioral terminology means that memory is described in terms of processes that are not directly observable. Psychologists speak of encoding, storage, retrieval, and information processing.

RETENTION

While memory refers to the set of processes involved in storing information, the specific process or state of storage is termed retention.

Measures of Retention

Three basic ways to measure retention are recall, recognition, and relearning.

RECALL

Recall refers simply to remembering or producing spontaneously the information requested, as must be done for an essay test. In responding to an essay item, one must search one's available recollections for the necessary information. Likewise, when encountering a new acquaintance, one must search one's past associations with the person to produce his or her name.

RECOGNITION

Recognition is the ability to recognize the correct information, as on a multiple-choice test. In choosing the correct answer on a multiple-choice test, one must scan the choices and identify the one that matches one's past information about this item. Thus, in recognition, two processes are undertaken and compared: a review of what is being perceived, and a review of what is remembered. When a match is found, we say recognition has occurred.

Recognition is also necessary in such mundane tasks as retrieving the correct coat or umbrella from a closet—finding one's own instead of taking someone else's—and such unusual tasks as eyewitness identification of crime suspects in a book of mugshots or a police lineup.

RELEARNING

Relearning requires that the material actually be relearned, for example, learning again a list of forgotten names. When the method of relearning is used, psychologists look for a savings score, measuring the extent to which the material is relearned more quickly than it had been originally learned.

For example, the less time one needs to relearn a list of names, the more of the list one must have remembered from the first lesson. The time saved represents one form of savings evident in relearning.

Comparing Measures

The sensitivity of a retention measure is its tendency to detect memory effects under various conditions.

Of these three measures of retention, recall is the least sensitive, that is, it requires the best retention. Relearning, on the other hand, is most sensitive, often showing savings even if none of the original material can actually be recalled. Recognition is less sensitive than relearning, but more sensitive than recall.

THE BIOLOGICAL BASIS OF MEMORY

The process of memory formation has been studied intensively at a number of biological levels.

Neural Activity

In terms of neuronal activity, there is evidence that activity at the synapses is particularly critical to memory. Certain complex biochemical molecules in synaptic regions of neurons have been suggested as being involved in the actual biological encoding of information in memory formation. This is much like the metallic particles in magnetic tape involved in encoding information for playback in tape recordings.

These biochemicals include various species of giant protein molecules as well as the nucleic acid, ribonucleic acid (RNA), closely related to the DNA that carries the genetic code.

It seems quite likely, however, that the formation of permanent memory involves the creation of new networks of neurons (what physiological psychologist Donald Hebb has termed cell assemblies) by the growth and alteration of synaptic connections between nerve cells in the brain.

Brain Structures

Various areas of the brain have been found to be important for the formation of permanent memories. These include the hippocampus (part of the limbic system, located beneath the lower temporal lobe), the amygdala (connected to the hippocampus and also part of the limbic system), the thalamus, and the cortex. Depending upon its extent and location, damage to these areas can cause anterograde amnesia, a type of memory failure (see Amnesia).

THEORIES OF FORGETTING

There are many theories of why forgetting occurs, ranging from common-sense explanations to those more solidly supported by research.

Decay Theory

DISUSE

A common explanation for forgetting is the notion of decay, which states that if information is not used it is gradually lost. The disuse theory of decay argues that information must be retrieved occasionally or it will be lost, as if through a process of atrophy.

One problem with disuse theory is that one frequently remembers events from one's past or information learned long ago and not thought of since. Disuse theory alone cannot explain why certain memories fade forever while others seem to be produced after long periods in well-preserved form.

MEMORY TRACES

Early and recent biological theories have attributed the decay of some memories to the slow loss of the actual brain substrate of the memory, termed the memory trace or engram, thought to be responsible for memory storage.

Memory trace theories might argue that some memories are retained though not retrieved for years because, when originally stored, they were exceptionally vivid, and so left stronger, deeper biological "traces," which were more easily aroused many years later.

MOTIVATED FORGETTING

While memory seems useful and forgetting a nuisance, it is important to consider the special case of unpleasant memories. In these instances one might be motivated to "forget" or be unable to retrieve certain memories to conscious review.

Freud, for example, considered such motivated forgetting to be an example of repression, a psychic defense mechanism (see chapter 15) that can occur when memories are painful or threatening. Repression is a process whereby unpleasant ideas—real memories as well as shameful fantasies— are moved from conscious consideration to storage in one's unconscious mind, where they will be unavailable to conscious efforts at retrieval.

Interference Theory

The above explanations for forgetting, while valuable, do not account for ordinary day-to-day forgetting. A more useful explanation is found in interference theory.

The basic idea in interference theory is that memories are not lost so much as they are inhibited, or interfered with, by other memories. There are two types of such interference, termed retroactive interference and proactive interference. Depending on the process assumed to be taking place, they are sometimes referred to respectively as retroactive inhibition and proactive inhibition.

RETROACTIVE INTERFERENCE

Retroactive interference occurs when later learning interferes, as if retroactively ("acting backwards"), with previous learning. For example, suppose that on Monday one studies Spanish and on Tuesday Italian. During a Spanish test taken on Wednesday intrusions are experienced from Italian words. Retroactive interference explains our inability to recall old memories as due to competition from new memories.

PROACTIVE INTERFERENCE

Proactive interference occurs when earlier learning interferes proactively ("acting forwards" in time) with later learning. Persistent habits provide good examples of proactive interference. Suppose one has lived for several years in an apartment with one kitchen drawer next to the sink where the tableware is always stored. The new apartment, however, has a bigger kitchen and the tableware is now stored in the drawer next to the stove. When hurried or preoccupied, one "forgets" this new plan and habitually seeks knives and forks in the wrong drawer, the drawer by the sink, which corresponds to the "old" storage place instead of the new one.

Proactive interference thus explains one's inability to acquire new knowledge or habits because of the powerful competition of old memories.

Cue-Dependent Learning and Forgetting

CUE-DEPENDENT RECALL

Cognitive psychological theories explain that when new information is learned (encoded), it is stored in the context of other information (cues) present at the moment. Recall is most effective when the person attempts to remember again in the presence of these cues. This is known as cue-dependent recall.

For instance, the recall of terms learned in a psychology class is best done in the room where the class is held and not, say, at the beach in the summertime. The classroom itself is a cue to effective retrieval.

Other cues can include mental associations made with the material at the time it is learned and even one's mood or state of mind (thus the term "state-dependent" remembering).

CUE-DEPENDENT FORGETTING

Cue-Dependent Forgetting. Cue-dependent forgetting refers to an inability to retrieve information when the other cues are not present. An example is trying to remember terms from psychology class while one is vacationing at the beach.

The Encoding-Specificity Principle. Implied by this process is its converse, the encoding-specificity principle. This principle asserts that recall is best in the presence of the cues that were originally present.

Mnemonics. Advantage can be taken of encoding-specificity to create powerful cues for specific items of information that one desires to memorize. Such strategies for memory are termed mnemonics, from the Greek word *mnemon*, "mindful."

Ancient Greek orators, for example, used the method of loci. They would imagine themselves walking through familiar places (in Latin, *loci*) like a building or garden. While memorizing, they would associate each object or room "encountered" in the building with a point to be made in their speech. Later, while giving the speech, they would imagine retracing their walk through the building and encountering these objects, reminding them of the points they wished to make.

A common mnemonic method used today is to think of silly rhymes or absurd images to associate with items in a list that must be set to memory. For instance, an English medical school limerick used to aid in memorizing the names of the twelve cranial nerves goes as follows: "On old Olympus' towering tops, a Finn and German viewed some hops." The first letter of each word in the limerick (O, O, O, T, etc.) is the same as the first letter of each cranial nerve (Olfactory, Optic, Oculomotor, Trochlear, etc.). Similarly, many college students memorize lists of structures or points by memorizing their initials in order and forming acronyms of those initials, easily reproducing and decoding the acronyms during exams.

STAGES OF MEMORY

For many years researchers have suspected that memory is not a single process, but involves more than one stage and thus more than one type of memory. Based on these thoughts, cognitive researchers Atkinson and Shiffrin in 1968 proposed what was to become one of the most successful theoretical models in the field of psychology.

According to the Atkinson-Shiffrin model, memory occurs in three major stages, termed the sensory storage (the sensory register), short-term memory (STM), and long-term memory (LTM). Information moves successively through these three stages if attention (focused awareness) is given to it. In the absence of attention, information tends not to move further into the system.

Sensory Storage

Sensory storage holds direct impressions of sensory events for short periods of time. There are different sensory registers for each of the senses. The visual register is termed the iconic memory, and the auditory register is termed the echoic memory. While the iconic memory lasts only about half a second, the echoic memory lasts several seconds or longer.

For example, in taking class notes, one is able, in a sense, to "hear" a sentence said by the instructor for several seconds after it is actually spoken, and is able to write it down. If the student involuntarily hears something else the instructor says in the meantime, however, the echoic memory of the first sentence is lost. Thus, like the memory of the front register of a hand calculator, sensory memory can easily be written over by new information. In fact, most information that enters the sensory registers is lost, otherwise one would be overwhelmed. What we attend to, however, moves on to the next stage of memory.

Short-Term Memory

The short-term memory (STM) has been called the workbench or desktop of the mind because it closely corresponds to conscious experience, and in particular to one's thoughts.

Most research on short-term memory has been done with auditory material, especially spoken words of one type or another.

CAPACITY LIMITATIONS

This memory is very limited in capacity, able to hold only about five to nine —the "magic number" seven plus-or-minus two—units of information at once. A seven- digit phone number, for example, is within this five-to-nine item capacity.

If the number of units goes higher, new information displaces, or writes over, existing units. Thus, it is easy to remember a seven-digit number long enough to dial the phone, but if someone asks us for a street address at the same time (requiring that we handle several more digits), we exceed our short-term memory capacity and lose at least part of the phone number.

CHUNKING

This limitation in capacity can be effectively expanded by a process termed chunking. In chunking, several units of meaningful information are packaged into each (short-term) rememberable unit in the short-term memory. For instance, the 12-digit sequence of numbers, 149217761941, can easily be remembered if the 12 digits are "chunked" into three foursomes, recognizable as three important dates in American history.

REHEARSAL

Information remains only briefly in short-term memory if it is not in use. In order to retain information such as a phone number for any length of time it is necessary to repeat it to ourselves, a process termed rehearsal. From a cognitive point of view, this amounts to reentering the information more quickly than it can fade from memory.

Moving information into long-term memory is equivalent to the creation of permanent memories. Attention is an important factor in the creation of such memories; what we pay most attention to is what we tend to remember best. In this vein there seem to be two types of rehearsal: maintenance rehearsal and elaborative rehearsal.

Maintenance Rehearsal. In maintenance rehearsal, information is merely repeated so that it is maintained in short-term memory until it is needed. For example, a phone number is repeated until the phone is dialed. This type of rehearsal requires little attention and is not likely to lead to long-term memory. Although one might repeat a phone number many times in attempting to dial past a busy signal, once the call has been made one is not likely to remember the phone number even a short time later.

Elaborative Rehearsal. A second form of rehearsal is elaborative rehearsal, in which one examines the unit of information, turning it over in one's mind and giving it special attention. This type of rehearsal tends to put information into long-term memory. It is the way one should study new material in order to remember it.

RETRIEVAL

Once in long-term memory, information tends to remain for a considerable length of time. To use it, however, it must be recalled (retrieved) back into short-term memory.

Long-Term Memory

In colloquial terms, when people talk about "memory" they are usually referring to long-term memory, the process of retaining and retrieving information anywhere from minutes to years, even a lifetime, after first encoding it.

CAPACITY

The capacity of long-term memory seems virtually unlimited. In time, information may be lost due to decay, but most problems in recall are the result of interference (see Forgetting).

ORGANIZATION

Even the most informal examination of long-term memory discloses that it is highly organized. Out of all the people we know, for example, it is possible to recall just those who live in this region, or who have red hair, or who are unusually tall, without laboriously sifting through our entire memory. How is it possible to scan the vast stores of long-term memory so efficiently if not for some system of organization, both in initial storage and in search and retrieval?

Networks. Cognitive psychologists have developed complex network models to explain this organization. Some of these models have been developed with the aid of computer simulations. These are based, for example, on the notion that networks of associations exist in long-term memory.

Schemata. Along these lines, research suggests that memories conform to familiar patterns, or schemata (schemas), learned from past experience. (This use of schemata is similar to the theory of Piaget, explained in chapter 12).

For instance, most kitchens are furnished with an oven, so it is easy to remember having seen an oven in a kitchen. In this example, one's schema of a kitchen facilitates the memory of a specific kitchen's properties or features.

Such schemata can also cause us to err, perhaps remembering having seen a stove when none was actually present (see below).

CATEGORIES OF LONG-TERM MEMORY

There are several ways that psychologists have categorized long-term or permanent memory. One way is to make a distinction between memory for different kinds of material, as in the distinction between episodic and semantic memory.

Episodic Memory versus Semantic Memory. Episodic memory is a record of specific events experienced and remembered. These include any episode that one can recall from his or her own life, including the events of the past few hours and days.

Episodic memories tend to fade, and in fact form only a small part of the total information available in permanent memory.

Most of what we can recall is in the form of general information, or facts, termed semantic memory. This includes everything from our own name, to the phone number where we work, to the name of the ocean on the western shore of the United States, and includes all of the facts we can recall.

While most if not all such information may at one time have been associated with a particular learning episode, the latter has long since been forgotten, leaving only the objective information. For example, you may not remember when you learned the significance of the year 1776 in American history, but this failure in episodic memory does not bar the semantic memory of knowing what is significant about that year.

Declarative versus Procedural Memory. Another useful division is between declarative and procedural memory. Declarative memory includes all information that can be spoken or written (declared). This includes virtually all the content of episodic and semantic memory.

Procedural memory includes learning that must be acted out as a procedure, such as riding a bicycle or operating a standard-transmission automobile. Procedural memory is obviously closely related to classical and instrumental conditioning.

CONSTRUCTIVE MEMORY

Though memories, when vivid, carry a strong feeling of truth (veridicality), considerable evidence suggests that in fact memories can be altered significantly by experiences that occur after their original formation. For example, suggestions made by other people can be incorporated into memory without our knowing it.

For example, how confident can one be that one's earliest memory was not, in fact, something that was originally related by a parent, or dreamed, or simply experienced later than in early infancy? The episodic details of the encoding may be lost, while the semantic substance of the memory is retained.

Well-established schemata can also play a role in memory distortion, causing one to recall things the way they are expected to be instead of the way they actually are.

Reconstructing Recall. Observations of distortions, misrecollections, and bias in recall have led psychologists to conclude that much of long-term memory may be constructive. This means that later events and knowledge can influence what one remembers or what one believes "must have" happened. For example, in answering the question, "What were you doing at 3:30 p.m. on January 5, 1990?," one might first use a calendar to reconstruct the information that the date was a Saturday, consider that it was winter and the semester had not yet begun, and so on, in order to "remember" what one "must have" been doing at that date and time.

Eyewitness Memory. Psychologists have studied this constructive aspect of memory as it effects eyewitness testimony in the courtroom. Such testimony is invaluable to the legal process, but it is important to bear in mind that it is far from reliable. Such factors as emotionality, distraction, and the wording of police questioning have all been shown to have a reconstructive (distorting) effect on eyewitness memory for detail and recognition.

AMNESIA: THE FAILURE OF MEMORY

Popular media and fiction frequently feature amnesia as a disorder that complicates characters' lives. In nonfictional life, amnesia (from the Greek *amnasthai*, "not to remember") is rare but fascinating.

There are many forms of amnesia, and few are well understood. Two types of particular interest are retrograde amnesia and anterograde amnesia.

RETROGRADE AMNESIA

Retrograde amnesia is the loss of memory for events just prior to any event that disrupts ongoing neural activity (such as a sudden blow or a mild electrical shock to the head).

This loss commonly covers only about a minute prior to the traumatic event, suggestive of the idea that only short-term memory is disrupted.

Other cases, however, can include longer periods prior to the event, sometimes half an hour, but in some cases as much as several hours or even days.

Retrograde amnesia usually encompasses loss of memory for events, rather than the amnesic's general knowledge. It does not involve loss of one's identity, a rare disorder known as a fugue state.

ANTEROGRADE AMNESIA

Anterograde amnesia is seen in certain instances of brain damage. New memories fade rapidly and are often lost within half an hour, if not sooner, though those formed prior to the damage remain unaffected. This suggests that it is not memory storage but the process of memory formation (encoding) that is affected in anterograde amnesia.

Strangely, anterograde amnesia often seems to involve only declarative memory, so that the same individual who cannot remember having practiced a skill (e.g., a video game) will nonetheless continue to improve at it daily, suggesting that procedural memory is intact.

Whereas learning involves acquiring new behaviors, memory involves saving information for later use. Memory retention is measured in three ways: recall, recognition, and relearning.

Research on the biological bases of memory have identified processes at the molecular and neural level of activity as important. Specific structures in the limbic system and temporal lobe of the cerebral cortex have also been implicated in memory.

Forgetting has been attributed to a process of decay over time, as a result of disuse or a fading of the biological traces of original memories. Psychoanalytic theory proposes that some forgetting is motivated, the explanation for the defense mechanism known as repression.

A more useful theory of forgetting argues that memories become irretrievable when they are inhibited or interfered with by earlier or later memories, respectively involving proactive or retroactive interference.

Cognitive theories suggest that remembering may be dependent on incidental cues at the time of encoding. Thus forgetting may be a function of the absence of such reminder cues. The encoding specificity principle states that memory is best in the presence of such original cues.

The effects of cues may be applied in mnemonic strategies for remembering, as in the method of loci, image associations, or memorizing initials that can be decoded for later retrieval.

The Atkinson-Shiffrin model of memory theorizes that there are three stages of memory with different processes of encoding, storage, and retrieval. Sensory storage involves retention of a sensory image, like a visual icon or auditory echo. Sensory storage is fragile because it is not energized by attention.

Attention can bring information into short-term memory, which has a limited capacity that can be extended through such procedures as chunking the material to be recalled, or rehearsing the material either to maintain it or elaborate on it for long-term memory storage.

Long-term memory, which may have no capacity limitations, is organized on the basis of networks of associations and schemata. Long-term memory may be distinguished into episodic versus semantic material, or declarative versus procedural material.

Long-term memory is susceptible to constructive processes, as original memories are distorted or augmented by later experiences or interpretations. Such tendencies have important implications for reliance on eyewitness testimony.

Amnesia, the failure of memory, is rare and little understood. Retrograde amnesia involves loss of memory for events up to half an hour before the traumatic event that caused it. Anterograde amnesia, observable in certain kinds of brain damage, involves the loss of newly forming memories and seems to affect declarative but not procedural memory.

Selected Readings

Anderson, J. F. *Cognitive Psychology and Its Implications, 3rd Edition*. New York: Freeman. 1990

Baddeley, A. D. *Memory: A User's Guide*. New York: Macmillan. 1982

_____*Human Memory: Theory and Practice*. Hillsdale, NJ: Erlbaum. 1990

Benne, B. *WASPLEG and Other Mnemonics*. Dallas, TX: Taylor Publishing Company. 1988

Glass, A. L. and K. J. Holyoak. *Cognition*. New York: Random House. 1986

Higbee, K. L. *Your Memory: How It Works and How to Improve It, 2nd Edition*. Englewood Cliffs, NJ: Prentice-Hall. 1988

Loftus, E. *Memory*. Reading, MA. Addison-Wesley. 1980

Neisser, U. *Memory Observed: Remembering in Natural Contexts*. San Francisco: Freeman. 1982

Smith, E. E. and D. L. Medin. *Categories and Concepts*. Cambridge, MA: Harvard University Press. 1984

Squire, L. R. *Memory and Brain*. Oxford, England: Oxford University Press. 1987

8

Thinking and Intelligence

*T*he information-processing approach to psychology characterizes human behavior as meaning-oriented. Early psychophysicists proposed an unconscious process from stimuli to response. This sequence can be summarized as $S \rightarrow O \rightarrow R$. In this conceptualization, S represents the stimuli or environmental changes that impinge on the sensory systems; O represents the organism and its internal sensory and perceptual processes; and R symbolizes the responses the organism makes as a consequence of stimulation.

Under the influence of behaviorism in the early 20th century, psychologists abandoned research into "O" (organismic) processes in favor of the directly observable "S" (stimuli) and R (responses). For this reason behaviorism came to be known as S-R psychology, emphasizing only the observable associations between these two processes without inferring the nature of the connection.

With the development in recent decades of artificial intelligence (systems and computers that process information), the new field of cognitive psychology has emerged and revitalized interest in unobservable organismic variables. The information-processing approach, one perspective of cognitive psychology, suggests that these "O" processes are a valid and appropriate subject for scientific research. Included among these are cognitive processes like perceiving, recognizing, thinking, imaging, and remembering. Many cognitive processes also take the form of "R" behaviors, influencing responses like problem-solving, decision-making, and language.

An understanding of thinking is essential to comprehending cognitive processes. The effectiveness of thinking contributes to intelligence, a quality considered central to most aspects of human performance.

THINKING

Thinking can be approached in terms of both its nature—types of thinking—and its forms and functions.

Types of Thinking

Thinking can be broadly distinguished into two kinds of processes, convergent thinking and divergent thinking.

CONVERGENT THINKING

Convergent thinking is focused, deliberate, directed thinking. It is the kind of thinking we undertake in order to recall an elusive idea, solve a problem, or make a choice. The term "convergent" implies that, although we may approach an issue from many different directions, eventually all these approaches "converge"—come together—on the same final solution or response.

DIVERGENT THINKING

Divergent thinking characterizes the undirected thinking of daydreaming and creativity. The term "divergent" implies that, from one starting point, subsequent thought processes may continue in different directions and culminate in different conclusions.

Daydreaming. Daydreaming, a form of conscious fantasizing, is considered by some researchers to be an altered state of consciousness. Daydreaming can be a form of escape, and daydreams may involve imagining alternate circumstances when we would rather be elsewhere. Individual differences have been found in the affect (pleasant or unpleasant) and vividness of daydreams.

Creativity. Creativity is the ability to produce novel and unique ideas. Creative problem-solving relies on divergent rather than convergent thinking. For example, creativity is demonstrated by coming up with many different uses for a simple object, like a brick or a toothpick. There is little clear relationship between creativity and performance on most intelligence tests. Formal education may inadvertently discourage creativity by emphasizing convergent thinking in traditional curriculum.

Components of Thinking

As a cognitive process, thinking bridges the gap between stimulation and response, and therefore it affects performance. Thinking is better understood through an examination of its components and applications.

Thinking involves two major kinds of components: images and concepts.

IMAGES

To answer the question, "What shape are a German shepherd's ears?" it is probably not necessary to review all your knowledge or memory about dogs, ears, or dogs' ears. It is most likely that you will simply picture a German shepherd, focus on this mental image, and produce the answer: "pointed."

Images are components of thinking in that they summarize and provide information. Specifically, an image is a mental representation of a sensory experience. Most imagery research has studied visual representations, although imagery can involve impressions of sound, taste, smell, and touch as well.

Images are useful in representing sensory details. They can also be used to mentally "arrange" the parts of a problem or puzzle. For example, in solving the riddle, "John is not as smart as Sue, but is smarter than Lee; who is smartest?" one may visualize a spatial ordering of John, Sue, and Lee along a "smartness" scale to produce the correct answer.

Individual differences have been discovered in ability to use imagery and in the vividness of imagery produced. Children may experience more accurate or vivid imagery than adults, who have learned to rely more on the propositional thinking of ideas and concept relationships.

CONCEPTS

All thinking requires concepts, mental representations of categories of experiences according to common features. The concept of "apple," for example, is really a category of many different examples, since real apples can be red, yellow, or green, sweet or sour, on a tree, in a basket of fruit or sliced and baked into a pie. The "common features" of all apples have to do with hard-to-describe qualities of taste and texture, origin, and form. The concept of "fruit" is a broader category, since it includes the concept of "apple" as well as many other, quite different concepts.

Concept Formation. Concepts are learned through experience. Children's first concepts are concrete, identified by sensory qualities. As we grow, we acquire more abstract or theoretical concepts by building on our earlier concrete ideas. For example, a young child may understand the concept of a "cow." Broadening on this concept, she may acquire the concepts of "farm" and "farm animals." A more abstract concept is "farming," and ultimately an older child will understand the concept of "agriculture," a completely abstract concept.

Children acquire concepts similarly to the way they acquire language. They apply labels and name things imitatively, like pointing and saying "dog." Through conditioning, children will generalize concepts (e.g., saying "dog" for other small four-legged animals like cats and pigs) as well as discriminate between them (e.g., saying "dog" for animals that play with them, but saying "horse" for animals that people ride on).

Types of Concepts. All concepts are not equally easy to learn or recognize. Researchers distinguish between conjunctive and disjunctive concepts. They also characterize some concepts as goal-derived. Finally, some cases are more typical of their concept categories than others.

Conjunctive versus Disjunctive Concepts. Researchers distinguish between easy-to-learn conjunctive concepts and harder-to-learn disjunctive concepts.

Conjunctive concepts are categories of things or ideas that share two or more common features simultaneously. For example, if you are shopping for "diet cola," you must choose from only those products featuring *both* desired qualities: a low-calorie diet formula, and a cola flavor. This is a relatively common and simple application of concepts in making everyday choices.

Disjunctive concepts are categories of things or ideas that share either one or the other of two specified features. For example, a dieter ordering from a restaurant menu may want to choose an item that is either vegetarian or low-calorie. This represents a broader selection than the conjunctive concept of "vegetarian and low-calorie." The disjunctive rule includes all vegetarian items, whatever their caloric content, and all low- calorie items, whether they are vegetarian or not. Given the larger range and unobvious connection, disjunctive concepts are harder to learn.

Goal-Derived Concepts. One feature that might characterize a concept category is the purpose or goal of a behavior. For example, the following very different items all "belong" together because they all fit in the concept category of "things necessary for writing a paper": pen; paper; typewriter; dictionary; desk lamp. Goal-derived concepts are categories of items linked by their connection to a common purpose.

Goal-derived concepts involve overlapping or intersecting other concepts. In the course of experience one learns that "pen" fits into the category of "things to write with" including pencil, crayon, and chalk, and that "dictionary" fits into both the category "books" (which includes other books) and the category "small, heavy objects" (which can include rock, bottle, hammer, and teapot). Thus goal-derived concepts are more complex, harder to learn, and more useful than simpler concepts in solving problems and making decisions.

Typicality. Some concepts include a broad range of examples, not all of which clearly "belong." Typical examples of a concept better summarize the features and qualities of the concept category. A robin is a typical example of the concept "bird." A chair is a typical example of the concept "furniture." Atypical examples are harder to agree on and do not as clearly "belong" in the category. A penguin is a bird, but it is not a typical bird. A wastebasket is a piece of furniture, but it is not a good example of the concept.

Functions of Thinking

REASONING

Philosophical approaches to human thought often identified human mental "faculties" or sets of abilities. Thomas Jefferson, for example, identified the three major human faculties as memory, imagination, and reason. He organized his personal library to represent corresponding sections (e.g., history, art, and science).

Reasoning relies on forms of logic, a system of rules for making correct inferences. The two best recognized types of reasoning are inductive and deductive reasoning.

Inductive Reasoning. Inductive reasoning begins with specific facts or experiences and concludes with general principles. For example, one day you observe a particular bird, a bluejay, building a nest. You next observe another kind of bird, a robin, also building a nest nearby. You might then inductively reason that all local birds have begun to build nests today. Since inductive reasoning makes inferences about an entire class based on only a few members of that class, it is an expedient but risky form of reasoning.

Deductive Reasoning. Deductive reasoning begins with general principles and applies these to particular cases. For example, you know that in spring birds begin to build nests, and that today is the first day of spring. You might then deductively reason that a particular bird you see in your neighborhood is commencing to build a nest somewhere. Deductive reasoning is more conservative than inductive reasoning and generally more reliable.

Analogical Reasoning. An analogue is a likeness in form or proportion; for example, an analogue wristwatch is equipped with a dial like a clock or sundial, while a digital watch displays digits but not a dial.

An analogy is an inference that two things or ideas that are similar in some ways share other qualities as well. Analogical reasoning involves forming a concept about something new based on its similarity to something familiar.

For example, in the analogy, "tines are to fork as teeth are to comb," one must first understand the relation between teeth and comb—that "teeth" are the serrations in a comb—in order to conclude that "tines" must be the word for the prongs of a fork.

Analogical reasoning takes commonplace forms as well. For example, if you turn down a friend's request to borrow your car because "the last time you borrowed something of mine you ruined it," you are drawing an analogy between the old behavior and the new request, and making your decision by carrying the inference forward.

PROBLEM-SOLVING

Problem-solving is one of the most obvious functions of thinking. Several processes have been proposed to account for effective problem-solving.

Insight. During World War I, Gestalt psychologist Wolfgang Köehler studied the practical problem-solving of chimpanzees. For example, a chimpanzee inside a cage reached without success for a banana out of reach just beyond the bars. There were two short hollow sticks, one thin and one thick, inside the cage, but neither was long enough to rake in the banana. Suddenly the chimpanzee seized the two sticks, assembled them by pushing the thin one partly into the thick one, and successfully used this new long tool to retrieve the banana.

Koehler characterized the chimpanzee's problem-solving discovery as an example of insight, the perception of a problem in a new way. Insight is often described as sudden or surprising, giving rise to the exclamation "Aha!" or "Eureka!" (I've found it).

THE GESTALT APPROACH

The Gestalt approach to perception emphasizes the search for meaningful patterns and interpretations in collected data or elements (see chapter 5).

Reorganization. Similarly, the Gestalt approach to problem-solving emphasizes the role of perception and interpretation in finding solutions. According to the Gestalt principle of reorganization, the solution to a problem depends on perceiving new relationships among its elements. Many paper-and-pencil brain-teasers are easily solved only when one eliminates assumptions about how lines must be drawn or how objects should be used.

Productive versus Reproductive Thinking. Gestalt theory also distinguishes between productive and reproductive thinking in problem solving. Productive thinking involves producing a new organization of a problem's elements, as in the insight solutions of Koehler's chimpanzees. Reproductive thinking applies past solutions to new problems. For example, having once learned to "assemble" sticks to form a rake, a caged chimpanzee might next reproduce this strategy by stacking boxes in a cage to reach a goal, when each box by itself is too short to do the job.

Set Effects. One problem with reproductive thinking can be the development of a set effect, a tendency to solve new problems by applying past habits and assumptions. A set effect can prevent one from perceiving a simpler solution than the familiar, tried-and-true but more cumbersome approach.

One type of set effect is functional fixedness, a perception that elements of a problem have fixed or inflexible functions and cannot be combined in new ways. For example, if you don't have a candle holder, how else can you safely prop up a lit candle? If you have aluminum foil handy, you can mold a sheet of it into a cuplike holder for a candle. But if your functional fixedness only allows you to think of aluminum foil as a covering or a wrapping, not a moldable substance, you will fail to find this solution.

THE INFORMATION-PROCESSING APPROACH

The information-processing approach analyzes problem-solving as a series of steps in a sequential process. Research suggests that problem-solvers pursue their tasks one strategy at a time.

Algorithms. One strategy for problem-solving involves using a procedure or formula guaranteed to produce a solution, known as an algorithm. For example, to calculate the area of a rectangle, multiply the length by the width. Like all formulas, this one for quadrangle area is an algorithm.

Algorithms are sure but not always expedient. For example, the algorithm for reassembling the anagram CINERAMA into another word would be to try every possible combination of letters until one makes sense. This would be a time-consuming procedure compared with the relatively quick payoff provided by the perception that the solution is the common term for a citizen of the United States.

Means-End Analysis. Another strategy for problem-solving is *means-end analysis*, a process of repeatedly comparing the present situation with the desired goal and reducing the difference between the two. This is the usual strategy for solving household problems like how to do laundry, how to prepare a meal, or how to dress a child.

DECISION-MAKING

Another function of thinking is decision-making. Many responses require making choices, often without prior experience or sufficient information to guarantee satisfaction. Decision-making strategies provide short-cuts and guidelines in such choices and crises.

Heuristics. A heuristic is a general solution strategy, like a rule of thumb, which often—but not always—applies and succeeds. Heuristics can take the form of familiar principles of spelling and grammar, like "i before e except after c." They can also make up more informal personal routines, like "I should brush my teeth before I sleep and when I wake up."

One kind of heuristic is called hill-climbing, in which one reevaluates the situation after taking each step closer to the goal (like looking back to see how far one has come while climbing a hill). An example of hill-climbing is the use of "process of elimination" when answering multiple-choice test items. Rule out each unlikely choice, until only the likely answer remains.

Another heuristic is to create subgoals by breaking a large goal into stages and each stage into objectives, working backwards from the ultimate goal, until one's immediate next step is clear.

Heuristics can help in decision-making by limiting the trial-and-error of undirected effort. They can also help to rationalize one's decision after the fact.

Framing. Decisions involve making choices among a set of alternatives. The alternatives may be presented in a biased or persuasive comparison, known as a frame. For example, consider the different impressions conveyed by these two alternatives:

> Alternative A: Would you invest all your money in a new business if you had a 50% chance of succeeding brilliantly?

> Alternative B: Would you invest all your money in a new business if you had a 50% chance of failing miserably?

The success-frame in A makes it seem more appealing than the failure-framed B, although the probability of success versus failure is the same for both.

Framing is sometimes used to create illusory comparisons, as when a television commercial claims that "no other brand works better." The implication of the frame is that the advertiser's brand works best, but it is just as likely that all brands work equally well (or poorly).

INTELLIGENCE

No single agreed-upon definition exists for intelligence, although most accept that it is a quality of the ability to acquire and use knowledge.

Theories of Intelligence

SCIENTIFIC VERSUS LAY DEFINITIONS

The meaning of intelligence is understood differently by psychologists and lay persons. Recent research shows that most laypersons think of intelligence as comprised of verbal ability, practical problem-solving ability, and social competence (e.g., being fair with others, having a social conscience).

In contrast, experts define intelligence as including verbal ability, problem-solving ability, and practical intelligence (e.g., being able to size up situations well)—but not the social competence that most laypersons apparently value.

SPEARMAN'S GENERAL FACTOR

At the beginning of the 20th century British psychologist Charles Spearman theorized that there is a general factor of intelligence, g, which functions as a source of energy for varied cognitive skills and performances. Many people also excel in particular areas of skill or talent, designated s. While s may be observed independently of a high level of *g*, *g* provides a richer foundation for *s* in people who have both kinds of ability.

THURSTONE'S PRIMARY MENTAL ABILITIES

The American psychologist L. L. Thurstone (1887-1955) relied on the findings of early intelligence testing to develop his idea of primary mental abilities. According to Thurstone, there are seven such abilities necessary for high-level test performance: spatial ability; perceptual speed; numerical ability; verbal meaning; memory; word fluency; and reasoning.

GUILFORD'S THREE-DIMENSIONAL MODEL

In 1967, J. P. Guilford presented a three-dimensional model of intellect. Guilford depicted his system as a cube-shaped structure, divisible into many smaller cubes. The three dimensions of this cube-shaped model represented three categories of intelligence test items: the content of an item (e.g., figures, meaning); the kind of operation the item required performing (e.g., evaluating, remembering); and the product resulting from applying a particular operation to that content (e.g., systems, transformations).

According to Guilford, there were four kinds of content, five possible operations, and six categories of products, yielding 120 identifiable intellectual abilities.

STERNBERG'S TRIARCHIC THEORY

In contrast with the early models of Thurstone and Guilford, recent work by Yale psychologist Robert Sternberg concludes that intelligence tests are not an appropriate source of information about the nature of intelligence. Sternberg's work has emphasized the importance of real-world problem-solving and reasoning, and encompasses a broader variety of skills than these earlier theories.

Sternberg's triarchic theory of intelligence describes three kinds of intelligence: componential, experiential, and contextual. Componential intelligence involves the ability to learn, acquire new knowledge, and use it effectively. Experiential intelligence is illustrated by adjusting well to new tasks, using new information, and responding effectively in new situations. Contextual intelligence involves wise selection of environments for one's efforts, adapting oneself or changing the scene as necessary. Contextually intelligent people enhance their strengths and overcome their weaknesses, and they work to achieve a good match between their skills and their settings.

In contrast with Spearman's original concept of one kind of intelligence, Sternberg argues that an individual exhibits several intelligences, which interact and are expressed in a variety of skills and abilities.

Intelligence Testing

The first intelligence test was designed by French psychologist Alfred Binet and his colleague Theodore Simon in 1905 as a means of placing schoolchildren in the appropriate grades in public school.

Since this first application to educational placement, intelligence testing has developed into a field and industry in its own right. Intelligence tests have varied in terms of their assumptions and applications.

INDIVIDUAL TESTS

Most intelligence tests were originally developed to be administered to one respondent at a time, or individually.

The Binet-Simon Scale. Binet and Simon's original test consisted of 30 subtests involving tasks that children of different ages should be able to perform. If a child could answer the questions that the average nine-year-old could answer, he or she was assigned a mental age (MA) of nine.

Each child's MA, as measured by the test, was compared with his or her actual chronological age (CA). When mental age exceeded chronological age (e.g., a seven-year-old with an MA of nine) the child was classified as bright, and assigned to a higher grade level. If CA exceeded MA, the child would be assigned to a lower grade level.

The Intelligence Quotient. German psychologist William Stern argued that a simple comparison between MA and CA—e.g., concluding that "MA> CA"—was insensitive to degrees of comparison.

Instead, Stern advocated using the ratio of MA to CA to measure intelligence. To eliminate decimal points, Stern's formula for this intelligence quotient (IQ) (since a quotient is the result of an arithmetic division) was: MA/CA x 100 = IQ. For example, a child with an MA of 9 and a CA of 6 has an IQ of 150, whereas one with an MA of 9 and a CA of 12 has an IQ of 75. When MA = CA, IQ = 100.

The Stanford-Binet Intelligence Scale. In 1916 (and several times since), Stanford University psychologist Lewis Terman (1877-1956) revised the original Binet-Simon scale of intelligence. Items that yielded little information were discarded, others were improved, and the resulting test, titled the Stanford-Binet Intelligence Scale, was restandardized on new populations of children.

The most recent version of the Stanford-Binet includes four designated areas, each with its own set of subtests: verbal reasoning; abstract value reasoning; quantitative reasoning; and short-term memory.

The Wechsler Tests. The individual intelligence test most often administered today is likely to be one developed by the late American psychologist David Wechsler.

Wechsler's scale consists of two subscales: a verbal scale, and a performance scale. The verbal scale includes questions and tasks involving information, arithmetic, and comprehension. The performance scale includes tests of picture arrangement, puzzle assembly, block design assembly, and identification of elements missing in pictures.

The Wechsler Adult Intelligence Scale-Revised (WAIS-R) is administered to individuals over age 16, while the Wechsler Intelligence Test for Children-Revised (WISC-R) is administered to school-age children.

GROUP TESTS

For the sake of expediency and time, many "intelligence" tests—often tests of achievement or of a particular skill like verbal ability—are designed to be administered in paper-and-pencil form to many individuals simultaneously. Best known among high-school and college students are the Scholastic Aptitude Test (SAT) and the American College Testing (ACT) program. Group tests are convenient and eliminate examiner bias. They are usually limited in the comprehensiveness of their results in comparison with individual tests.

ISSUES IN INTELLIGENCE TESTING

Heritability. Because intelligence, though not well-understood, is considered important in education and employment, the assumptions and uses of intelligence testing are often controversial. One issue concerns whether intelligence, as a human trait, is more a product of heredity or environment. The so-called heritability factor (inherited degree) of intelligence is of concern in determining the fair use of tests for educational and employment advancement.

Related to heritability is the question of the relation between race and intelligence. Research to date is inconclusive about the degree to which one's race or ethnicity "determines" one's possible intelligence.

Culture and Fairness. Regardless of whether intelligence is influenced by inherited traits or race, there is no doubt that culture influences what is considered to be intelligent, at least among laypersons.

One problem with traditional intelligence tests may be their reliance on verbal items and measures. If a test is written in English, a non-native speaker of English may be disadvantaged in that evaluation.

In response to the concern that intelligence tests be "culture-fair," psychologists have developed and used nonverbal measures of performance that are less affected by a particular language. Such culture-fair tests include the Progressive Matrices test, the Goodenough-Harris Drawing Test, and Cattell's Culture-Fair Intelligence Test.

Thinking is the most familiar form of cognition. Convergent thinking involves directing thought to a single solution, while divergent thinking begins with a challenge but may progress in any of several different directions. Daydreaming, an altered state of consciousness, is one form of divergent thinking. Creativity is another form of divergent thinking.

The essential components of thoughts are images and concepts. Concepts develop from concrete to abstract, and categorize items and experiences according to common features. Conjunctive concepts are easier to identify and learn than disjunctive concepts. Some items are good or typical examples of a concept; others are atypical and are harder to remember or categorize.

Reasoning can be either inductive or deductive. Analogical reasoning approaches new information by identifying its likeness to similar familiar information.

Problem-solving can sometimes occur quickly, as in the experience of insight, but more often employs strategies to reach a solution. The Gestalt approach to problem-solving emphasizes the value of perception, such as in reorganizing the elements of a problem, productive thinking, and reproductive thinking. The information-processing approach to problem-solving argues that the process is undertaken step-by-step in sequence, utilizing such strategies as algorithms or means-end analysis.

Decision-making involves choosing among alternatives. Heuristics or simple guidelines can simplify decision-making. Some decisions will be affected by the wording or conditions that frame the problem.

Intelligence refers to the ability to acquire and use information. Laypersons' definitions of intelligence differ from those of scientists. Psychologists vary in their definitions as well. Spearman conceptualized intelligence as a general factor, g, in contrast with specific skills and talents he labeled s.

With the advent of intelligence testing, the theories of Thurstone and Guilford defined intelligence in terms of test performance. Thurstone conceived of primary mental abilities, while Guilford proposed a three-dimensional model of intellectual abilities. More recently Sternberg's triarchic theory of intelligence argues that intelligence has practical, real-world manifestations as well as consequences for test-performance.

Intelligence testing began with educational placement tests developed by Binet and Simon. Their test was later revised by Terman as the Stanford-Binet scale. The concept of IQ was introduced as more sensitive to intelligence than a mere comparison of mental with chronological age. The tests developed by Wechsler include both performance and verbal subscales. Group tests are more expedient than individual tests but not as comprehensive or detailed.

Modern intelligence testing is evaluated in terms of its cultural fairness, as well as assumptions about the heritability of IQ.

Selected Readings

Anderson, J. R. *The Adaptive Character of Thought*. Hillsdale, NJ: Erlbaum. 1990

Best, J. B. *Cognitive Psychology*. St. Paul, MN: West Publishing. 1989

Bransford, J. D. and B. S. Stein. *The IDEAL Problem Solver: A Guide for Improved Thinking, Learning, and Creativity*. New York: Freeman. 1984

Gilhody, K. J. *Thinking*. London: Academic Press. 1988

Hunt, M. *The Universe Within: A New Science Explores the Human Mind.* New York: Simon and Schuster. 1982

John-Steiner, V. *Notebooks of the Mind: Explorations in Thinking.* Albuquerque, NM: University of New Mexico Press. 1985

Lewis, D. *Thinking Better.* New York: Holt, Rinehart and Winston. 1983

Mayer, R. E. *Thinking, Problem-Solving, and Cognition.* New York: Freeman. 1983

Nisbett, R. E. and L. Ross. *Human Inferences: Shortcomings of Social Judgement.* Englewood Cliffs, NJ: Prentice-Hall. 1980

9

Psychological Assessment: Personality and Intelligence Testing

Psychological assessment is a process designed to measure characteristics of individuals or groups. Assessment procedures involve gathering samples of responses or behaviors for description of present characteristics and/or prediction of future ones. The most common type of assessment is psychological testing; other techniques include observation, interview, and rating.

DEVELOPMENT OF PSYCHOLOGICAL TESTING

Psychological testing and assessment has its origins in an interest in individual differences, which led to the development of specific tests for educational placement and psychological characteristics.

Individual Differences

Sir Francis Galton (1822-1911) maintained a lifelong interest in individual differences in abilities. His convictions about the origins of individual differences were apparently influenced by ideas about physiognomy (see chapter 1).

Galton sought to identify key physical differences between "eminent" British citizens and their undistinguished, anonymous countrymen. He believed that the "eminence" of successful statesmen and scholars could be traced to such physical distinctions as head size, distance between the eyes, length of nose, and hand-grip strength.

Galton failed to take into account important differences in education and environment (nurture) as well as inherited physical traits (nature), and failed to confirm his hypothesis. Nonetheless his early efforts mark the beginning of psychology's continued interest in assessing individual differences.

Intelligence Testing

In 1905 the French educator Alfred Binet (1857-1911) was asked by the French government to devise a means of classifying students for entry into a new nation-wide public education system. Binet and his colleague Theophile Simon (1873-1961) developed a test of age-graded items—questions to answer, problems to solve—for students to respond to, rather than measuring their head size or visual acuity. This was the forerunner of what we now call the intelligence test.

In 1916 Lewis Terman (1877-1956), on the faculty of Stanford University, revised the original Binet-Simon test, dubbing the new version the Stanford-Binet. The Stanford-Binet test score was expressed as an Intelligence Quotient (I.Q.). The I.Q. is calculated by dividing the respondent's mental age by his or her chronological age, then multiplying by 100 (to get an integer): $IQ = MA/CA \times 100$ (see also chapter 9).

Both the Binet-Simon and the Stanford-Binet tests were designed to be administered to one respondent at a time. After the outbreak of World War I, however, there emerged a need for a system for testing large numbers of military inductees to make appropriate leadership and task assignments. One psychologist, James McKeen Cattell (1860-1944), involved himself in this effort despite his personal opposition to America's entry into the war. Cattell had been Wilhelm Wundt's first laboratory assistant at Leipzig. In his career he pursued psychometric studies (measurement of psychological characteristics) as well as founding and editing several influential journals, including *Psychological Review*. The standardized tests so familiar to American college students are a modern legacy of the work of Cattell and other early assessment developers.

Personality Assessment

One of the most well-known psychological assessment techniques is the inkblot test. Swiss psychiatrist Hermann Rorschach (1884-1922) first employed subjects' interpretations of inkblot shapes as keys to dimensions of personality. In 1935 American psychologist Henry A. Murray (1893-1988) and his colleagues developed the Thematic Apperception Test (TAT), a technique in which a subject examines and tells stories about each of a series of pictures. Both the Rorschach and the TAT are termed projective techniques because the subject is assumed to project his or her own needs and character onto an ambiguous test stimulus—one which can be interpreted in different ways—in developing a story or description.

The best known objective technique for assessing personality is the Minnesota Multiphasic Personality Inventory (MMPI), developed by two University of Minnesota faculty members in 1943. The MMPI consists of 550 true-false items, whose reponse pattern reveals the respondent's scores on various personality traits first diagnosed among a large clinical population, a group of patients in a setting like a clinic or psychiatric hospital.

The Sixteen Personality Factor Inventory (16PF), a personality inventory standardized on a normal population, was developed in 1950 by Raymond B. Cattell (b. 1905) and his colleagues, who conducted a sophisticated mathematical analysis of many personality traits into a profile of sixteen basic personality "factors."

CHARACTERISTICS OF GOOD TESTS

To be useful, a psychological assessment should have the same properties as a physical measurement: reliability, validity, and objectivity. Tests provide a good illustration of these principles.

A reliable test produces a similar value or score each time a person takes it (unless the person has changed in some way between testings). A valid test measures what it is designed to measure. An objective test is unaffected by the attitudes or biases of the person giving the test.

Psychological tests also should be standardized by administering them to large, representative samples of people. The scores generated by the standardization group can be used to determine norms, patterns of responses characteristic of different types of people.

Reliability

A synonym for reliability is "consistency". A reliable test gives consistent results each time a person takes it, unless the person has changed in some way between administrations. Such consistency in the absence of change is necessary for the test to detect real change when it occurs.

Three forms of reliability are test-retest reliability, alternate form reliability, and internal consistency.

TEST-RETEST RELIABILITY

After a test is developed, it is given to the same group of people repeatedly over a period of months. Results are used to identify parts of the test needing revision. The process is repeated until the test produces a reasonable level of consistency across testing occasions. This consistency across testing sessions constitutes test-retest reliability. A similar process is used with other types of assessments, such as observations, interviews, and projective measures. Assessments made by several "raters" are compared to identify parts of the assessment associated with inconsistent results.

ALTERNATE FORM RELIABILITY

Whenever more than one form of a test is developed, data must be collected to ensure that test takers would earn relatively similar scores on either form. Alternate-form reliability, then, is a measure of the equivalency between forms.

INTERNAL CONSISTENCY

On the other hand, internal consistency is a measure of reliability within a test. Internal consistency analyses determine if test takers receive similar scores on different items designed to tap the same knowledge, ability, or skill.

Validity

A synonym for validity is "accuracy." A valid test measures what it was intended to measure.

CONSTRUCT VALIDITY

Some tests are designed to measure constructs, characteristics such as intelligence that cannot be defined objectively. Construct validity is determined by comparing scores on the test with performance on other well-researched measures of the same construct.

CRITERION VALIDITY

Tests also can be designed to predict performance on another measure called a criterion. College entrance exams provide an example of this criterion-validity procedure. To determine if SATs are a valid predictor of success in college, SAT scores from a group of entering students would be compared to their later college GPAs to determine if the scores predict college success.

Standardization and Norms

When tests are standardized, individual test results can be compared to the test performance of specific types of people in the standardization group. Norms are patterns of test scores characteristic of particular ages, grades in school, genders, occupations, or psychiatric classifications. Tests designed to compare individual performance to the performance of others in a group are called norm-referenced tests.

TYPES OF TESTS

Tests can be grouped into several broad categories. Personality tests measure personal qualities, sometimes referred to as traits. Achievement tests measure what a person has learned. Aptitude tests are designed to predict future behavior, such as success in school or job performance. Intelligence tests measure verbal and/or nonverbal skills related to academic success. Interest inventories are used to help individuals make effective career choices.

Personality Tests

Personality tests are either objective or projective.

OBJECTIVE TESTS

Objective tests present specific questions or statements that are answered by selecting one of a set of alternatives (e.g. true or false). Objective tests traditionally use a "paper-and-pencil" format which is simple to score reliably. Although many objective tests ask general questions about preferences and behaviors, situational tests solicit responses to specific scenarios.

The MMPI. The Minnesota Multiphasic Personality Inventory (MMPI) is the leading objective personality test. Its hundreds of true-false items cover a broad range of behaviors. A major advantage of the MMPI is the incorporation of validity scales designed to detect possible response bias, such as trying to present oneself in a socially desirable way.

PROJECTIVE TECHNIQUES

Projective personality tests use ambiguous stimuli into which the test taker presumably projects meaning. This indirect type of assessment is believed by many to more effectively identify a person's real or underlying personality.

Scoring Projective Techniques. Because the test taker is free to respond in any way, rather than being required to select an answer from a set of alternatives, projective tests can be difficult to score.

To ensure reliability, projective tests must be accompanied by a specific set of scoring criteria. Projective tests are more reliable and valid when scoring focuses on the way the questions are answered (structure of responses) rather than the content of the answers.

Two leading projective tests are the Rorschach and the Thematic Apperception Test (TAT).

The Rorschach Test. In the Rorschach, individuals are asked to describe in detail their impressions of a series of inkblots. Scoring involves analysis of both the structure and content of responses.

The Thematic Apperception Test (TAT). In the TAT, individuals construct stories to describe a series of pictures. TAT analysis traditionally focuses on the role played by the main character in each story.

Aptitude and Achievement Tests

Aptitude and achievement tests are used most often in educational and occupational decisions. These two types of tests differ in purpose and theoretically, therefore, in focus.

Achievement tests are designed to assess current level of performance; aptitude tests are designed to predict future performance. Practically, however, the prediction of future performance often involves some attention to current level of performance. For this reason, achievement tests can be misinterpreted as measures of aptitude. Such use of achievement tests can be potentially discriminatory toward those individuals who have had less opportunity to achieve in the area tested.

Intelligence Tests

Intelligence tests measure verbal and/or performance (nonverbal) skills. These tests are designed to measure a person's potential or aptitude for intellectual performance. A long-term goal of intelligence testing is the development of a culture-free test that is valid regardless of cultural background. Two examples of popular intelligence tests are the Stanford-Binet Test for children and the Wechsler Adult Intelligence Scale (WAIS).

THE STANFORD-BINET

Traditionally, the Stanford-Binet contained age-graded items in a variety of skill areas. Items were coded according to the average age at which children succeed on those items.

A child taking the Stanford-Binet would be classified according to age level achieved (mental age or MA). The child's mental age was compared to the child's chronological age (CA) to produce an intelligence quotient or IQ, using the formula: $IQ = MA/CA \times 100$. This procedure set the IQ score of the average child at 100.

Recent revisions of the Stanford-Binet have abandoned this ratio scoring procedure in favor of a point scale similar to that used in Wechsler tests (see WAIS below). The average IQ, however, remains at 100.

THE WAIS

The WAIS uses 11 subtests—6 verbal and 5 performance (nonverbal) to generate 3 IQ scores: a verbal IQ (VIQ), a performance IQ (PIQ), and a full-scale IQ (FSIQ) representing overall level of performance. The WAIS, and Wechsler tests developed for other age groups, use a point scale where points are earned for each correct answer. Standardization of Wechsler tests determines the scale for converting raw score (points earned) to an IQ score. The average IQ arbitrarily is set at 100.

ISSUES IN INTELLIGENCE TESTING

Years of study indicates that IQ is not necessarily constant over the life span. Although infant intelligence tests are available, IQ scores do not begin to distinguish between those likely to be high or low ability until about age 5. Intelligence test score is reasonably stable from age 12 to adulthood, but wide fluctuations in test scores are still possible.

Although IQ tests were designed to predict success in school, school achievement is greatly influenced by other factors such as interest, motivation, family support, and the quality of instruction. Even greater care must be exercised when using IQ score to predict other outcomes, such as occupational success. Occupational success reflects the additional influences of personality and specialized talents. Nevertheless, people in professional or managerial careers traditionally have a higher average IQ than people in unskilled jobs.

Intelligence tests were conceptualized as a pure measure of intellectual potential, free from the influence of wealth or privilege. Some critics argue that test performance in fact is greatly influenced by type of upbringing, social background, and education. There is continuing debate over whether these tests measure inherited ability, which is genetically determined, or learning, which incorporates the effects of experience. Although there is research to support both points of view, critics contend that intelligence tests have become instruments for discriminating against lower social class or minority group children.

Interest Tests

Interest tests are used in vocational counseling to assist people with the process of career choice. Individual responses are compared to those of successful members of different occupational groups. Interests typically are stable enough by the end of high school to permit reliable measurement and valid prediction. Two major interest inventories are the Strong Vocational Interest Inventory and the Kuder Preference Record.

Psychological assessment measures characteristics of individuals or groups. The historical development of psychological assessment began with an interest in individual differences, and continued with applications in educational placement and identifying personality characteristics.

Good assessment techniques should be reliable, valid, objective, and standardized. Reliable tests yield consistent results across time, sessions, and conditions. Valid tests measure what they are supposed to measure. Objective techniques are free from bias or influence. To apply tests properly, it is important to know the group or groups who provided the original norms by which the tests were standardized.

Different types of tests have been developed to measure different qualities and abilities. Personality tests can be objective like inventories or subjective like projective techniques. They seek to identify stable personality patterns in responses. Achievement tests assess current performance levels, while aptitude tests seek to predict future performance. Intelligence tests measure both verbal and nonverbal skills. Interest tests are used in vocational counseling to assist with career development and choices.

Intelligence tests have been developed during several decades of research and application. Several forms are widely used today. The Stanford-Binet, for example, is used to identify a child's IQ. The WAIS uses several subtests to determine a raw score that can be converted to an IQ scale. Current issues in intelligence testing include gauging appropriate age ranges for testing, distinguishing between school and non-school achievement, and eliminating bias in test construction and administration.

Selected Readings

Anastasi, A. *Psychological Testing, 5th Edition*. New York: Macmillan. 1982

Day, J. D. and J. G. Borkowski,. *Intelligence and Exceptionality: New Directions for Theory, Assessment, and Instructional Practices*. Norwood, NJ: Ablex. 1987

Gould, S. J. *The Mismeasure of Man*. New York: W. W. Norton. 1981

Jensen, A. R. *Bias in Mental Testing*. New York: Free Press. 1980

Kail, R. and J. W. Pellegrino. *Human Intelligence: Perspectives and Prospects*. New York: Freeman. 1985

Kline, P. *Personality Measurement and Theory*. New York: St. Martin's Press. 1983

Linn, R. L. *Intelligence: Measurement, Theory and Public Policy*. Urbana, IL: University of Illinois Press. 1989

Lyman, H. B. *Test Scores and What They Mean, 4th Edition*. Englewood Cliffs, NJ: Prentice-Hall. 1986

Sattler, J. M. *Assessment of Children, 3rd Edition*. San Diego, CA: Jerome M. Sattler. 1988

10

Motivation and Emotion

A central question for both professional and amateur psychologists concerns why people behave as they do. An interest in this question has led to research and theory about motivation, the process of energizing and directing goal-oriented behavior.

A related interest in less observable processes has developed work on emotion, the subjective experience of motivation, and the feeling that accompanies motivation.

Both motivation and emotion are constructs, processes which cannot be directly observed or studied but whose antecedent conditions (causes) and consequences (outcome behaviors) can be so researched. Many other topics—such as learning, cognitive processes, and perception—are also constructs in the sense that they cannot be directly studied, but they can be inferred to occur as processes between the factors that cause them and the behaviors they bring about.

MOTIVATION

Motivation is a process that both energizes and directs goal-oriented behavior. A number of theories have been developed since the early years of scientific psychology to explain how behavior is both energized and directed.

Theories of Motivation

Theories of motivation have been developed and modified to reflect prevailing assumptions about human nature and the effects of the environment on behavior.

INSTINCT THEORY

The influence of dualism on early psychology provided a temptingly simple answer to the question of why people behave as they do. Because dualist views of human nature supported the idea of free will, the dualist "theory" of motivation succintly asserted that people choose their courses of action.

This view presented problems for scientific psychologists, especially as research identified indisputable environmental influences on behavior. Given the mechanistic influences on early psychology, a more appealing theory of motivation explained human behavior as being, like animal behavior, governed by instincts. Instincts are innate, goal-directed sequences of behavior; they are more complex than simple reflexes but are impervious to the influence of learning and experience.

The concept of instinct enjoyed great popularity and support in the late 19th century. Two very different instinct theories of motivation were developed by the psychoanalyst Sigmund Freud and the functionalist William James.

Sigmund Freud. Freud's view of instincts was very broad, almost on the order of the later concept of a drive (see below). In Freud's view, human behavior was motivated by two biologically energized instincts, respectively termed Eros, the life instinct, and Thanatos, the death instinct. The life instinct was considered to be the basis for sexual motivation, while the death instinct underlay aggressive motivation.

For Freud, these instincts and most of their subsequent motivations remained a part of each individual's unconscious. In contrast, most other theories of motivation emphasize explanations for conscious motivation.

William James. In line with his functionalist perspective, James emphasized the survival value of instinctive motivation. He argued that humans were born with a score of instincts—such as fear, sociability, cleanliness, and love—which underlay all more complex behavior.

Critics assailed instinct theories of motivation for merely labeling yet failing to explain behavior. Moreover, instincts were not observable and could not be subjected to empirical testing or behaviorist evaluation.

DRIVE THEORY

By the 1920s psychological research reflected the values of behaviorism, and instinct theories of motivation were abandoned in favor of the construct of drive.

A drive is a motivational force that energizes goal-directed behavior. The concept of force is more general than the specific sequence of behaviors involved in instinct. A drive is hypothesized to motivate not a single specific behavior but an entire class of behaviors, all connected to the same basic need. Thus one's hunger drive could account for eating many different things in varied circumstances, as well as accounting for related non-eating behavior, such as restlessness before mealtimes.

A need is a physiological requirement of an organism, for a resource, for example, or for balance among bodily processes. The experience of a need was hypothesized to be unpleasant. The drive produced by this need would act as a signal for behavior to gratify the need. Thus drive theory explains behavior in terms of a motivation for drive-reduction. An animal that needs food will experience the hunger drive, and this will motivate eating behavior until the drive is reduced.

HULL'S THEORY OF MOTIVATION

Learning theorist Clark Hull incorporated this need-produced concept of drive into an equation for motivated behavior. In Hull's equation, the probability of a given behavior is a function of three factors: (1) the drive the organism experiences as a result of a need state; (2) the incentive, the value of the external stimulus that will reduce the need state; and (3) habit strength, the organism's practice or past experience with, or ability to perform, the behavior.

Hull's equation can be summarized as $B = D \times I \times H$, where B refers to the behavior, D to the drive state, I to the size of the incentive, and H to habit strength.

The stronger these three factors are, the greater will be the likelihood that the organism will perform the behavior in question. Alternatively, if any of these factors drops near zero in strength, so will the likelihood of the given behavior.

The Neobehaviorist Perspective. Hull's view of motivation is considered neobehaviorist rather than strictly behaviorist, because it relies on the operation of intervening variables like drive, incentive, and habit strength, instead of observable conditions and responses. Each intervening variable is assumed to be determined by an observable antecedent condition (a stimulus or influence). Likewise, the result of the interaction of the intervening variables is assumed to be an observable, measurable aspect of behavior.

MASLOW'S HIERARCHY OF MOTIVES

Humanistic psychologist Abraham Maslow (1908-1970) had orginally been enthusiastic about behaviorism, but he became disillusioned with its limited view of human aspirations. His conception of human motivation exceeded a purely biological or survival-oriented view. For Maslow, while biological motives were clearly essential to survival, other motives were just as essential to ultimate human development and productivity. He ranked human motives in a hierarchy of motives, an ordering of needs that must be satisfied in human behavior.

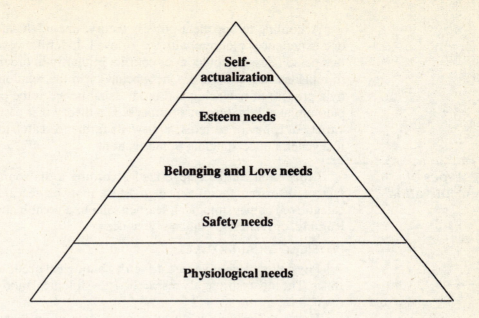

Fig. 10.1 Maslow's Hierarchy of Needs

As depicted in Figure 10-1, this hierarchy of motives is usually arranged as a pyramid, with the most basic physiological needs, such as hunger and thirst, at the bottom.

After these are satisfied, safety needs take precedence, including physical security and freedom from pain and fear.

Next in importance are belongingness needs, needs to be accepted and loved by others, and to have a place or territory of one's own.

Beyond these are the esteem needs, including both the esteem (appreciation) of others and self-esteem.

At the top of the pyramid Maslow placed need for self- actualization, the motivation to live up to (actualize) one's potential to be fully human.

OPPONENT-PROCESS THEORY

Most modern researchers believe that motivation is too complex to be explained by a single theory. Therefore, much motivation research focuses on individual motives, such as hunger, achievement motivation, and curiosity. Opponent-process theory is one modern theory of motivation that embraces a broad view of motivation but is more modest than traditional single-concept theories. Theorist Richard Solomon argues that many acquired motives (learned motives) arise from the interplay of two opposing processes in the brain.

According to opponent-process theory, one might fall in love because one experiences pleasure with the beloved. Later, however, one stays with that person despite boredom or conflict primarily in order to avoid the pain of breakup and loneliness. One's behavior in the relationship is motivated by a process of balancing and progressing between the opponent forces of pleasure and pain. Opponent-process is a theory that promises to explain a variety of behavior patterns, and awaits further research to confirm its value to a general understanding of motivation.

Types of Motivation

Motivation can be categorized according to its sources as well as the factors theorized to influence it. Most motives researched can be thus categorized as physiological, learned, due to a combination of biology and learning, or related to human effectance.

PHYSIOLOGICAL MOTIVES

Physiological motives are driven by biological needs and internal bodily states. The most thoroughly researched physiological motives are hunger and thirst.

Hunger. Early research on hunger focused on localizing (identifying physical origins for) the sensations and energy that drive eating behavior. Classic research by Walter B. Cannon (1871-1945) initially concluded, erroneously, that the stomach contractions that accompany hunger pangs are themselves the physical stimulus for eating behavior.

Later research rejected this simplistic localization in favor of a more physiological explanation. Hunger is generally cyclical, corresponding to the rhythms of homeostasis, the bodily balance essential to healthy function. When nutrients are needed to fuel the body, the individual feels hungry; when one is well-nourished, one feels sated and disinclined to eat further.

Brain research has identified the "location" of the body's hunger signals as cells within the hypothalamus, a part of the limbic system that is integrally involved in motivation and emotion.

Cells in the lateral hypothalamus (LH) (the sides of the structure) appear to function as a "start" center, sending signals to "eat" when the concentration of glucose, a simple sugar, in the bloodstream is low. Conversely, cells in the ventromedial hypothalamus (VMH) (a front, central region of the structure) function as a "stop" center, indicating satiety, a level of adequate glucose concentration.

Together, the LH and VMH comprise a lipostat, a brain center that measures the nutrient level of the bloodstream and regulates eating behavior to maintain that ideal balance, or setpoint.

Some research suggests that individuals with eating disorders may be suffering the effects of an altered setpoint, feeling hungry when they are physically sated (obesity), or feeling sated when they are physically starving (anorexia).

Research comparing obese with normal weight individuals indicates that eating behavior is influenced by *external factors* as well as by hunger (an internal state).

Obese individuals (whose body weight is 20% above ideal body weight for their height and build) are more influenced than normal-weight individuals by the smell, taste, and texture of food. Their eating behavior is also more influenced by time (e.g., whether it appears to be mealtime) and sensory access to food (e.g., seeing a bag of snack food close at hand) than is that of normal-weight individuals.

Across weight levels, people's eating behavior is strongly influenced by social factors, including cultural preferences and aversions to certain foods, norms for which foods are served for specific mealtimes, and the role of food in accompanying social activities. For humans, eating is a complex behavior, strongly but not exclusively influenced by internal signals of hunger.

Thirst. Like eating, drinking is a behavior strongly but not exclusively influenced by a physiological drive, in this case the thirst drive.

Early attempts to localize thirst as triggered by dryness in the mouth and throat were abandoned in favor of a physiological explanation. Thirst is regulated by two *bodily fluid balances*: the fluid within the body's cells, and the fluid between the body's cells.

In the first case, high intracellular (within-cell) sodium levels dehydrate cells, causing stimulation of receptor cells in the hypothalamus. This "drink" center activates the thirst drive and we engage in drinking behavior. At present it is unclear whether and where there is a "stop drinking" counterpart in the body to signal that fluid levels have been restored.

A second thirst regulator, sensitive to the functioning of the kidneys, appears to monitor extracellular (between-cell) fluid levels. This regulator interacts with the first one to produce the internal signal of thirst.

Like eating, drinking behavior is strongly influenced by learned, individual, and cultural factors. *Social factors*—including peer pressure and advertising—can affect drinking behavior, especially for fluids other than water (the only fluid that "quenches" thirst). *Environmental cues* also affect what we drink and when, as iced tea may sound refreshing in the summer, while hot chocolate is the beverage of choice for winter weather.

LEARNED MOTIVES

Many behaviors can be explained in terms of learned motives, motives acquired through classical or operant conditioning. In particular these appear to be social motives, motives for behavior that concerns relationships with others.

The learned motives include aggression, affiliation, and motives for achievement and power.

Aggression. Aggression is any behavior intended to harm another. Instrumental aggression uses harm to achieve another goal (e.g., attacking another to obtain food), while hostile aggression intends harm as its sole purpose.

Freud argued that aggressive behavior is the motive expressed by the unconscious *death instinct*. According to psychoanalytic theory, human nature is inherently aggressive, but aggressive impulses can be relieved through catharsis, a vicarious release of emotion, such as watching a violent film or fantasizing about harming an enemy. Research, however, has failed to support the contention that watching aggressive stimuli reduces rather than enhances aggressive behaviors.

Another instinct theory of aggression has been proposed by ethologists like Konrad Lorenz who argue that aggression in nonhuman species is usually tied to territorial protection and survival.

A more recent theory of aggression posits its cause as frustration, failure of one's efforts to reach a goal. According to *frustration-aggression* theory, frustration always results in the impulse to aggress, and aggression can always be traced to the experience of frustration.

If the target of intended aggression is unavailable or retaliatory, one may displace aggression by harming an object or person other than the original target.

In a revision of the original theory, frustration is theorized to lead not directly to aggression but to anger, a readiness to behave aggressively. Anger in turn may give way to aggressive behavior if triggered by such social and environmental influences as attack, pain, and extreme heat.

Undoubtedly much aggressive behavior is *learned*, through both direct and indirect reinforcements (operant conditioning) and through the lessons of modeling (observational learning), such as when a child who has wrongly hit another child (an aggressive behavior) is spanked by an adult (another aggressive behavior).

Affiliation. Both humans and nonhumans often exhibit a preference to affiliate, or be physically close to others of their own species. Classic research by Stanley Schachter in 1959 studied whether affiliation is a response to fear. Schachter led some young women to believe that, as part of a psychology experiment, they would experience intense pain, while others were told the experience would involve no pain. When asked where they would prefer to wait while the experiment was set up, those who expected pain expressed a strong preference to wait with other women. Those who expected no pain expressed no such affiliative preference.

One explanation for this "misery loves company" effect is that affiliation gives us the opportunity for social comparison, an evaluation of how our own beliefs and behaviors compare to those of others. The less sure we are of the validity of our own thoughts and actions, the more we rely on and are reassured by our similarity to others.

Achievement Motivation. One factor in an individual's success is that person's need to achieve, a need to excel and overcome obstacles. Such achievement motivation is theorized to function independently of any desire for reward or response to incentives.

Some individuals interpreting stimuli in the Thematic Apperception Test (TAT) tell stories that are significantly higher in success and achievement imagery than those of others. These individuals have been found to behave in achievement-oriented ways when presented with tasks and problems. Achievement-motivated behavior is characterized by ambitious but realistic goal-setting. It has been linked to child-rearing practices that emphasize encouragement and independence.

Another factor in success may be an individual's *need for power*, the need for recognition by or influence over others. Measurements of the need for power have been related to a variety of behaviors, from American presidents' effectiveness to patterns of control and abuse in personal relationships.

EFFECTANCE MOTIVES

Many behaviors appear early enough in human development to seem inborn, and yet they seem more varied in expression and direction than physiological motives. Among these are behaviors motivated by activity, exploration and curiosity, and manipulation. Some researchers have termed these effectance motives because they comprise an individual's abilities to function within and have an effect on his or her environment.

Activity. Contrary to the predictions of drive-reduction theories of motivation, both humans and animals appear more likely to seek and display activity than an inert, nonstimulated, or satisfied state. Research indicates that general activity levels may be higher when specific drives increase. For example, a hungry caged rat runs more and faster in a treadmill as a regularly schedule mealtime approaches. This suggests that general activity may be energized by the arousal of specific drives.

Exploration and Curiosity. There may be a motivational "need to know," stimulated especially by uncertainty and mystery. Animals will learn when reinforced only by opportunities to explore the environment. Humans rate scenic views as more aesthetically pleasing when they include "mystery," whether a partially obscured view or a disappearing pathway. Gestalt principles of perception (see chapter 5) also suggest that humans value meaning, closure, and understanding, and that we may undertake behaviors in search of these qualities.

Manipulation. There is some evidence that people have stimulus needs, needs for sensory stimulation, as well as needs aimed at reducing sensations like hunger and thirst. One such stimulus need is evident in manipulation, touching and grasping behavior, which is observed only in primates like humans and apes.

COMBINATION MOTIVES

Research on nonhumans concludes that much of their behavior is explained by either physiological or learned motives. Human behaviors are more complex and less clearly categorized. Combined motives are explanations for human behavior that involve both physiological and acquired influences. Two of these are sex and contact needs.

Sex. In animals sexual behavior is demonstrably influenced by physiological factors like hormones and bodily rhythms (e.g., the estrous cycle of females preparatory to mating). For nonhumans sex could be considered a physiological drive.

For humans however sex does not function as a clearly physiological drive. While survival of the species depends on sexual behavior and reproduction, survival of the individual does not. Human sexual behavior is motivated by learned and individual as well as physiological factors.

In both males and females *testosterone* is the hormone that influences sexual behavior. It does not appear to "drive" sexual behavior, however, although testosterone levels are correlated with such activity.

Many animals have been found to secrete *pheromones*, scented glandular substances that may externally influence sexual response in the opposite sex. Although some research supports similar effects among humans, the role of such substances is yet unclear.

The number and nature of stimuli that can activate human sexual behavior is almost infinite. Although *cultural norms* exist for sensory impressions that are considered erotic (sexually arousing), no specific formulas have been identified as having aphrodisiac effects.

Gender differences have been identified. Men respond more than women to visual stimuli. Women are aroused by similar stimuli at a slower rate than men. Women are influenced more by the mood and setting of material, while men favor close-ups of sexual acts. Gender differences in sexual behavior, like other gender differences, may be fewer than similarities. They are likewise explained better by a combination of biology and cultural influences than by either set of factors alone.

Contact. Among many nonhuman species, young animals *imprint* onto older animals, usually their mothers, a process of restricting their social behaviors to the imprinted object. A newly hatched chick will follow and try to cuddle with the imprinted object, whether or not it is a hen, and will show distressed behavior when prevented from making such contact. Interrupted imprinting may result in some social confusion when the animal is older.

Primates, including humans, are dependent on parental care when young, but they develop more complex, learned behavior *attachment* than the imprinting of simpler species. Classic research with infant monkeys has indicated the need for physical contact in healthy development. Given the choice between a wire- mesh milk dispenser and a soft, cuddly "mother" who did not dispense milk, baby monkeys chose to spend all their non-nursing time clinging to the comfortable surface.

Being deprived of physical contact has been associated in both humans and primates with illness, poor development, and failure to attach. Contact and physical access appear to be important in attachment to significant others in infancy, and perhaps throughout life.

EMOTION

Emotion is, like motivation, a construct, a process that is hypothesized to explain unseen connections between observable stimuli and responses. Emotions are subjective experiences, feelings that accompany motivational states. Several theories have sought to explain emotional processes, development, and expression.

Theories of Emotion

YERKES-DODSON LAW

Arousal. One approach to emotion emphasizes the role of arousal and its effects on behavior. The Yerkes-Dodson Law, named for its developers, explains that every task involves an optimal level of arousal. When arousal is too low or too high for a particular task, performance suffers. In general, an increase in one's arousal leads to improved performance on simple tasks but reduced performance on complex tasks.

The Yerkes-Dodson law suggests that the effects of emotional arousal will vary with the nature of the task and performance in question. This explains why mild fear, such as of an approaching deadline, might arouse one individual to do a better job than otherwise on a familiar (simple) assignment, while causing another to work more slowly and make more mistakes on a novel and ill-prepared (complex) task.

Lie Detection. The relationship of general arousal to emotion is central to assumptions about the usefulness of polygraphy, the general term for measurements such as so-called lie detection. Subjects in such tests respond to verbal questions while ongoing measurements are made of various physiological arousal effects, such as heart rate, blood pressure, and sweat gland activity (hence the term polygraph from *poly*, "many," and graph "written record"). The assumption of polography is that lying requires effort and causes measurable arousal.

Polygraphy is more a business than a science, and while many employers rely on lie detectors for tests of workers' honesty, there is no consistent scientific evidence to support its use for such purposes.

JAMES-LANGE THEORY

In the late 19th century, William James formulated a theory of emotion similar to that proposed about the same time by Danish psychologist Carl Lange. The so-called James-Lange theory of emotion proposes that emotions are experienced in the following sequence: (1) an emotional stimulus is presented, causing one to experience (2) physiological reactions, which are (3) consciously experienced as an emotion.

For example, when one encounters a growling wild animal (emotional stimulus), one feels a faster heartbeat, widening eyes, and a physical urge to flee (physiological reactions). As one becomes aware of these changes, one experiences the feeling of fear (emotion).

CANNON-BARD THEORY

Walter Cannon and Philip Bard disputed the James-Lange theory, arguing that the brain plays a more important role in producing emotion than simply experiencing it.

The Cannon-Bard theory of emotion asserted that an emotional stimulus simultaneously triggered both the bodily changes and the conscious awareness of the emotion being experienced.

To use the above example, according to the Cannon-Bard theory, an encounter with a snarling wild animal (emotional stimulus) would simultaneously lead one to feel the heart pounding and muscular tension (bodily changes) and to realize that one was experiencing fear (emotion).

SCHACHTER-SINGER THEORY

In 1962 Stanley Schachter and Jerome Singer conducted classic research identifying a cognitive process in emotional response. In their experiment, subjects received injections of either epinephrine, an arousing drug, or an inert saline solution. Subjects were then taken to a room where a confederate acted either extremely angry or euphoric. Subjects were observed and later asked to describe their emotional state. Results indicated that subjects who were aroused by the drug but unaware of its effects were most likely to adopt the emotional label of their angry or euphoric companions, and to behave likewise.

Schachter and Singer concluded that emotional experience requires two factors: (1) a state of physiological arousal, and (2) a cognitive interpretation or labeling of that state as an emotion. Arousal without a label is not an emotion; a label without arousal does not lead to emotional behavior.

Despite some problems with Schachter and Singer's cognitive theory of emotion, it is an influential approach in both research and application.

Types of Emotion

According to Robert Plutchik, humans and animals experience eight basic categories of emotions that motivate adaptive behavior: fear, surprise, sadness, disgust, anger, anticipation, joy, and acceptance. These are arranged in order in a circle, with adjacent emotions (e.g., fear and surprise) being functionally alike and opposing emotions (e.g., fear and anger) being functionally opposite.

In addition, emotions can combine to produce new hybrid emotions (e.g., joy + acceptance = love, surprise + sadness = disappointment).

In Plutchik's model, emotions can vary in intensity as well. For example, the most intense form of anger is rage, and the least intense form of anger is annoyance.

Plutchik's model has been applied to observations of emotional development in young children in determining the functions and effectiveness of different types of emotions.

Emotional Expression

Because emotion is a construct, it is not directly observable. In conducting research on emotion, psychologists usually observe and make inferences about expressions of emotion.

Although the study of verbal expression of emotion—saying what one is feeling—is most direct, it is also subject to the bias and distortion of self-report. For this reason researchers are more likely to study nonverbal expressions of emotion.

FACIAL EXPRESSIONS

Universal Expressions. Evolutionary theorist Charles Darwin originally proposed that facial expressions of emotion have specific survival value and are part of our biological heritage. This would explain such phenomena as the universality of a smile as a facial sign of happiness.

Modern research by Carroll Izard suggests that this evolutionary history of emotion can be read in the distinctive (and not-yet- learned) facial expressions of infants.

Cross-cultural research by Paul Ekman and colleagues has indicated that, while cultures vary in many norms for facial expressions of emotion, six emotions are universally recognizable: happiness, sadness, fear, anger, disgust, and surprise.

Individual Differences. There is considerable individual variation in facial affect or the facial expression of emotion. In one study by Ross Buck, subjects who acted as "senders" examined emotionally arousing visual stimuli, pictures of scenes and events that aroused various emotions. While they viewed these stimuli, a video camera focused on each sender's face transmitted the face alone to another room where a subject acting as a "receiver" watched.

Results indicated gender differences in both sending and receiving: the emotions of female senders were more accurately identified by receivers, and female receivers more accurately identified senders' emotions.

In addition, senders who were hard to "read" (i.e., whose faces showed little emotional expression) were found to experience higher measurable levels of physiological arousal than senders whose faces were expressive and easy to "read." In other words, poker-faced people seemed to be "internalizing" their emotional experiences, while expressive-faced "externalizers" showed less internal arousal. This finding has led to speculation that facial expressions are causally related to physiological arousal.

NONVERBAL COMMUNICATION

Beginning with therapists' observations that clients indicated effect and resistance with body language, psychologists in recent years have studied various forms of nonverbal communication.

In addition to facial affect, research has focused on patterns in tone of voice, eye contact, gesture, body position and posture. These channels of nonverbal communication indicate such factors as immediacy (the tendency or wish to be physically close to others) and status (social rank).

Open body positions—with arms uncrossed and upper body relaxed— are associated with positive affect and acceptance, while closed body positions—crossed arms and legs, upright posture—are associated with negative affect and rejection.

Interpersonal distancing is also employed as a form of nonverbal communication to indicate intimacy and reciprocation in interactions and relationships.

Motivation energizes and directs goal-oriented behavior. Early theories of motivation utilized the concept of instinct as the explanation for much of human behavior. Later, drive theories argued that physiological needs give rise to drives, general forces that motivate behavior. Hull's theory of motivation posited behavior as a function of drive, habit strength, and incentive. Maslow's humanistic approach supported a hierarchy of motives, with certain levels of need being more basic than others in driving human action. Finally, opponent-process theory describes motivation as a tension between opposing forces, such as pleasure and pain, in driving behavior.

Most theories of motivation categorize different types of individual motives, including physiological, learned, effectance, and combination motives.

Physiological motives include hunger and thirst. Early attempts to localize hunger in stomach sensations were abandoned, and later research identified the hypothalamus as the site of hunger motivation and the regulation of eating behavior. Eating is also influenced by external factors like cultural norms and sensory impressions.

Thirst has also been traced to hypothalamic function, where signals of intracellular dehydration prompt drinking behavior. Kidney function also affects the sensation of thirst from extracellular dehydration. As is true of eating, drinking behavior is affected by external forces as well, including social factors such as advertising and pressures to conform.

Learned motives are acquired through classical and operant conditioning. Early instinct theories proposed that aggression is an innate human tendency, an expression of a Freudian death instinct, or an adaptive mechanism of survival. Later theories argued that aggression is a response to frustration, either directly or through the experience of anger. Social learning theory argues that aggressive behavior is reinforced by experience and taught by punitive models.

Affiliation is sought under conditions of uncertainty and fear. Being with others provides social comparison of appropriate behaviors and reduces some forms of anxiety.

Successful people may have a greater need to achieve than others. Achievement motivation can be measured with projective techniques and verified in performance. A need for power has also been related to authoritative and even aggressive behavior.

Effectance motives prompt behaviors that make one competent and effective in one's environment. General activity, exploration, curiosity, and tactile manipulation have all been related to greater competence and efficacy.

Combination motives are produced by a combination of physiological and learned or experiential influences. Sexual behavior in humans can be traced both to physiological sources like hormonal activity and psychological sources like cultural values and individual preferences. Another combination motive for humans is contact. Like other primates, we have a need for contact comfort both for survival and attachment formation in infancy and later development.

Emotion is a subjective awareness of experienced motivation. Emotional arousal is originally physiological arousal. According to the Yerkes-Dodson Law, arousal affects performance in an enhancing way for simple tasks and adversely for complex tasks. Effortful activity such as lying may be reflected in increased arousal, although research has not supported the application of this assumption in the operation of polygraphs or lie detectors.

The James-Lange theory posits that emotion is experienced when a stimulus elicits a physiological response, which is then interpreted by conscious awareness as an emotion. The Cannon-Bard theory claims that both physiological arousal and conscious awareness are produced simultaneously by an emotional stimulus. Work by Schachter and Singer suggests that emotion has two components, a level of physiological arousal and a cognitive interpretation or label of this arousal as due to emotion.

Plutchik's theory of emotions categorizes a circle of emotional responses that vary in intensity, and are combined to form new emotions.

Studies of emotional expression have focused on facial affect in identifying the human development of emotional expression and universal features of emotional experience. Individual differences and gender differences have been identified in nonverbal sensitivity and expression. Other aspects of nonverbal communication include body language, quality of voice, and eye contact.

Selected Readings

Deci, E. L. and R. M. Ryan. *Intrinsic Motivation and Self-Determination in Human Behavior.* New York: Plenum. 1985

Franken, R. E.. *Human Motivation.* Monterey, CA: Brooks/Cole. 1982

Geen, R. G. and E. I. Donnerstein,(Eds.). *Aggression: Volume I: Theoretical and Methodological Issues* and *Volume II: Issues and Research.* New York: Academic Press. 1983

Izard, C. E., J. Kagan and R. B. Zajonc (Eds.). *Emotion, Cognition and Behavior.* New York: Cambridge University Press. 1984

McClelland, D. C. *Human Motivation.* Glenview, IL: Scott, Foresman. 1985

Mook, D. G. *Motivation: The Organization of Action.* New York: Simon and Schuster. 1987

Scherer, K. R. and Ekman, P. (Eds.). *Approaches to Emotion.* Hillsdale, NJ: Erlbaum. 1984

Spence, J. T. (Ed.). *Achievement and Achievement Motives.* New York: Freeman. 1983

Tavris, C. *Anger: The Misunderstood Emotion.* New York: Simon and Schuster. 1983

11

The Life Cycle

The province of developmental psychology is the life cycle, the period of constant change between conception and death.

The modern discipline of developmental psychology evolved from child psychology, which studies changes in physical, cognitive, social, and personality functions from birth through adolescence. There has been, however, increasing interest in development before birth, the prenatal period, and development after adolescence, the adult years.

Some developmentalists now prefer to be called lifespan psychologists, a term that underscores the life long capacity of humans to grow and change.

Developmental psychologists seek to describe the typical patterns of change that occur over time. Once patterns have been identified, developmentalists attempt to explain these changes through psychological theory. An important element of developmental psychology is the study of how factors other than age affect development, since age alone cannot capture the extent of differences between people.

THE HEREDITY-ENVIRONMENT QUESTION

Background   Historically, psychologists have debated the relative importance of heredity ("nature") and the environment ("nurture") in human development.

G. Stanley Hall, one of the first developmental psychologists, represented a rather extreme position on the side of genetics. Strongly influenced by Darwin's evolutionary theory, Hall saw human development as a case of "ontogeny recapitulates phylogeny," meaning that the development of the individual reflects the evolutionary development of the species. Hall saw

125

development as influenced not only by the genes of one's family but by the broader genetic inheritance we possess as members of the human race.

This view was challenged in the early 20th century by the environmentalists, led by the behaviorist John B. Watson. Watson and other behavioral psychologists believed that development was the cumulative result of our experiences, and that genetics did not predispose individuals to particular developmental outcomes. The environmentalists' rejection of genetic predispositions had great appeal in a democratic society. This environmentalist view dominated American psychology for several decades.

The Crucial Interaction

Today there is less emphasis on the question of which factor, heredity or environment, determines development. Most psychologists view development as the result of an interaction of heredity and environmental factors. Behaviors and characteristics are seen as resulting from the combined effect of genetic inheritance and experience. Although some psychologists attempt to determine the relative amount of each influence, usually as a percentage (the heritability ratio), many believe that each factor affects the other to produce a result not equal to the sum of the two influences.

THE ROLE OF GENETICS

Genes are the basic elements of genetic transmission. A chromosome is a chain formed by a combination of nearly 20,000 genes. Chemically, genes consist of deoxyribonucleic acid, usually abbreviated DNA, which contains codes for synthesizing the proteins that form the body and guide its functioning. In essence, DNA defines our genetic inheritance.

Mature reproductive cells or gametes—sperm for males and ova for females—have 23 chromosomes each. At conception, a fertilized egg is formed with 23 pairs of chromosomes, one member of each pair having been contributed by each parent. From this point on, all body cells except gametes contain the same 23 pairs of chromosomes.

Dominant and Recessive Genes. Because each cell contains pairs of chromosomes, each cell contains pairs of genes. Many genes come in two forms differing in potency. The more powerful form is called the dominant gene. The weaker form is called the recessive gene. The code of the recessive gene will be expressed only if its dominant counterpart is absent.

Genotype and Phenotype. The actual genetic pattern mapped in the chromosomes is the child's genotype. Even though a child inherits 23 chromosomes from each parent, only identical twins have the same genotype. Different "genetic messengers" are carried in the chromosomes of each gamete, so that it is virtually impossible for children produced by the same two parents to have identical genotypes. Identical twins, however, are formed from the fertilization of a single egg that subsequently splits and develops into two separate people.

The apparent characteristics exhibited comprise the child's phenotype. Even identical twins may exhibit different phenotypes depending on the environment in which they are reared. Although height is in part dictated by genetics, for example, identical twins reared under different nutritional conditions may differ phenotypically in adult height.

Direct and Indirect Influences. Hereditary factors can affect behavior directly. For example, color blindness can result from a hereditary defect that prevents detection of certain hues. But heredity also can influence behavior indirectly. A person with particularly long fingers may become a pianist because this genetic feature facilitates acquiring a particular behavior.

Studying Genetic Influences. Much of our information about the role of heredity comes from the study of twins. Identical twins (from one fertilized egg or zygote, thus "monozygotic") have the same genotype and a common environment. Fraternal twins (from two fertilized eggs or zygotes, thus "dizygotic") are no more similar genetically than siblings, but they do share a common environment. When monozygotic twins are similar in a characteristic and dizygotic twins are not, psychologists infer that this characteristic reflects the effects of genetics.

Twin studies indicate a genetic element in certain psychiatric disorders, such as manic-depressive disorder and schizophrenia (see chapter 16).

Some personality characteristics, such as sociability and introversion-extroversion (see chapter 14), also are likely to be genetically influenced. Perhaps the most widely researched attribute, intelligence test score, appears to have a significant genetic component. However, many psychologists question the assumptions of twin research, and the role of genetics in development is still hotly debated.

THE ROLE OF ENVIRONMENT

Environment is a potent influence affecting every aspect of development and behavior. The language we learn, our religious and cultural values, and many personality traits are all influenced by environmental factors.

Psychological Characteristics. Although intelligence may have a genetic component, intellectual ability clearly is affected by such environmental variables as education and social class.

A genetic propensity for schizophrenia (a severe behavior and thought disorder) may exist, but exhibiting schizophrenic behavior also depends on environmental factors such as stress. Moreover, research indicates that environment can even affect the outcome of specifically genetic characteristics.

Phenylketonuria. One such example is phenylketonuria (PKU), which results from a hereditary defect. People with the PKU gene lack the enzyme responsible for metabolizing a basic amino acid (phenylpyruvic acid). The build-up of this acid produces mental retardation.

Once a technique for identifying the PKU gene was developed, people with PKU could be identified in infancy and placed on special diets to prevent accumulation of the acid and ensure normal development. The environment—in this case, diet—can alter the outcome of a specific genotype.

THE PRENATAL PERIOD

Stages of Prenatal Development

The prenatal period lasts roughly 280 days and is divided into three stages: (1) the germinal stage, (2) the embryonic stage, and (3) the fetal stage.

THE GERMINAL STAGE

Conception marks the beginning of the first prenatal stage, the germinal stage. Conception involves fertilization of an ovum (egg) by a sperm and usually occurs in a Fallopian tube. During the next 10-14 days, the zygote (fertilized egg) repeatedly divides as it travels to the uterus. The divisions are mitotic, meaning that the cell merely replicates itself. The mass of cells that implants in the lining of the uterus is therefore a mass of undifferentiated cells, each one exactly like the others.

THE EMBRYONIC STAGE

When the cell mass implants, the embryonic stage begins. For the next six weeks, the cells differentiate in both structure and function.

Some cells develop into protective structures, including the placenta, the umbilical cord, and the amniotic sac. The placenta is the protective organ that surrounds the embryo and facilitates nourishment and waste elimination. The umbilical cord carries blood containing nutrients from the mother to the embryo via the placenta. It discharges wastes from the embryo to the mother by the same route. The amniotic sac surrounds the embryo in a suspension of fluid called amnion.

Other differentiating cells develop into the actual body structures. By eight weeks past conception, a rudimentary form of each body structure is present, although many of them are nonfunctional.

THE FETAL STAGE

The fetal stage begins when a basic form of each structure is present. For the remaining 32 weeks, cells continue to divide and differentiate to produce functional body structures and to increase the size and weight of the fetus. Development proceeds in a cephalocaudal (literally "head to tail" or head-to-

toe) fashion. This is why the newborn's head is so large relative to the rest of the body at birth.

The fetus is still totally dependent on the mother for nutrients and discharge of wastes.

Problems in Prenatal Development

Although the course of prenatal development is genetically determined, the developing child is susceptible to problems resulting from the uterine environment. Because the blood supplies of mother and child interact, substances in her blood can be passed into the child's body. The placenta functions as a primitive filtration system, but many substances, including drugs and viruses, can enter the child's bloodstream and affect the course of prenatal development. For example, smoking during pregnancy is associated with low birth weight and prematurity; the viral infection rubella (German measles) is associated with blindness and deafness.

INFANCY

Neonatal Behavior

Infancy spans the first two years, beginning with the newborn (neonatal) period (first month). The newborn infant is amazingly competent. Although the cerebral cortex is not yet mature, newborns exhibit a variety of inborn, coordinated motor behaviors called reflexes. The sucking reflex enables the infant to operate a nipple, while the rooting reflex permits the infant to locate a nipple in spite of poor vision. If an object touches a newborn's cheek, the head automatically "roots" or turns in the direction of that object.

Newborns also have well developed senses of hearing and smell that can be used to identify people.

Physical and Motor Development

The first two years of life continue the rapid course of growth begun prenatally. Body proportions change as the legs and arms grow to "catch up" with the head and trunk. Development of muscles and the motor centers of the cortex enable the infant to reach, grasp, sit, crawl, walk, and vocalize. The order of these physical and motor changes is surprisingly regular throughout the world, and they are viewed as evidence of the role of maturation, growth due to aging rather than learning.

Cognitive and Language Development

Infancy is when the symbolic function emerges. Psychologists use the term symbolic function to refer to representational activities, such as language and thought. Infants learn that certain combinations of sounds represent the names of people and objects. They develop memory or the capacity to represent mentally the world around them with images or sounds. These skills provide the basis for learning language and for developing thought and reasoning.

By the age of two, most infants can communicate in two- to three-word sentences, can sort familiar objects into groups, and have a basic understanding of cause-effect relationships (as in "If I cry, then Mommy will do what I want").

Social and Personality Development

Personality and social behavior also develop. As early as two months of age, infants demonstrate stable patterns of reaction to objects and events, referred to as infant temperaments.

By six to eight months, infants form attachments with significant people in their environments, such as parents, siblings, or child care workers.

By two years, most infants look forward to opportunities to interact with other children.

CHILDHOOD

Childhood is the period from about two to twelve years. Although physical growth slows markedly, changes in behavior emerge almost daily. Individual differences in skills and abilities emerge, providing a dramatic illustration of the effects of varying genetic endowment and experiences.

Physical and Motor Development

Overall growth declines to a slow but steady rate by age five to six. Improvements are seen in gross and fine motor coordination and in eye-hand coordination. By age five, children can catch a ball, cut with scissors, and write letters and numbers. Children also begin acquiring their permanent teeth around five or six.

Individual differences in skills are common during this period. Depending on their experiences, children can become proficient at tasks such as playing the piano, playing soccer, or playing Nintendo.

Cognitive and Linguistic Development

COGNITION

Cognitively, children develop progressively more sophisticated memory and reasoning skills. Although children between two and five clearly can pay attention and learn, they often fail to recognize what they need to know and how to use information to their advantage. As a result they may approach learning tasks in an unsystematic, hit-or-miss fashion.

They also tend to be less than objective when analyzing the world around them. Children between two and five often reason egocentrically, meaning that they use their own experiences and points of view to interpret the world around them. At this age, their thinking tends to be rigid and categorical.

In contrast, children between five and twelve are better able to focus on the relevant features of a learning task, and to understand objectively the causes and effects of events around them (see discussion of Piaget's theory, chapter 12). Thinking becomes more logical and flexible.

LANGUAGE

On the other hand, children practically master their native languages between two and five years of age. The ungrammatical two- to three-word sentences of the infant are rapidly replaced with longer, more grammatical sentences containing pronouns, modifiers, and suffixes.

By five to six years of age, children's language is not only grammatical but demonstrates awareness of pragmatic issues such as focusing on a topic, taking turns in a conversation, and adding information to resolve ambiguities.

Social and Personality Development

Childhood presents extensive opportunities to interact with peers, and these social interactions have important implications for the child's developing sense of a personal and social self.

SOCIAL BEHAVIOR

Children demonstrate a variety of social patterns, from being shy and insecure around others to being the leader of the pack. Popular children typically are self-confident, competent, and socially skillful. They know how to play, and other children enjoy their company. Children who are unable to join a group or who are very aggressive are usually left to themselves.

SELF-IMAGE

Ages Two to Five. Children form a self-concept and basic sex-role between two and five years of age. At age five, most children's self-descriptions are categorical (e.g., in terms of age, gender, behavioral patterns) and greatly influenced by the messages they receive from other people. Much to the dismay of many parents, sex-roles at this age—the behavior patterns children consider appropriate for one gender or the other—are typically stereotyped. This means children have inflexible, narrow definitions of what is considered feminine and masculine. For two- to five-year-olds, both patterns of self-concept and of sex-role are likely to reflect the categorical thinking characteristic at these ages.

Ages Five to Twelve. Between five and twelve years, children's self-concepts and sex-roles begin to broaden. They are more likely to describe themselves in terms of psychological attributes (e.g., nice, smart) and to evaluate themselves relative to their peers. This social comparison process is influential in the establishment of a sense of self-esteem.

PERSONALITY DEVELOPMENT

Many psychologists see personality development as progressing through a series of stages. (See Table 11.1 below.)

Psychosexual Stages. Psychoanalysts, led by Freud, point to the importance of a series of psychosexual stages where children must learn to control

Table 11.1: Psychosexual Stages of Development		
Stage	**Ages**	**Characteristics**
Oral	0-1 year	Focus on mouth as region of pleasurable stimulation, nourishment, contact with mother.
		Adult fixation: oral gratification sought when stressed; excessive eating, drinking, or smoking.
Anal	2-3 years	Focus on elimination functions as sources of personal physical control, in conflict with limits of toilet training.
		Adult fixation: excessive efforts to be neat, clean, tidy in stress, or "explosive" rejection in the form of sloppiness, overspending.
Phallic	3-6 years	Focus on genitals and self-stimulation as pleasurable activity. Curiosity about sex differences. Attachment to opposite sex parent and rejection of same sex parent, resolved by identifying through gender role with same sex parent.
		Adult fixation: selfish behavior, especially in relationships and sexual intimacy.
Latency	6-12 years	Hiatus in psychosexual associations with erogenous zones while child is preoccupied with school and peer relations. (No zone of focus, no fixation).
Genital	12+ years	Focus on genitals and other features as aspect of relationship with appropriate intimate partner. Necessary for mature experience of love. (No associated fixation).

their instinctual biological impulses and act in appropriate ways. At each psychosexual stage—named for the body's erogenous zones or regions associated with physical pleasure—the resolution of this conflict between instinct and social mores shapes later personality.

For example, children subjected to stress during toilet training (the anal period) may develop into compulsively neat adults. See Table 11.1 for a list of Freud's psychosexual stages.

Psychosocial Crises. Neo-Freudians (innovators on the work of Freud) like Erik Erikson (b. 1902) propose that psychosocial issues are central to personality development. Erikson sees the social world, particularly our need for social approval and belonging, as more influential than our need to control instinctual urges. At each psychosocial stage (see Table 11.2), the child

Table 11.2: Psychosocial Crises		
Crisis	**Ages**	**Choice or Decision Involved**
Trust vs. Mistrust	0-1 years	Can my parents and environment be trusted, or is my future insecure?
Autonomy vs. Shame and Doubt	2-3 years	Can I control myself and be physically competent, or must I doubt my abilities?
Initiative vs. Guilt	3-5 years	Am I encouraged to meet new challenges, or am I unworthy and incompetent?
Industry vs. Inferiority	6-12 years	Am I productive and useful to myself and others, or am I powerless and inadequate?
Identity vs. Role Confusion/ Diffusion	12-19 years	Can I identify and develop my unique but meaningful roles, or is my distinction and social role unclear?
Intimacy vs. Isolation	20s and 30s	Can I form an intimate, loving relationship with another, or must I remain lonely and incomplete?
Generativity vs. Stagnation	30s to 50s	Can I be productive and creative in my work and relationships, or is my life stagnated, routine, and unpromising?
Integrity vs. Despair	60s+	Can I come to terms with the approach of my own death, or do I feel despair over the disappointments in my life?

* The abbreviation "vs." = versus, meaning "against" or "or," indicating the choice Erikson sees as implicit in each psychosocial crisis.

encounters the need to make a choice or decision about his or her relationship with the social world. The child acquires either a positive social attitude or a negative one, depending on experiences. For example, two- to four-year-olds (in the crisis of autonomy versus shame and doubt) who are encouraged to become independent develop a sense of autonomy. Conversely, those who are reprimanded for asserting their independence are likely to doubt their competence.

ADOLESCENCE

Adolescence is the stage between childhood and adulthood, roughly from twelve to eighteen.

The Role of Culture

As a stage of development, adolescence is greatly influenced by one's culture. In more primitive societies, for example, the transition from childhood to adulthood is rapid and marked by traditionally prescribed rites of passage (puberty rites). In American and European societies, the transition period has been steadily increasing over the past 100 years, giving rise to a specific adolescent subculture. In addition, the conflicting signals regarding when one truly becomes an adult contribute to a variety of stress-related problems.

Physical and Physiological Development

Adolescence is associated with both sexual maturation (puberty) and an overall growth spurt. Both of these result from a sequence of hormonal changes initiated by the hypothalamus and orchestrated by the pituitary gland (see chapter 3).

THE TIMING OF PUBERTY

There are group and individual differences in the ages when these changes occur. For example, changes generally appear earlier in girls than boys, and earlier in southern as compared to northern climates.

At present the mechanism determining the actual timing of the changes is unknown. It is clear, however, that being an individual at either extreme of the age range for one's group is psychologically stressful.

THE GROWTH SPURT

Girls typically begin the height and weight growth spurt around age 10, reach a peak at about 12, and decelerate markedly by 14. The spurt occurs almost two years later in boys; thus, girls are typically taller and heavier than boys from about age ten and a half to thirteen.

The growth spurt also changes both body proportions and body shape, a source of embarrassment and concern for many adolescents. Arms and legs grow rapidly, sometimes producing a temporary awkwardness or clumsiness. Chest and shoulder tissue grows rapidly in boys, as does hip and thigh tissue in girls. Adolescents concerned about these changes in body build may diet or exercise compulsively in an effort to regain what they view as an attractive shape. Serious eating disorders such as *anorexia* (abnormal fasting and self-starvation) may emerge at this stage.

SECONDARY SEX CHARACTERISTICS

In girls, enlargement of the breasts is usually the first external sign of impending puberty. The age of onset of menstruation, along with the age of onset of other physical changes, has been steadily decreasing for the past 100 years. Most girls today reach menarche, the first menstrual cycle, within six months of their 13th birthday, as compared to between ages 15-17 a century ago.

Boys typically begin their growth spurts at about twelve and a half. Impending sexual maturation is marked by enlargement of the testes, scrotum, and penis and the development of pubic hair. This is followed by enlargement of the larynx and thickening of the vocal cords, producing a transitional period in which the voice may "crack."

Cognitive Development

Adolescence is characterized by increases in ability to generalize, handle abstract ideas, and reason logically and consistently. These changes may reflect the emergence of a specific cognitive stage (see discussion of Piaget's theory, chapter 12) or the result of accumulating knowledge that expands one's capacity for making distinctions and inferring relationships.

Research indicates that the most intellectually competent adolescents are well-educated, come from families that are small in size and economically secure, and have parents who encourage learning and provide individual attention.

Social and Personality Development

Becoming an adult requires establishing new relationships with parents and peers, and developing a sense of personal identity.

PARENTAL VERSUS PEER INFLUENCE

Some psychologists conceptualize the tasks of adulthood as a process of separation-individuation, a process of distancing oneself from parents and establishing a sense of individuality. Much has been written over the years about the "generation gap" (the perceived divergence between adolescents' values and those of their parents) and the tendency of adolescents to be over-influenced by their peers.

Research indicates that, in fact, parents and peers influence different spheres of adolescent life. Adolescents do experience and give in to peer pressure to conform, especially around puberty; but peers tend to influence adolescent decisions about superficial matters like dress, language, and recreation. Parents usually continue to influence adolescent values and long-term goals. In fact, the basic values of most adolescents' friends are quite similar to those of their parents, possibly because adolescents' friendship choices are influenced by values learned at home.

SEXUALITY

With the onset of puberty, adolescents become sexual beings. The past twenty-five years have seen marked changes in adolescent sexual attitudes and behavior. Most adolescents now view premarital sex as acceptable if it occurs within the context of a loving relationship. By age 19, two-thirds of adolescent girls and four-fifths of adolescent boys have had sexual intercourse.

IDENTITY

Sexuality can be viewed as part of establishing a more adult identity. Erikson saw adolescence as precipitating an identity crisis, a period when one reevaluates oneself with an eye toward entering the adult world.

Adolescence brings dramatic physical and cognitive changes that can disrupt childhood self-image. Adolescents must come to terms with their adultlike bodies and with the impending tasks of adulthood. Cognitive changes enable the adolescent to consider relationships between "who I am" and "who I want to be." Typically, establishing an identity involves adopting a sense of personal values and making an initial vocational decision. Adolescents who are unable to resolve these issues are viewed as experiencing diffusion, an incomplete sense of identity.

ADULTHOOD

Modern Perspectives on Adult Development

The adult years have only recently become a popular research area for developmental psychologists. In part this interest reflects changing demographic trends. A significant increase in population occurred in the United States during the so-called "Baby Boom," a period of highly increased birthrate between 1946 and 1964. The social and economic consequences of the aging of the "Baby Boomers" born then has underscored the importance of understanding development during adulthood.

Psychologists and sociologists who specialize in the study of older adults (those 60 years of age and older) are called gerontologists.

Physical and Physiological Development

Adults reach their physical peak between 18 and 25 years of age. For most adults, physical decline is slow and gradual. By middle age there are noticeable changes in skin tone, hair, reaction time, and sensory functions (e.g., vision, hearing). Although some of these changes reflect the natural ageing process, environmental factors such as lifestyle, diet, exercise, and emotional stress clearly influence the extent of decline.

Between 47 and 52 most women experience menopause, the result of a dramatic decrease in the production of female hormones. Although menopause may bring physically uncomfortable sensations (e.g. "hot flashes") and psychological stress, its negative effects are frequently exaggerated.

Cognitive Development

The 20s bring improvements in ability to learn new skills and information, solving problems requiring speed and coordination, and shifting between problem solving strategies. By middle age the speed of problem solving declines, often producing a decline in scores on tests including timed problems. Performance on recall tasks often suffers, although recognition memory remains quite good.

Environmental factors play a central role in cognitive changes in adulthood. Educated adults who live and work in stimulating environments, and who maintain a social network, typically show little overall cognitive decline until very late in life.

Physical health also influences cognitive performance. Problems such as hypertension, hardening of the arteries, and neurological disorders such as Alzheimer's disease contribute to earlier cognitive decline.

Social and Personality Development

SOCIAL PATTERNS

The adult years in most cases are characterized by stability in social behavior. Adults who are socially and sexually active in their 20s tend to maintain those patterns into their 60s. Social isolation becomes a more serious problem with advancing years. It is associated with both poor health and declines in cognitive functions.

ADULT PERSONALITY DEVELOPMENT

Although psychologists once assumed that personality was stable from adolescence on, current researchers and theorists see adulthood as a time of continuing personality development. Erikson, one of the first lifespan theorists, sees adults as confronting the tasks of establishing intimacy with others, a sense of generativity or lasting accomplishment, and a sense of personal integrity.

Other theorists, such as **Daniel J. Levinson** and **Gail Sheehy**, see adults as alternating between periods of stability and periods of transition. These transitions are "passages" during which adults must adapt to changing abilities and expectations. Many must cope with the potentially stressful events of children leaving home (the "empty nest"), retirement, and caring for aged parents. Overall, however, most people successfully adapt to the changes of the adult years.

Developmental psychologists seek to describe the patterns of change that characterize human behavior through the lifespan. A central issue in developmental psychology is the relative contributions of heredity and the environment, or the nature-nurture controversy. While most modern theories emphasize the interaction of these influences, genetics plays an undeniable role in development. Twin studies have been useful in identifying the effects of genetics in physical and psychological processes. Environmental influences are also important, however, and such factors as diet and culture can be critical in all stages of development.

Prenatal development involves three stages of physical growth: the germinal stage, the embryonic stage, and the fetal stage. Throughout these stages the individual is wholly dependent on the mother for nourishment and waste elimination.

Infancy is a time of rapid growth although neonates are surprisingly competent, being born with many reflexes and sensory operations. Physical development proceeds in a cephalocaudal (head-to-toe) direction, and motor development likewise proceeds in a sequence whose regularity attests to the role of maturation. The symbolic functions of language and thought emerge in infancy, including memory, speech production, and basic cause-effect understanding. Infants demonstrate stable temperaments and form attachments to significant others.

During childhood physical growth slows but behavior changes almost daily. Motor coordination improves and children develop varying skills. They develop the ability to remember and reason, if still unsystematically. Older children have better attentional focus and learning skills. Younger children think in rigid, stereotyped ways about objects and people, including themselves and their sex roles, but this gives way to broader concepts and flexibility in later childhood. Freudian theory charts childhood development through a series of psychosexual stages, while Erikson's theory of psychosocial crises suggests a series of lifelong choices or decisions and their consequences.

Adolescence is marked by the physical changes of puberty, the development of secondary sex characteristics, and the growth spurt toward young adulthood. Adolescents are capable of greater cognitive feats and benefit greatly from supportive environments. In the processes of separation and individuation, adolescents must deal with the influences of both parents and peers, achieve some sense of personal sexuality, and survive an identity crisis in order to avoid the perils of diffusion.

Recently developmental theorists have focused more attention on adulthood than was formerly true. Most physical changes and limitations are gradual and not necessarily negative. There may be some reduction likewise in the speed or quality of cognitive functions, but environmental factors appear to be more important than the ageing process in these changes. Some cognitive decline is also a function of disease rather than of ageing itself. Adult social behavior is more stable than in other stages of the life cycle, although social isolation can be a problem with advancing age. Some theorists see the adult personality as focused on generativity, while others see adulthood as a time of transition versus stability. Though there are predictable and unpredictable challenges, most adults adapt successfully.

Selected Readings

Bower, T. G. R. *Development in Infancy, 2nd Edition.* San Francisco: W. H. Freeman. 1982

Cole, M. and Cole, S. *The Development of Children.* New York: W. H. Freeman and Company. 1989

Conger, J. J. and Peterson, A. C. *Adolescence and Youth, 3rd Edition.* New York: Harper and Row. 1983

Hoffman, L. W., S. G. Paris, E. Hall, and R. Schnell. *Developmental Psychology Today.* New York: Random House. 1988

Lerner, R. *Concepts and Theories of Human Development, 2nd Edition.* New York: Random House. 1986

Scarr, S., R. A. Weinberg, and A. Levine. *Understanding Development.* San Diego: Harcourt Brace Jovanovich. 1986

Schaie, K. W. and S. L. Willis. *Adult Development and Aging, 2nd edition.* Boston: Little, Brown. 1986

Sprinthall, N. A. and W. A. Collins. *Adolescent Psychology.* New York: Random House. 1988

12

Developmental Processes I: Cognitive and Linguistic Development

Developmental psychologists explore the changes that occur over time in a variety of human processes, including physical, motor, language, cognitive, social, emotional and personality processes. Thus, developmental psychology is not simply a topical area in psychology; it is a unique approach to the study of all psychological processes.

DEVELOPMENTAL PARADIGMS

Many developmental psychologists approach the study of psychological change from a particular perspective or paradigm. Since each paradigm is characterized by its own themes and assumptions about the nature of development, different psychologists focus on different aspects of developmental change. Focusing on certain aspects implies lack of attention to others, so no single theory or line of research can by itself capture the complexity of human development. Those who are most successful at explaining developmental change adopt an ecclectic or multi-dimensional perspective.

Psychoanalysis versus Learning Theory

In the early 20th century, two perspectives dominated American psychology and thus the study of developmental processes. The psychoanalysts, led by Sigmund Freud, focused on factors in early childhood that presumably affected the structure and functioning of adult personality. Physical and physiological maturation was seen as precipitating a series of psychosexual crises or conflicts between the expression of instinctual drives and the pressures of socialization.

The learning theorists, following the lead of behaviorist John B. Watson, rejected the notion that development was determined by maturational crises. Exponents of learning theory stressed the role of environment in shaping responses to objects and events. Development was viewed as the accumulation of sets of behaviors through specific experiences.

The Cognitive-Developmental Perspective

Although both of these perspectives currently exist in somewhat modified form, a third perspective has assumed a major role in developmental psychology. This cognitive-developmental view, alternately referred to as the genetic-structural perspective, reflects the influence of the late Swiss psychologist Jean Piaget (1896-1980).

Cognitive-developmental psychologists focus on the way thoughts and behaviors are organized. These psychologists view development as the emergence of a series of structures and rules, or operations, which are used to organize thought and behavior. As the word "genetic" implies in its alternative label, the cognitive-developmental perspective assumes that maturation plays a major role in developmental change.

Thematic Distinctions

Underlying these three perspectives are different assumptions about the causes and nature of developmental change. Learning theorists see development as the product of experience, whereas psychoanalytic and cognitive-developmental theorists emphasize the role of maturation.

Learning theorists view developmental change as gradual and continuous, referred to as quantitative change. In essence, children acquire more and more complex responses over time. In contrast, proponents of psychoanalytic and cognitive-developmental theory see developmental change as discontinuous or occurring in a series of stages that produce qualitative change. In this view, children literally acquire different types of responses over time.

The contrast between these assumptions can be illustrated by examining available theory and data on several areas of development. This chapter reviews the development of cognition and language. The next chapter reviews social and moral development.

COGNITIVE DEVELOPMENT

The most comprehensive account of cognitive development is the work of Jean Piaget. A proponent of the genetic-structuralist view, Piaget proposed that cognitive development was the result of an adaptation process. Just as animals adapt their appearance or behavior to a changing environment, Piaget saw the child as adapting cognitively as his or her world expands. This adaptation requires formulating new rules and structures to organize knowledge, to reason, and to solve problems.

Piaget's Theory

To Piaget, intelligence is the result of adaptation to one's environment. In its simplest sense, adaptation is the maintenance of an equilibrium or state of balance between the organism and the environment. When the child encounters a new object, a new idea, that balance is disrupted. This loss of equilibrium impels the child to grow cognitively and so come to understand this new element.

ASSIMILATION AND ACCOMMODATION

Adaptation involves two complementary processes: assimilation and accommodation.

Assimilation. Assimilation occurs when new information is incorporated into existing knowledge and is dealt with through existing behaviors. A breast-fed infant can assimilate a bottle nipple, identify it as a nipple, and operate it through the existing sucking routine.

Accommodation. Accommodation occurs when new information produces a reorganization of existing knowledge and the acquisition of new responses. A 10-month-old infant given a cup of milk learns that milk also comes in a container without a nipple, and to drink the infant must use a behavior other than sucking.

Both processes are necessary for cognitive or intellectual growth. Children must integrate new information into existing knowledge and expand existing knowledge to encompass new and different elements.

ORGANIZATION

Along with our biological propensity to adapt comes a propensity to organize information. Adaptation and organization are called Piaget's functional invariants, processes characteristic of and operating similarly in all humans.

Piaget calls the units into which people organize information schemas or schemata (a schema is a summary of knowledge about a particular concept). Adaptation, then, involves incorporating information into existing schemata (assimilation) and modifying existing schemata (accommodation).

Table 12.1: Piaget's Stages of Cognitive Development		
Stage	**Ages**	**Tasks and Characteristics**
Sensorimotor	0–2 years	Overt behavioral schemata; circular reactions; egocentrism; development of *object permanence*; emergence of symbolic function.
Preoperational	2–5 years	*Preconceptual phase:* Symbolic schemata; language; still egocentric. *Intuitive phase:* More logical thinking, decline in egocentrism; still no operational ability.
Concrete Operations	6–12 years	Mastery of *conservation*, hierarchical classification; concrete, present-oriented thinking; trial-and-error problem-solving. Operational ability limited to concrete concepts.
Formal Operations	12+ years	Abstract thinking, hypothesis testing; logical reasoning. Formal operational ability develops.

Piaget's Stages

Piaget proposed that intelligence develops through a sequence of four cognitive stages maturationally related to age. Children progress through the stages as they experience uncertainty (disequilibrium) and attempt to adapt their understanding of the world to reduce uncertainty (restore equilibrium).

Progress through the four stages is reflected not only in intellectual growth but also in language, social, and emotional development. (See Table 12.1 for a summary of Piaget's stages).

THE SENSORIMOTOR STAGE (BIRTH TO TWO YEARS)

For Piaget, the sensorimotor stage is composed of six substages, whose accomplishments are summarized here.

During the sensorimotor stage, children's understanding of the world is based totally on their sensory and motor interactions with it. Schemata at this stage are all organized systems of overt behavior. The earliest schemata are composed of basic reflexes, such as sucking, through which children explore the world around them. As the body and brain mature, children become better able to control and direct their movements and to coordinate sensory and motor information. Schemata expand to include coordinated voluntary actions.

Sensorimotor development is characterized by a series of behaviors called circular reactions, seemingly meaningless repetitions of chance events that catch an infant's eye. To Piaget, circular reactions represent the emergence of intelligent action. Through these interactions with objects, children learn how to learn by combining different actions, such as "grasp" and "look," and varying the actions used with an object, such as "suck" or "shake."

Children learn to discriminate between and classify objects based on their perceptual properties, such as "feels smooth," and the ways they respond to motor actions, such as "it rolls."

Linking actions with objects to produce reactions—for example, kicking a mobile to make it spin—leads to a basic understanding of cause-effect relationships.

A child at this age is *egocentric*, unable to conceptualize a world existing outside him- or herself that is affected by the actions of others.

Sensorimotor children also lack an appreciation of the permanence of objects. To the young infant, "out of sight is out of mind." The disappearance of an object is not troublesome; attention moves rapidly elsewhere. However, after a child's first birthday, the protests often made when mother leaves the room or a toy is taken away demonstrate the emergence of the concept of object permanence. The child "knows" these things or people continue to exist "somewhere," and expresses this in demanding to have them "back." This is a major achievement of the sensorimotor stage.

The other major achievement of the sensorimotor stage is the emergence of the *symbolic function*, the ability to represent objects and events mentally. This representational skill is important for observational learning and language acquisition, as well as the ability to think and solve problems.

THE PREOPERATIONAL STAGE (TWO TO FIVE YEARS)

The preoperational stage is divided into two substages: the preconceptual phase (two to three years of age) and the intuitive phase (four to five years).

Preconceptual Phase. Preconceptual children are capable of symbolic schemata, rather than being limited to the behavioral schemata of infancy. They can organize information mentally by thinking about the properties of objects and events or about the relationships between them.

Language appears, and children begin to draw pictures that represent things. However, they tend to be egocentric in that they use their own experiences and ideas as the basis for this organization. Thus a drawing of three trees of different sizes is said to depict the "daddy," "mommy," and "baby" tree. Although they understand the concepts of classification and causality, their egocentrism interferes with appreciation of more objective systems for organizing information. To a three-year-old, a bird cannot be a bird if it cannot fly. The sun goes down to make it dark so we can sleep. These interpretations seem perfectly logical to the preconceptual child.

The Intuitive Phase. In the intuitive phase, thinking begins to become more logical and objective. Classification and problem solving skills improve, and egocentrism begins to decline.

However, intuitive phase children still cannot represent a series of actions mentally and thus cannot solve problems requiring attention to sequences.

THE CONCRETE OPERATIONAL STAGE (SIX TO TWELVE YEARS)

It is during the stage of concrete operations that the ability to use logic matures.

Concrete operational children are much less egocentric and are more objective about the world around them. Their representational skills have improved to the point that they can follow a sequence of actions and coordinate information about more than one dimension of an object or event.

Concrete operational children have mastered the idea of *conservation*, understanding that changes in the appearance of objects do not necessarily imply changes in properties. For example, one cup of fruit juice is the same amount (the amount is conserved) whether it is poured into a tall thin glass or a short squat cup.

Concrete operational children have also mastered *hierarchical classification*, as in understanding that the class of "birds" may have two subgroups, "flying birds" and "non-flying birds."

They are able to use logical rules or *operations*, such as addition and subtraction, and to see relationships between rules, such as subtraction being the opposite of addition. Thinking at this stage is present-oriented and tied to concrete, physical evidence. Although much of their problem solving is often trial- and-error, their performance improves greatly.

THE FORMAL OPERATIONAL STAGE (AGE 12 THROUGH ADULTHOOD)

In formal operations, thinking becomes more abstract, systematic, and probabilistic. Adolescents are able to think hypothetically (making guesses about explanations for events), to consider possibilities, and to imagine future outcomes of present actions.

Adolescents learn to solve problems by systematically generating and testing hypotheses, a far cry from the more random trial-and- error approach of childhood. They can use past experiences and present events to assign probabilities to possible outcomes, and they can reason deductively.

This type of logical reasoning is the basis of the scientific method (see chapters 1 and 2). It also contributes to the self-absorption shown by many adolescents. Being able to think in such abstract, hypothetical ways is a two-edged sword that can lead to various preoccupations: "Should I abstain from sex?", "Are drugs really bad?", and "Is there a God?"

Evaluating Piaget's Theory

Piaget proposed his four stages as representing an invariant sequence of changes maturationally tied to age. Recent research indicates that although the sequence of changes is reliable, the changes do not necessarily represent separate, distinct stages of development. Children may show features of several stages at a given point in development.

Children also can be taught certain concepts, such as conservation, at ages when Piaget assumed their conceptual skills were too immature.

In addition, Piaget appears to have underestimated the abilities of infants and young children and overestimated the abilities of adolescents and adults. Using different types of tests, other researchers have demonstrated object permanence almost six months before Piaget's proposed age and conservation in four- to five-year-old children. Testing of adolescents and adults indicates that formal operations is not a universal outcome of development. The ability to reason in formally operational ways is highly dependent on environmental factors such as culture and education.

LANGUAGE DEVELOPMENT

Theoretical Overview

When children first begin to speak, they utter only short sentences of two to three words. Later, sentences become longer and their structure becomes more complex. Psychologists who believe that development is continuous suggest that these changes reflect gradual increases in the child's ability to remember words and to use them grammatically in sentences. No special predisposition for learning language nor fundamental change in the child's knowledge of language is assumed.

Other psychologists maintain that these changes reflect fundamental changes in the child's organization of language information. These individuals see language acquisition as a movement through a series of qualitatively different stages. Although the sequence of these stages is maturationally determined, environment may influence the rate at which a child progresses through them.

Theories of Language Acquisition

LEARNING THEORY

B. F. Skinner offered a learning theory explanation for language changes using the principles of operant conditioning (see chapter 6).

In this view, children are reinforced first for making sounds, then for combining sounds, and later for using these sound combinations as words in appropriate contexts. (From chapter 6 this can be recognized as an application of shaping.) Parents and others continue conditioning language behavior by later reinforcing children's combinations of words in grammatical sentences.

SOCIAL LEARNING

Many psychologists see operant conditioning as an unlikely explanation of language change. Children learn language so quickly that it is difficult to imagine enough conditioning experiences occuring in such a short time. Social or observational learning theorists have expanded the traditional learning account by including the process of imitation. In addition to being reinforced for appropriate language behavior, children imitate the language of the models around them.

Although the inclusion of imitation reduces the hypothetical amount of time needed for learning language, research indicates that children are limited in ability to imitate language that is more sophisticated than their usual speech. In addition, children in different cultures appear to show similar patterns of change in language behavior, even though the extent of their contact with adult speakers varies. These cross-cultural regularities have led other psychologists to look to biology and maturation to explain language development.

THE LANGUAGE ACQUISITION DEVICE

Noam Chomsky claims that humans have an innate (inborn) ability for language acqustion. This human predisposition for learning language, like the human predisposition to walk upright on two legs, results from our species' genetic heritage. It is independent of our level of intelligence or our frequency of contacts with adult speakers. This genetic ability or language acquisition device (LAD) enables us to learn any human language once we have contact with its sounds and can control our vocal apparatus.

Cortical Function. Although psychologists have not yet discovered any "language genes," biological factors clearly influence language behavior. Specific areas of the cerebral cortex (see chapter 3) control language production and comprehension, as is obvious from the changes in language behavior following damage to these areas (e.g., as a result of stroke or head injury).

Infants do not begin to develop language until the brain has reached a certain level of maturity, and language learning is generally easiest during the period of rapid brain growth.

MATURATIONAL SEQUENCES AND STAGES

Psychologists also see maturation reflected in studies of children's language behavior. Infants from a variety of environments, though they ultimately learn different languages, all begin by babbling the same sound combinations (e.g., "bababa" or "deedee"). The sequence of language changes, from babbling to words to sentences, is remarkably similar cross-culturally. And milestones in language development are correlated with milestones in motor development, a finding interpreted as a sign of the importance of neurological maturation.

The maturational quality of language, and the appearance of a predictable sequence of changes, is the focus of the cognitive-developmental view of language. Roger Brown and his colleagues have proposed that language acquisition involves progression through a series of stages. Each stage is characterized by a new set of rules and skills that organize the child's language knowledge and permit production of utterances exhibiting new forms and levels of complexity.

Major Features of Language Development

Although psychologists still debate the precise roles of conditioning, imitation, and maturation in language acquistion, much is currently known about the characteristics of children's language behavior.

Most developmental psychologists see language development as reflecting an interaction of maturation and experience, with maturation playing a central role in infancy and experience becoming increasingly influential over time.

There are a variety of systems for categorizing the course of language development. The following sections describe what cognitive-developmental psychologists see as qualitatively different types of language behavior. In each stage description, note instances where children's language fits better with a maturational learning perspective.

PREBABBLING PHASE (BIRTH TO SIX MONTHS)

During the first three months of life, infants communicate primarily by crying. They lack sufficient neuro-muscular development to control their vocal apparatus and produce individual speech sounds. But crying is an effective means of communication. Experienced parents and observers can discriminate between cries associated with such states as hunger, pain, or fear.

Toward the end of this phase infants begin making speech-like sounds including the vowels "a" and "e." The sounds are often referred to as cooing. Language behavior at this age does not vary across cultures.

BABBLING PHASE (SIX TO 12 MONTHS)

By six months of age, infants expand their speech sounds to include the consonants "m," "b," "d," and "p." The order of emergence of speech sounds, or phonemes, is determined to a great extent by the infant's motor abilities. The vowels "a" and "e" are produced in the back of the mouth and require little motor control. The consonant "m," for example, simply requires closing the lips and allowing air to vibrate in the nasal cavity. Compared to later phonemes, such as "r" or "t," early phonemes require minimal control of the lips, tongue, and air passages. These developments are cross-culturally regular.

By eight months, infants begin to combine sounds and repeat combinations over and over, producing such common babbles as "mama" and "dada." Infants six to eight months old will babble endlessly to themselves in bed or while crawling around; the babbles do not appear to be efforts to communicate with others. Although initially all infants produce the same babbles, beginning at eight months the variety of sounds produced changes to better match the sounds commonly occurring in the language the infant hears.

The period from eight to twelve months is characterized by continuing changes in phoneme production and increasingly word-like babbles.

FIRST WORDS (12 TO 18 MONTHS)

Semi-Words. The first words children use are idiosyncratic and typically are not the words they have heard other people use. These invented words or semi-words, approximations of adult words, demonstrate the creative quality of language production and underscore the belief that child language is not simply an imitation of the language of adults.

Specificity versus Generalization. Children learn words at an intermediate level of specificity first, such as "dog" rather than "animal" (more general) or "Buster" (more specific).

Children 12-18 months often over-generalize words, as in calling a cow a "dog." Such behavior implies that early words are defined in terms of perceptual features, such as "four legs," "brown and white," and "has a tail."

Holophrastic Speech. First words are often used as holophrases at this age, single words used to convey whole thoughts (or words meant to be "whole phrases"). The word, combined with intonation, gestures, and context, functions as a sentence would for an adult. Context is therefore important. For example, a child who says "sock" in a whiny voice, while waving arms and indicating bare feet, means something quite different from a child who says the same word, with the same intonation and gestures, but is wearing socks.

EARLY SENTENCES (18 TO 24 MONTHS)

Telegraphic Speech. Children typically begin producing two- to three-word sentences at 18-24 months. These sentences are telegraphic in that they contain only the minimum number of words important to expressing the underlying idea, similar to the spare style of a telegram whose cost is calculated by the word.

Function words (e.g., articles and prepositions) and grammatical suffixes are eliminated even in speakers of languages that require suffixes to identify parts of speech (e.g., German or Russian). The universality of telegraphic speech clearly implies maturational constraints on children's language behavior.

Expansion. Intonation, gestures, and context are still important to interpreting children's speech at this age. Adults often engage in expansion, repeating a child's telegraphic sentence in its complete grammatical form. When asked to imitate a complete sentence, children usually continue to produce a telegraphic version of the modeled sentence.

Baby Talk versus Adult Speech. Although expansion does not explain how children move from telegraphic speech to grammatical speech, exposure to grammatical speech at this age is important for later language development. Children exposed primarily to "baby talk" do not advance to the next stage as quickly as children exposed to more adult grammar.

EMERGENCE OF GRAMMAR (AGES TWO TO FIVE)

By the age of two, children may have a vocabulary of 250-300 words. Between the ages of two and five, children acquire the function words (e.g., prepositions and modifiers) and suffixes necessary for grammatical speech.

Over-Regularization. An important distinction in grammar is the difference between regular and irregular words. Some words are regular in that they are changed according to standard rules that apply to many other words. For example, the plural of "hand" is "hands," and the past tense of "walk" is "walked." In contrast, other words are irregular, and are changed in unique ways rather than "according to the rules." For example, the plural of "foot" is "feet," and the past tense of "go" is "went." The distinction between regular and irregular words is difficult to grasp, and children often over-regularize irregular words (apply common rules to words that are exceptions to those rules). For example, a child might form the past tense of "go" by adding the regular ending, producing "goed."

Cognitive-developmental psychologists see over-regularization as a reflection of the child's active attempt to organize language information, and to formulate and test language hypotheses. It is unlikely to reflect either the effects of operant conditioning or modeling, and is a cross-cultural phenomenon.

Communication. Children also are learning more about the pragmatics of language, the social rules of communication. Listening skills, topic focus, taking turns in conversations, and politeness all improve during this period.

REFINEMENT OF LANGUAGE (BEYOND AGE 5)

Children at age five are amazingly competent speakers of language. Beyond age five, most language changes involve increasing vocabulary and mastering the fine points of grammar and syntax, the rules for combining words into meaningful sentences.

Children become able to produce longer sentences with more complex grammatical structures and to understand passive and embedded sentences. The child's environment, including the family, mass media, involvement in reading, and school, greatly influence rate of progress and level of sophistication attained. At this age, experience clearly surpasses maturation as a determinant of language behavior.

*D*evelopmental psychologists explore human changes over time, providing a unique approach to the study of psychology. Early influential paradigms in developmental psychology were psychoanalytic theory and learning theory. More recently, cognitive-developmental theory has provided its own perspective, emphasizing the roles of operations and maturation in individual development. Different paradigms emphasize either continuous, quantitative change or discontinuous, qualitative change in the lifespan.

Piaget's theory of cognitive development is one of the most influential approaches in developmental psychology. According to Piaget's theory, children adapt and maintain balance through the processes of assimilation and accommodation. In growing from infancy to adulthood, children develop their cognitive abilities through a sequence of stages. In the sensorimotor stage infants rely on behavioral schemata and must acquire a sense of object permanance. In the preoperational stage, children develop better language, rely on symbolic schemata, and master conservation and hierarchical classification. In the concrete operational stage children develop trial-and-error problem solving and concrete logic. Finally, in the formal operational stage, children develop abstract reasoning and hypothesis testing.

Language acquisition has been explained in terms of operant learning, imitative social learning, a uniquely human "language acquisition device," and the interaction of maturation with developmental stages. As language develops, children move from crying, to babbling, to first words, to early sentences, and finally to more and more sophisticated use of grammar.

Selected Readings

Boden, M. *Jean Piaget*. Harmondsworth, England: Penguin Books. 1979

Bruner, J. S. *Child's Talk: Learning to Use Language*. New York: Norton. 1983

Flavell, J. H. *Cognitive Development, 2nd Edition*. Englewood Cliffs, NJ: Prentice-Hall. 1985

Garvey, C. *Children's Talk*. Cambridge, MA: Harvard University Press. 1984

Kail, R. W. *The Development of Memory in Children, 3rd Edition*. San Francisco: Freeman. 1990

Reich, P. A. *Language Development*. Englewood Cliffs, NJ: Prentice-Hall. 1986

13

Developmental Processes II: Social and Moral Development

Theories of cognitive development and language acquisition (see chapter 12) consider children as thinking beings. Children are also social creatures from the moment of birth. An understanding of development is incomplete without a consideration of how interaction with others is developed. This chapter examines social interactions, including play and aggression, and the development of a sense of the morality of actions.

Research and theory on social and moral development reflects the three major developmental paradigms introduced in chapter 12: psychoanalysis, learning theory, and the cognitive-developmental perspective.

Learning theorists emphasize the role of experience in development. They view developmental change as continuous and quantitative.

In contrast, psychoanalytic and cognitive-developmental theories emphasize the role of physical maturation in other spheres of development. They conceptualize developmental change as discontinuous, occurring in discrete, qualitatively-different stages.

These distinctions in paradigms (experience vs. maturation) and themes (quantitative vs. qualitative), already reflected in theories of cognitive and linguistic development (chapter 12), are likewise evident in various theories of social and moral development.

SOCIAL DEVELOPMENT

The human animal, like other primates, is a social creature. Beginning in infancy, children are interested in contact with other people. In fact, the psychiatric disorder known as early infantile autism is diagnosable in infancy because children with autism do not shift to being more interested in people than in objects.

Two topics of current interest to developmental psychologists are the nature and function of children's play, and the development of aggressive behavior.

Play

Play is an important mechanism of socialization. Children learn to adjust to the realities of the social world through play experiences, particularly through social play with peers. Play provides children with opportunities to learn about and test different roles, to confront the expectations of others, and to adapt to group norms. In addition, play has important consequences for both cognitive and personality development. Involvement in imaginative or "pretend" play is correlated with overall level of cognitive functioning in later childhood, and success in social play with peers is a predictor of likelihood of later emotional disturbance.

THEORIES OF PLAY

The Ethology of Play. Ethologist Konrad Lorenz has suggested that play is an integral part of the evolution of the species. To Lorenz, play is a biologically-based behavior, an outgrowth of the instinct to explore and learn about the environment. The activity of play provides the species with the knowledge necessary for its members to adapt to changing circumstances, and therefore to survive and prosper. In an evolutionary sense, then, play is important to the overall development of the species. Play not only provides the animal with information; it also helps refine and sharpen cognitive skills. This instinctual behavior generates the experiences necessary for the development of both the individual and the species.

The Developmental Role of Play. Erik Erikson (see chapter 11) views play as important to the child's psychological development. Erikson sees play as one of the major functions of the ego and as central to ego development. The ego is the part of the psyche involved in establishing a sense of reality and enabling the individual to cope with the stresses of the social world.

Children's play, to Erikson, is not simply a form of recreation, like the play of adults. Instead, play is a mechanism for dealing with life experiences, for self-teaching and self-healing. In play, children can safely express their fears and frustrations. They can make up for the defeats they experience in the real world. The child who fails at a task in the outer world can retreat into what Erikson calls the "safe island" that play provides and can overcome feelings of failure or inferiority within his or her own set of boundaries. Erikson views the progression in play—from focus on self to play with others—as a demonstration of play's importance to both social and personality development.

The Structure of Play. In addition to theorizing about the functions of play, psychologists have researched the structure of play. Jean Piaget (see chapters 11 and 12) identified three forms of social play that occur between ages two and six and illustrate the child's increasing ability to interact constructively with others.

In this perspective, children's play is viewed as a window to their developing social and cognitive skills, their ability to conceptualize and create shared experiences.

FORMS OF PLAY

Parallel Play. At two to three years, most children enjoy playing in the company of other children. On close examination, however, it appears that these children often play alongside one another but engage in different activities. This is referred to as parallel play. The children play in close proximity, but there is no theme, no cooperative effort. One may be drawing with a pencil on paper, while the other is building a tower with blocks.

Piaget sees parallel play as reflecting cognitive constraints on children's ability to understand and create shared experience. Nevertheless, parallel play is an important first step toward later social play.

Associative Play. By three to four years of age, children often play in groups of several people. While they appear to be playing together, they are more likely to be playing with the same materials as the others but using them in different ways. While such associative play is a "shared" experience, it does not necessarily involve the theme and cooperative effort characteristic of later social play.

For example, several children may be building with blocks, but each builds a separate creation. Cognitive maturation has proceeded to the point where children can begin to share and cooperate but not yet participate in a common and truly interactive experience. When asked to describe how they are playing together, one reports making a spaceship, one a firehouse, another a circus. Although playing together, the children do not coordinate their efforts.

Associative play sometimes produces behavioral contagion, activities that "catch on" and are copied by others who observe it. For example, a few children will be building with blocks and suddenly all the children in the area want to build with blocks.

Cooperative Play. Between the ages of four and six, children begin to demonstrate cooperative play. It is not uncommon to see one four-year-old pushing another on a swing, or children on a see-saw together. These activities, requiring coordinated actions on the part of two or more children, exemplify the principle of cooperative play.

Board games and team sports, favorites of the over-six age group, require a basic facility with cooperative play. To Piaget, cooperative play indicates significant cognitive and social maturation. Children now can conceptualize, create, and enjoy shared experiences.

Aggression

In contrast to play, aggression is viewed as detrimental to development. Aggression is usually defined as any behavior intended to harm others. However, it is important to distinguish between types of aggression and to differentiate typical patterns of aggression from those likely to be more pathological.

Aggressive behavior is a good demonstration of the effects of both maturation and experience.

FORMS OF AGGRESSION

Aggression can be either physical or verbal. Hitting, kicking, and yelling are all forms of physical aggression, whereas name- calling and other forms of insult are verbal aggression.

Aggression also can be either exploratory, instrumental, or hostile in nature. *Exploratory aggression*, as its name suggests, is aggression that occurs carelessly or incidentally to exploration. For example, an infant pokes a child in the eye while trying to grab an eyelash.

Instrumental aggression occurs when aggression is used as a means to an end, such as hitting a child in order to retrieve a treasured toy.

Hostile aggression has as its primary goal specifically injuring another person. It is often retaliatory, an action in response to a real or imagined hurt.

DEVELOPMENTAL TRENDS IN AGGRESSION

Prior to the age of four, most children are aggressive and most of their aggression is physical. Exploratory aggression is common during the first two to three years. Instrumental aggression begins at 18-24 months as children's exploratory behavior enables them to learn cause-effect relationships associated with behaviors such as hitting, kicking, and biting. Typically, aggression peaks at about four years and then begins to decline.

The aggression of children over four becomes more verbal and more retaliatory. Name-calling and other forms of teasing predominate among five- to seven-year-olds. Children aged five to six are more likely to defend themselves when attacked by responding in kind. By six to seven years, most children begin to acquire alternative ways of resolving conflicts, and aggressive outbursts become infrequent.

INDIVIDUAL DIFFERENCES IN AGGRESSION

Children clearly differ in the extent to which they demonstrate aggression. Gender, stress, and social influences are all factors in individual differences in childhood aggression.

Gender. Beginning around age four, boys show more physical aggression, while girls are more likely to be verbally aggressive, including threats to "tell on you." Aggression also shows more stability for boys than for girls. Both of these patterns have been related to sex-role stereotypes.

Stress. As with adults, level of aggression in children is influenced by frustration and threats to one's sense of security. Children whose lives are chaotic often evidence high levels of aggression, as do children whose lives are in transition (e.g., experiencing divorce).

There are scant data to support a biological predisposition to aggression; it appears more likely to result from learning and experiences. Children who fail to learn alternative ways of dealing with frustration and conflict are likely to demonstrate higher levels of aggressive behavior.

Social Influences. Aggression has a complex relationship to popularity with peers and thus to opportunities for social interaction. Submissive children, who fail to defend themselves or retaliate when attacked, tend to be unpopular. On the other hand, children who frequently explode and exhibit uncontrolled aggression toward everyone also are unpopular. Popular children are somewhat aggressive, but their aggression is controlled and focused. They are also able to be assertive without resorting to aggression, and to employ a variety of nonaggressive strategies to resolve conflicts with others.

MORAL DEVELOPMENT

Moral development is the process by which children acquire knowledge of right and wrong. Developmental psychologists have studied this process as well as how this knowledge affects children's behavior.

Early Theories

Early developmental theories proposed different processes to underlie moral development.

PSYCHOANALYTIC THEORY

Psychoanalytic theory proposed that morality resided in the superego, a part of the psyche formed through identification with the same sex-parent during preschool. (For a review of the psychoanalytic structure of the personality, see chapter 14). This identification was an attempt to reduce anxiety created by the central conflict of the phallic stage of psychosexual development: the Oedipal conflict (for boys) and the Elektra conflict (for girls). (See chapter 11 for a review of the psychosexual stages of development.)

Freud proposed that the intrinsically sexual nature of the human animal led to unconscious childhood desires for exclusive control of an opposite-sex parent. Such desires placed children in direct competition with same-sex parents, and thus produced high levels of anxiety. By identifying with the same-sex parent, and becoming like that parent, children protected themselves from possible retaliation by that parent.

It is difficult to evaluate the psychoanalytic proposal empirically since both the phallic conflict and its resolution through identification occur unconsciously. Although children and adults do differ in superego strength, a psychoanalytic construct, it is difficult to relate superego strength to specific experiences or use it to predict obedience to rules or values.

LEARNING THEORY

Learning theory proposed that morality or a set of values was a meaningless concept. Instead, children acquire patterns of responses to specific situations based on their experiences with reinforcement, punishment, and models. This doctrine of specifity predicts that children will not necessarily act in morally consistent ways in different situations.

There appears to be some validity to this proposal. Although current research indicates that children can evaluate situations and explain why a course of action is "right" or "wrong," there is little relationship between a child's stated values and his or her behavior.

Cognitive-Developmental Theories

Cognitive-developmental theories focus on the emergence of moral judgment or reasoning, the child's ability to understand and apply concepts of "right" and "wrong" to specific situations.

PIAGET'S THEORY

Piaget proposed two stages of moral development maturationally tied to concrete operational and formal operational thinking.

Before Moral Development. Until the age of six, children are viewed as premoral, lacking awareness or appreciation of the existence of a system of rules for regulating behavior. Piaget saw this characteristic as a natural outgrowth of the egocentrism of the preoperational child.

Moral Realism. The first true stage, called moral realism or morality of constraint, coincides with the entrance to concrete operations. Children recognize the existence of rules and codes for behavior, but they lack a real understanding of their nature. Rules are seen as universal, unchangeable, and primarily functioning to limit behavioral options.

The rigidity of concrete operational thinking leads to belief in the importance of unbending adherence to rules and swift retribution for transgressions.

Moral Relativism. The second stage, moral relativism or morality of cooperation, coincides with the onset of formal operations. Thinking becomes more flexible and abstract, enabling children to understand rules as a cooperative effort to create a useful system for behavior regulation. The emphasis is on restitution for wrongdoing, the restoration of property or rights affected by a transgression.

Critiquing Piaget's Model. Piaget's theory is important as an initial effort to describe the development of moral reasoning. As research progressed, however, it became clear that the two-stage model was unable to capture the variety of judgments seen in childhood, adolescence, and adulthood.

KOHLBERG'S THEORY

Lawrence Kohlberg noted that there was not the age-related consistency in moral judgments predicted by Piaget's theory. In fact, when confronted with "moral dilemmas," word problems posing two possible courses of action, some subjects in each age group could reason in ways to support either choice.

There were, however, definite patterns in the types of reasons generated. Kohlberg subsequently developed a model of moral reasoning containing three levels of moral development, each containing two stages (see Table 13-1).

Kohlberg's stages were viewed as sequential and universal across cultures, tied both to cognitive development and social experiences. Although Kohlberg's theory has been criticized recently by Carol Gilligan as biased against women, it remains the dominant model of moral development today.

The Preconventional Level. In Level 1, the preconventional level (age four to 10 years), children's reasoning does not reflect an awareness of rules as a system with inherent benefits to those who use it. Thinking reflects an emphasis on the physical consequences of actions and the power of authority figures.

At Stage 1, the *obedience and punishment* orientation, children make choices based on the principles of avoiding punishment and obeying authority figures.

In Stage 2, *naive hedonistic and instrumental* orientation, choices are governed by the principle of self-satisfaction ("hedonism," or seeking pleasure and avoiding pain), and satisfying the needs of others who are important in the life of the child.

Table 13-1: Kohlberg's Stages of Moral Development	
Ages	**Level, Stage and Orientation**
4-10	**Level 1: Preconventional**
	Stage 1: Obedience and punishment orientation
	Stage 2: Naive hedonistic and instrumental orientation
10+	**Level 2: Conventional**
	Stage 3: Good boy/good girl orientation
	Stage 4: Law and authority orientation
13+	**Level 3: Postconventional**
	Stage 5: Social contract orientation
	Stage 6: Universal ethical principle orientation

The Conventional Level. At Level 2, the conventional level (beyond 10 years of age), reasoning reflects not only the pressure to conform for personal gain but also a loyalty to codes of behavior based on a sense of belonging to a family or society. Doing "the right thing" becomes an end in itself.

In Stage 3, the *good boy/good girl* orientation, children make choices reflecting a desire for the approval of others.

At Stage 4, *law and authority* orientation, the decisions reflect a sense of "duty" to obey recognized authority and the avoidance of actions that might undermine the social order. According to Kohlberg's research, most adolescents and adults demonstrate some form of Level 2 thinking.

The Postconventional Level. Level 3, the postconventional level, probably can be attained only by adults who are formal operational and have had experience both with freedom of choice and the effects of the lack of such freedom. Individuals at this level are guided by concern for the rights of the individual rather than loyalty to the group.

In Stage 5, *social contract* orientation, concern is focused on balancing the value of social stability with the rights of the individual. Morality is viewed as a social contract in which individuals derive benefits from compliance with rules. Rules can and should be adjusted when adherence to those rules fails to protect the rights of individuals.

At Stage 6, *universal ethical principle* orientation, decisions are based on conscience and principles such as justice, reciprocity, human rights, and personal dignity. Violation of principles, rather than laws, is condemned.

GILLIGAN'S CRITIQUE

Psychologist Carol Gilligan has criticized Kohlberg's research and theory on the grounds that his assumptions—and thus his conclusions—are sexist. Specifically, Kohlberg had found that, in explaining their judgments that certain "moral dilemmas" were decided rightly or wrongly, girls and women reasoned at a lower level of moral development than boys and men.

For example, should a man steal an expensive drug to save the life of his sick wife if he cannot afford to pay the pharmacist's price? Kohlberg found that boys and men tended to say yes, because human life is more important than money or property. But Kohlberg found that girls and women gave less absolute answers, and did not cite the "principle" that life is more valuable than property.

Gilligan's criticism of Kohlberg suggests that males and females are taught different values as they develop, not different levels—higher versus lower—of the same values or principles.

Specifically, Gilligan argues that boys and men are taught to value independence, autonomy in identifying the important principles of moral decision-making. Girls and women, however, are taught to value relationships and connections with others as being of lasting importance. Thus many girls and women responded to the drug theft dilemma by suggesting that the thief and the druggist cooperate to find a solution to their problem, rather than forcing the thief to take drastic action alone.

Gilligan's research serves as a reminder that developmental theories, like all theories, may be subject to the biases and expectations of the theorist. An important function of psychological research is to examine and question the value of past theories in applying them to present observations and experience.

Children are social creatures, and studies of social development—particularly children's play and aggressive behavior—have provided clues to broader developmental processes. Theories of play have examined its ethological value, its developmental role, its structure, and its developmental forms. Studies of aggression have examined its forms, developmental trends in aggression, and individual differences in its development and expression.

Studies of moral development examine how children learn to make decisions about what is right or wrong. Psychoanalytic theory explains moral thinking in terms of the operation of the superego. Kohlberg's theory argues that moral thinking develops over a series of stages in three levels: preconventional, conventional, and postconventional moral thinking. Gilligan has criticized Kohlberg's theory in terms of sexism, and suggested that the genders are educated to pursue different values, not different levels of the same moral principles.

Selected Readings

Eisenberg, N. *The Development of Prosocial Behavior*. New York: Academic Press. 1982

Gilligan, C. *In a Different Voice: Psychological Theory and Women's Development*. Cambridge, MA: Harvard University Press. 1982

Kohlberg, L. *Essays on Moral Development, Volume I*. New York: Harper and Row. 1981

Rest, J. R. *Moral Development: Advances in Research and Theory*. New York: Praeger. 1986

14

Personality

In the long history of psychology as a human interest, personality has been one of the most enduring subjects. Personality is defined as an individual's characteristic pattern of behavior, thought, and emotion. The word personality derives from the Latin persona, or "mask." Many theories of personality suggest that an individual adopts a strategy for behaving from one situation to the next, similar to putting on a mask, although it represents one's "real" self rather than a false face.

PERSONALITY DEVELOPMENT

Personality is influenced by biological as well as psychological factors. Theories of personality have both described and explained the development of personality.

Biological Influences

Are personality tendencies inherited? The popular observation of "like parent, like child," may have support in physiological research.

GENES

The genetic "map" for the nervous system is of course inherited. Insofar as nervous system operation is a function of its anatomy, consequent behavior may show inherited influences.

One example of a genetic influence on personality is the function of a biochemical, monoamine oxidase (MAO), which regulates certain neurotransmitters' concentration in the brain. Low levels of MAO have been associated with a high degree of sensation-seeking, a readiness to take risks and try new behavior.

Other examples of genetic influences on personality are supported by twin studies in which identical twins, separated at birth and raised in separate households, have been found to resemble each other in significant ways as adults.

GENDER

One's biological gender—whether one is anatomically male or female—will have consequences for the physical changes and hormonal influences every individual experiences. However, the effects of gender are usually confounded (blended or confused) with those of gender role, the set of behavioral norms a culture considers standard for individuals of a given gender.

Thus it is difficult to discern whether men are more aggressive than women because of being male (gender) or acting masculine (a learned gender role). Similarly, it is not clear that women are more nonverbally sensitive than men because they are born female (gender) or have learned to act feminine (gender role).

Experiential Influences

Experience plays an undeniable role in personality development and structure. Experiential factors can be found in family influences, cultural norms, and the physical and social environment.

FAMILY

The structure and nature of one's family plays a crucial role in an individual's personality development, especially during one's childhood. Direct family influences include parents' attitudes and practices concerning childrearing, such as support, affect, and discipline.

Another family-related factor thought to influence personality development is *birth order*, one's place in the sequence of children. For example, oldest children have been found to outnumber other birth-order categories in some indices of success and achievement. Oldest children, as the firstborn, may be parents' "experimental" children and learn to work harder for the approval that comes more easily to later-born children.

CULTURE

One's culture or society develops norms, prescriptive patterns of behavior, that are communicated to every individual. Rewards are given for conforming to the norms and penalties for violating or deviating from them.

An example is the relative value of a trait like "independence" in American society. While independence is considered an important value—e.g., the American celebration of the Fourth of July as Independence Day—children may not learn many acceptable ways of behaving independently without violating other cultural norms like "respecting one's elders" and "obedience to authority." Classic social psychological research (see chapter

18) suggests that cultures do differ with respect to values and norms, and that these differences can be measured in individuals' behavior.

ENVIRONMENT

An important environmental influence on personality development is stress, the demands to which an individual must adapt. A child raised in an isolated rural farm family must deal with the stresses of family responsibility, chores, loneliness or boredom, whereas one raised in a small apartment in a big city will have to face crowding, anonymity, and crime.

Even individuals raised in the same families and environments bring different genetic and temperament factors to bear on their situations. This helps to explain why siblings can be so different despite similarities in their experiences.

Most developmental theories of personality consider personality to be the product of an interaction between genetic and biological influences (nature) and experiential influences (nurture).

Persons and Situations

CONSISTENCY

Most personality theories explain behavior in terms of the influence of stable personality traits and patterns. However, personality is not manifested in a vacuum. Observable behaviors are usually responses to situations, circumstances that provide the context for behavior. Psychologist Walter Mischel has argued that people's behavior across situations fails to show the consistency and reliability to be expected of personality. In essence, personality traits are poor predictors of behavior.

Alternatively, Mischel argues, people's behaviors are shaped by the rewards and punishments provided by their social situations (see Social Learning Theory).

RECIPROCAL DETERMINISM

Psychologist Albert Bandura suggests that persons and situations interact in a mutually influential process called reciprocal determinism. Situations shape persons' behaviors in ways that may endure. Then these behavior patterns influence both the selection and impact of future situations.

As long as one can select his or her situations, it is possible that behavior in those situations will be very similar from one occasion to the next. But this illusion of consistency, argues Mischel, is not proof that the entity called "personality" exists.

DESCRIPTIVE THEORIES OF PERSONALITY

As this chapter reveals, numerous theories have been proposed to explain personality. These theories can be broadly classified into two categories: theories that *describe* personality, and theories that account for the *development* of personality.

Whether it is descriptive or developmental, a theory of personality must account for two paradoxical ideas: (1) the commonality or similarity of experiences and behaviors that is observed across individuals, despite their uniqueness; and (2) the individual differences among people despite this commonality.

This section summarizes prominent descriptive theories of personality. There are two kinds of descriptive theories: type theories and trait theories.

Type Theories

FOUR-HUMORS THEORY

The earliest recorded personality "theory" was a type theory, a model of the categories of personality descriptions. This was the four-humors theory adapted by the early Roman physician Galen, based on the ideas of the ancient Greek physician Hippocrates (see chapter 1).

According to four-humors theory, the human body produced and required four humors or bodily fluids to function: blood, yellow bile, black bile, and phlegm. An imbalance among these humors would cause physical or psychological illness.

Excessive levels of any one humor could be diagnosed by specific moods or personality tendencies. An excess of blood caused one to be "sanguine" or cheerful. Too much yellow bile caused one to be "bilious" or angry. Black bile (in Greek, *melancholia*) caused one to be extremely sad. And a predominance of phlegm would make one "phlegmatic" or lethargic and apathetic.

Such excesses could be corrected by the process of bloodletting, a practice popular through the Middle Ages of opening a vein to "release" the excess humors. Bloodletting was usually done by barber-surgeons, whose tools-of-the-trade were scissors and scalpels. Their nonverbal sign of trade, a white arm trailing a spiral of blood, can be recognized in the modern barber shop pole.

CONSTITUTIONAL THEORY

Although no modern psychologist takes seriously the predictions of four-humors theory, the idea that one's physique has an impact on personality has remained popular.

American psychologist William H. Sheldon (1899–1977) popularized such a notion with his constitutional theory of personality. According to Sheldon, people's physical bodies could be classified in three body types or somatotypes: the *ectomorph*, a tall, thin, fragile frame with a large head; the *mesomorph*, a muscular, athletic, thick-necked body; and the *endomorph*, a soft, rounded, overweight body. While few people would be classified as "true" types, everyone could be graded or scaled according to each morphological type.

Each of Sheldon's somatotypes is associated with a predominant personality tendency or orientation. Ectomorphs were cerebrotonic: cerebral, introverted, and self-conscious. Mesomorphs were somatotonic: active, risk-oriented, and adventuresome. And endomorphs were visceratonic: sociable, fond of food, people, and comfort.

Sheldon's original theory is no longer popular, but it has influenced recent work on temperament and personality.

CONTEMPORARY TYPE APPROACHES

The type approach is popular among laypersons because it simplifies understanding commonalities and individual differences. For this reason, type theories of personality continue to be developed for modern applications.

The Type A Personality. A recent example of the type approach is the profile of the Type A personality, a behavior pattern characterized by impatience, concern with time and punctuality, anger, and perfectionism. First described in the 1970s, the Type A profile is interesting because it has been linked to a higher risk of cardiovascular disease like heart attacks. Unlike early somatotype theories, however, the Type A personality is thought to be the cause, not the consequence, of this susceptibility to heart disease. (See chapter 15 for further details on the consequences of Type A behavior).

The Myers-Briggs Type Indicator. Based loosely on psychoanalytic theorist Carl Jung's theories of personality, the Myers-Briggs Type Indicator is a paper-and-pencil personality inventory that categorizes respondents along four dimensions: introverted-extroverted; sensing-intui-ting; thinking-feeling; and perceiving-judging. A respondent's pattern of answers is categorized along these four choices based on its resemblance to others' answers. For example, an "ENTJ" profile characterizes someone who is extroverted, intuiting, thinking, and judging.

Originally published in 1943 by Katharine C. Briggs and Isabel Briggs Myers, and revised several times since then (most recently in 1987), the Myers-Briggs is more popular as an informal self-assessment experience than a formal diagnostic tool. For example, management trainees may complete the Myers-Briggs to discover their individual management "styles" and identify better strategies for working with others.

Trait Theories

Another descriptive approach to personality is the trait approach. A trait is a relatively stable personality tendency. Words like "generous," "ambitious," "aggressive," and "shy" are all examples of traits.

GORDON ALLPORT

American psychologist Gordon W. Allport (1897-1967) believed that the trait was the best unit of analysis for the study of personality. For Allport an individual's traits were part of his or her nervous system, and thus basic to his or her behavior.

In research with a colleague, H. S. Odbert, Allport identified almost 18,000 trait words in the English language, testifying to their importance in behavior and society.

Allport distinguished among cardinal traits, central traits, and secondary traits. *Cardinal traits* are rare but so central to one's personality that they influence virtually all behavior. For example, an extremely selfish person may convey this characteristic in all he or she does. *Central traits* are often but not always detectable in behavior, such as shyness which is not evident when one is with friends or family members. *Secondary traits* come into use in particular situations but not general behavior. For example, one may behave aggressively when absolutely necessary but avoid doing so as under normal circumstances.

PERSONALITY FACTORS

Raymond B. Cattell. Psychologist Raymond B. Cattell (b. 1905) applied a mathematical procedure called factor analysis to a narrowed-down list of 200 personality traits. Results of this analysis showed that the many different trait terms sorted into 16 basic *personality factors.* For example, the different terms "persevering," "determined," "responsible," "ordered," "attentive" and "stable" are all slight variations of the same basic personality factor.

Five-Factor Theory. Still other efforts to reduce the load of terms that encumber trait theories have suggested that there are even fewer then 16 basic personality factors. One set of five factors has been repeatedly confirmed in recent research: extraversion; agreeableness; conscientiousness; emotional stability; and intelligence.

DEVELOPMENTAL THEORIES OF PERSONALITY

As popular as type and trait theories are for their simplicity and familiarity, they fail to explain whether and how an invididual's personality develops and changes across situations as well as across the lifespan. Most theories of personality begin by addressing its development and apply these concepts in describing and predicting behavior.

There are three broad categories of developmental personality theories: psychoanalytic theories; humanistic theories; and learning theories.

Psychoanalytic Theories

Most psychoanalytic theories begin with the work and ideas of Sigmund Freud (1856-1939), the Viennese physician who originated psychoanalysis, an approach to therapy, human nature, and personality theory that emphasizes the role of unconscious motivation in conscious behavior.

The best-known concepts in psychoanalytic personality theory were developed by Freud himself. In addition, important contributions were made by Freud's followers and students, who went on to develop important variations. These include the theories of Carl Jung, Alfred Adler, Erik Erikson, and Karen Horney.

SIGMUND FREUD

Sigmund Freud was trained in medicine and specialized in the treatment of "nervous disorders" such as hysteria (conversion disorder), a pattern of physical symptoms with psychogenic (psychologically-originating) causes.

In the course of his practice and research, Freud built upon mechanistic ideas of the physical bases of behavior, as well as early ideas of levels of consciousness.

Basic Concepts. According to Freud, all human behavior is driven by two basic, antagonistic, biological instincts: the life instinct (Eros) and the death instinct (Thanatos), which respectively emerge in the motives of sex and aggression.

These instincts are not part of conscious deliberation but reside in the larger region of the mind that is unconscious, unavailable to conscious reflection and memory. Between the conscious and the unconscious minds is a preconscious level where ideas and images remain accessible to consciousness before they are retrieved (e.g., memories).

The relationship among these Freudian concepts of levels of consciousness is often depicted as a largely-submerged iceberg, emphasizing that the "visible" personality ("above the surface") is but a small part of one's total personality and motivation.

Much of one's unconscious motivation is antisocial and selfish and violates the laws of civilized society. When such ideas are consciously considered, one experiences anxiety, an overwhelming feeling of dread similar to fear. To avoid anxiety, one represses unwanted thoughts, feelings, or memories, pushing them beyond conscious access into the unconscious.

When life experiences are threatening or frustrating, an individual is strongly motivated to defend against possible anxiety by employing defense mechanisms, behavior patterns that reduce the symptoms of anxiety but do not necessarily eliminate the sources of the conflict. For a review of basic defense mechanisms, see chapter 15.

Personality Structure. One of Freud's most enduring contributions to a popular understanding of personality is his theory of the structure of personality. According to Freud, the individual at birth has no personality or public "persona" yet. The infant is completely selfish and motivated by the pleasure principle, the drive to seek physical pleasure and satisfaction. This is embodied in a part of the personality known as the *id* (Latin for "it").

In the course of early childhood discipline the child develops ideas of right and wrong, permitted and forbidden behavior. The understanding that some acts are wrong comprises one's conscience, while the gradual understanding of what is good and socially rewarded becomes one's ego ideal (idealized self). Together the conscience and ego ideal make up the *superego*. The superego guides and shapes the primitive id, inducing guilt when one has behaved selfishly or badly, and permitting a sense of pride when one has behaved well.

Between the selfish urges of the id and the almost unrealistic admonitions of the superego, one develops an *ego*, a self that is largely visible (in contrast with the completely unconscious id and the partially unconscious superego). The ego abides by the reality principle, effecting compromise that will satisfy some of the id's demands while not violating too many of the superego's constraints.

For example, when one meets an attractive new person, one's id might commence sexual fantasies and urge aggression, while one's superego pretends disinterest and advises escape. One's ego might effect a compromise by remaining in the situation but acting with restraint, perhaps starting a conversation or asking the other person for a date, without making any aggressive advances.

It is important for these different personality components to develop in balance. A powerful id or weak superego may result in unchecked antisocial behavior, such as criminal activity. A weak id or powerful superego may result in personally ineffective behavior, self-denial, and unrealistic standards of behavior.

Psychosexual Development. For Freud, the psychic energy of unconscious motivation originated in biological growth. In the course of early life, as our bodies change, we associate pleasure with the stimulation of different parts of the body. From infancy to adolescence our development is guided by experiences associated with these erogenous zones. Freud referred to this development, through changing associations of physical pleasure, as psychosexual development.

There are five stages of psychosexual development: the oral stage (the first year), during which pleasure is associated with the mouth; the anal stage (ages two and three), when toilet training conflicts with one's desire to control one's own body; the phallic stage (ages three to six), when the child associates pleasure with genital manipulation, and becomes interested in the opposite sex; a latency period (ages six to 12), during which the child focuses more on activity (e.g., school) than physical pleasure and parental discipline; and finally the genital stage, from puberty through adolescence, when genital pleasure is associated with pleasing another—a partner of one's own choosing—rather than oneself. (See chapter 11 and Table 11.1 for more information about the psychosexual stages of development).

CARL JUNG

Carl G. Jung (1885-1961) was once thought of as Freud's "crown prince of psychoanalysis" before he broke with his mentor over differences in their theories. Jung's interests in symbolism and mysticism have made his ideas enduring and popular today.

Personal versus Collective Unconscious. Jung differentiated within the unconscious mind between a personal unconscious and a collective unconscious.

One's personal unconscious contains one's own repressed thoughts, forgotten experiences, and undeveloped ideas—any of which can be triggered into recall by new sensations.

The collective unconscious consists of memories and behavior patterns inherited from one's ancestors. Among the thought forms stored in the collective unconscious are *archetypes*, ideas and memories that people have had in common from primitive human origins. Archetypes form the basis for many universally recognizable symbols. They explain why myths and fairy tales are so similar across vastly different times and cultures worldwide.

Anima and Animus. Two other archetypes, the anima and animus, represent an unconscious level of gender. Every woman's personality includes an animus, her male traits, and every man's personality includes an anima, his female traits. These are important in successful interaction with members of the opposite sex, since they provide a degree of recognition and empathy.

Extroversion versus Introversion. Jung categorized personalities into two types based on attitudes toward others. Introverts are unsociable, withdrawn, and concerned with their private worlds. Extroverts are outgoing, interested in participation in external events and involvement with others.

Rational versus Irrational People. Jung also categorized people according to their use of reason in guiding their actions. Rational people think and feel, making decisions on the basis of ideas, emotions, and value judgments. Irrational people base their perceptions on sensations and intuitions, relying on surface impressions or unconscious insights.

ALFRED ADLER

While Jung's theories resemble Freud's in many ways, those of another Freudian disciple, Alfred Adler ((1870-1937), differed obviously.

Power as Motivation. Freud's model of personality emphasized the value of physical pleasure and biological satisfaction, while Adler argued that a more important goal in human behavior is the achievement of competence or power. One implication of this is the use of the defense mechanism of compensation, efforts to overcome real or imagined personal deficiencies. A popular Adlerian image is that of the French dictator Napoleon, compensating for shortness in physical stature by becoming politically "tall" as emperor.

In cases where compensation fails and one becomes defeated as well as disillusioned with oneself, Adler blames an inferiority complex, a paralyzing fixation on one's inadequacies.

Striving for Perfection. Beyond childhood concerns with power and domination, Adler argued, adult life is characterized by striving for perfection, efforts to become personally superior as well as make one's society better. Early in life one develops guidelines and personal meanings that influence one's style of life. Specifically, an individual composes a set of goals that make up his or her fictional finalism, the values he or she believes in and pursues, whether they are attainable or not.

ERIK ERIKSON

Erik Erikson (b. 1902) is sometimes referred to as a "neo- Freudian" theorist because his own theories build in such innovative ways upon those of Freud. Erikson's best-known elaboration on Freudian theory is his sequences of psychosocial development. Unlike Freud's five stages of psychosexual development, which cover the period from birth through adolescence, Erikson's sequence maps psychosocial "crises" that one encounters throughout the life span.

The eight stages of Erikson's sequence are: trust versus mistrust; autonomy versus shame and doubt; initiative versus guilt; industry versus inferiority; identify versus role-confusion; intimacy versus isolation;

generativity versus stagnation ; and integrity versus despair. (For details on Erikson's stages, see chapter 11 and Table 11.2).

KAREN HORNEY

Based on her experience as a therapist in both Germany and the United States, Karen Horney (1885-1952) argued that sex and physical pleasure had been overemphasized as motivating forces in personality.

Anxiety as Motivation. Instead, Horney posited that the noxiousness of anxiety was a more basic motivator of behavior. In contrast with Freud's characterization of anxiety as based in sexual conflict, Horney pointed out that anxiety has many other sources. For example, young children are dependent for survival on their parents, a relationship that must prepare one for both satisfaction and disappointment. In response to the anxiety of this dependency, children build up defensive ways of reacting, first to their families and ultimately to the world.

Neurotic Trends and Relationship Types. For Horney, the defensive behaviors people develop can become neurotic trends, patterns that work as defenses only at the cost of independence. Neurotic trends were characterized by three types of personality, revealed in people's personal relationships. The *compliant type* of individual approaches and submits to others in an effort to gain their approval. The *aggressive type* attacks and moves against others rather than approaching them. And the *detached type* withdraws and moves away from others. These trends are neurotic because they become inflexible traps from which individuals cannot escape or develop freely and independently.

Humanistic Theories

Psychoanalytic theories of personality development generally portray human motivation as self-interested and uncivilized unless socially acceptable roles and outlets are provided.

In contrast, humanistic theories of personality assume that human nature is essentially positive, productive, and growth-oriented, and that people would develop in healthy ways if they knew how.

WILLIAM JAMES

The early functionalist theorist William James (1842-1910) developed a four-part theory of the self that is considered to be an early influence on humanistic theory.

According to James, one's self is a collection of four "selves": a material self that includes one's physical body and material possessions; a social self that consists of how one is viewed by others; a spiritual self, one's psychological faculties, including reasoning and feeling; and the pure ego, maintained in one's ongoing awareness or stream of consciousness.

ABRAHAM MASLOW

The work of Abraham Maslow (1908-1970) has powerfully shaped humanistic theories of personality.

Hierarchy of Motives. Maslow's hierarchy of motives (see chapter 10) proposes that human motivation is founded in needs, but that these needs range from basic physiological survival to social needs like belonging and esteem, and ultimately to a distinctly human need for self-actualization. (See Figure 10- 1).

Self-Actualization. Maslow focused his research on the phenomenon of self-actualization by studying friends, acquaintances, and historical figures whose lives seemed to embody the principles of productiveness, self-acceptance, dignity, and appreciation of the world. He observed that the achievement of self-actualization is often marked by peak experiences, feelings of ineffable happiness and peace in the course of one's life activities.

CARL ROGERS

Carl Rogers (1902-1987) is known for his humanistic approach to therapy (see chapter 17) as well as his contributions to humanistic personality theory.

Self-Actualizing Tendency. Rogers has argued that each individual possesses a genetic "blueprint" for his or her life's potential, and a biological urge propels him or her forward to realize it, a drive he calls the self-actualizing tendency. Thus self-actualization is not only possible for every human, it is natural and would be universal if all people were encouraged and assisted in this process.

Positive Self-Regard. The difficulty in actualizing oneself originates in an unrealistic or unhealthy self-concept or self-image. One's self-concept develops from childhood as a result of the regard or treatment others provide.

When one experiences conditional positive self-regard, the positive self-concept has been made conditional on certain behaviors. When these conditions are violated, one's self-regard is not positive.

Instead, Rogers argues, an individual must feel unconditional positive self-regard, a positive estimation of self-concept that is not conditional on any specific behaviors or bargains with others.

When one accepts oneself positively and unconditionally, one closes the gap between one's present self-concept and one's ideal self (similar to Freud's ego ideal), and becomes a fully-functioning person, self-directed, independent but respectful of others, and open to experience.

Learning Theories

Both psychoanalytic and humanistic theories portray human personality as naturally driven, whether by biological impulses or a self-actualizing tendency. Unlike these are the learning theories of personality. These apply basic principles of learning to the development and function of personality.

While there is no "behaviorist theory of personality" per se, the behaviorist approach to learning (e.g., that of B. F. Skinner [1904-1990]) has been extended to the phenomenon of personality.

In this view, personality is a consistent pattern of behavioral responses across time and situations. An individual, motivated by needs, acts upon the environment and is either reinforced or punished by the consequences. The consequences provided by one's social and physical environment will thus shape one's personality.

REINFORCEMENT THEORY

Learning theorists John Dollard (1900–1980) and Neal E. Miller (b. 1909) have identified as reinforcements those consequences which reduce a drive or satisfy a need. Behavior that is consistently reinforced will be consistently emitted. For example, if a child wants a parent's attention, she might throw a tantrum. The parent might spank or criticize the child in an effort to stop the tantrum, but if the parent pays any attention to the child, the tantrum behavior has been reinforced, and the child has "learned" to behave this way in the future.

Dollard and Miller agree with psychoanalytic theorists that the early childhood years are important to personality development, though for reasons of training rather than psychic sensitivity. They further explain conflicts between child and parent as due to inconsistencies in reinforcement and punishment. As one example, a parent might sometimes punish a child for "making a mess" with food or crayons but at other times praise the child for being creative or "cute."

One implication of reinforcement theory for personality development is that unsuccessful personality patterns can be changed through learning. A shy or victimized person can learn to be assertive by engineering rewards (e.g., self-respect, others' cooperation) for behaving in an assertive manner.

SOCIAL LEARNING THEORY

In a lifetime, most of a person's social experience will involve other people besides his or her parents. Most others will not design a consistent schedule of reinforcement or punishment to "train" someone into developing a particular personality pattern. For this reason some theorists argue that most social learning relies not on reinforcement and punishment but on less direct processes.

A leading proponent of social learning theory, Albert Bandura (b. 1925), has implicated *modeling* as a powerful process in personality development. In modeling, an individual observes another's behaviors and their consequences, imitating actions and vicariously identifying the consequences.

By observing others' actions and their consequences, Bandura says, people develop *performance standards*, behavioral goals and expectations. Thus a girl whose father values achievement and praises it in his wife and children will learn to set ambitious, achievement-oriented standards for her own performance.

Experiencing success in meeting one's own performance standards will develop one's sense of *self-efficacy*, a feeling of competence and self-control.

Persons and Situations. Social learning theory has gained popularity because of its simplicity and applicability. However, it has also been criticized for being a "personality theory without the person." One response to that criticism is that personality depends not on the consistency of behavior across experiences and situations but on its flexibility.

*P*ersonality is the individual's pattern of behavior, thoughts, and feelings. There is evidence that personality is influenced by both biological factors, such as genes and gender, and experiential factors, including the influences of family, culture, and environment. The concept of personality is controversial in that it involves analyzing the relative influence of persons and situations. Personality theories must account for the commonality of personality among individuals as well as individual differences despite those commonalities.

Most personality theories explain both the development and the function of personality, although some are primarily descriptive. Descriptive theories include both type theories and trait theories. Type theories categorize personality patterns into a finite number of profiles, such as the ancient four-humors theory, Sheldon's constitutional theory, and contemporary type approaches such as the Type A profile and the Myers-Briggs personality scale. Trait theories examine the meanings and patterns of trait descriptions of personality. Among these are Allport's identification of cardinal, central, and secondary traits; R. B. Cattell's 16-factor theory of personality; and the theory that all traits can be summarized in five factors.

Developmental theories of personality include psychoanalytic, humanistic, and learning theories. Psychoanalytic theories are based on the original ideas of Freud and his followers' subsequent elaborations. Freud's basic concepts include the role of unconscious motivation, the power of anxiety, the structure of the personality, and the development of personality through five psychosexual stages.

Jung's theories posit the influence of both a personal and collective unconscious, the gender-related influences of anima and animus, and typing persons along introversion-extroversion and rational-irrational functioning.

Adler's theory emphasizes the importance of power and competence in personality development, influencing such behaviors as compensation and the inferiority complex. For Adler, each individual strives for perfection by following a unique style of life and pursuing the goals of a fictional finalism.

Erikson's innovation on Freud's sequence of psychosexual development resulted in a model of lifelong psychosocial development.

Horney proposed that anxiety was a more basic motivator than pleasure, and that its sources were more varied sexual conflicts. In defending against anxiety, people may develop neurotic trends of responding to others by being compliant, aggressive or detached. These trends can entrap one by curtailing freedom and independence.

In contrast with the assumptions of psychoanalysis, humanistic theories conceptualize human nature as productive and oriented toward growth and health. William James's original self theory proposed several levels of selfhood. Maslow's theory proposes a hierarchy of motives whose ultimate human goal is self- actualization. Rogers's approach to therapy and theory characterizes the self-actualizing tendency as biological in orgin. The key to a fulfilled self is unconditional positive self-regard.

Learning theories of personality apply the principles of operant conditional and observational learning to personality development. Dollard and Miller extend Skinner's concept of reinforcement contingencies to explain how personality is shaped over time. Bandura's social learning approach emphasizes the power of observational learning and modeling in influencing the consistency of personality over situations.

Selected Readings

Byrne, D. E. *An Introduction to Personality.* Englewood Cliffs, NJ: Prentice-Hall. 1981

Hampson, S. E. *The Construction of Personality: An Introduction, 2nd Edition.* London: Routledge. 1988

Mindess, H. *Makers of Psychology: The Personal Factor.* New York: Human Sciences Press. 1988

Phares, E. J. *Introduction to Personality, 2nd Edition.* Glenview, IL: Scott, Foresman. 1988

Rogers, C. R. *A Way of Being.* Boston: Houghton Mifflin.(1980

Skinner, B. F. *Beyond Freedom and Dignity.* New York: Bantam/Vintage. 1982

15

Stress and Conflict

Stress and conflict are a normal part of life, and healthy behavior involves the ability to cope and adapt. Psychologists make a distinction between behavior that successfully defends and copes and behavior that fails to adapt and resolve conflict. The latter category, disordered behavior, will be examined in chapter 16. The present chapter first examines the nature and sources of stress, and then the behavioral strategies with which people respond to stress.

THE CONCEPT OF STRESS

Stress is any demand or set of demands requiring adaptation. The word "stress" derives from the Latin *stringere*, "to stretch." The term implies a stretching of physical and psychological resources to meet demands placed on an organism.

Research on Stress

Modern research on stress began with observations that many physical illnesses, termed *psychosomatic* disorders, were partially caused by psychological factors. The most common psychosomatic disorders are ulcers, hypertension (high blood pressure), migraine headaches, and various skin ailments. For example, an executive may understand that her ulcer is aggravated "by worrying," although worry itself must be physically processed to create her symptoms.

ILLNESS AND TRAUMA

In the late 1930s the Canadian physiologist Hans Selye discovered a pattern of physical symptoms emerging among animals subjected to a variety of stressors. Regardless of the nature of the stress—whether injection of a mild irritant or subjection to extreme cold—the animals showed the signs of excessive endocrine activity and gastric ulceration. Selye's research led to identification of the *general adaptation syndrome* (The Stress Response, below).

Selye's work suggested that the psychophysical connection in psychosomatic disease was stress and the body's response to it.

ENVIRONMENTAL STRESS

Modern work on stress has gained popular interest because of numerous identifications of environmental stressors. Both daily hassles (like commuting and crowding) and traumatic experiences (like natural and technological disasters) have been linked with subsequent symptoms of stress. For example, victims of hurricane damage may show increased physical signs of stress months after the crisis has passed.

The Stress Response

In his research with animals, Selye identified three stages of a general adaptation syndrome, a physiological and psychological pattern of symptoms in the wake of a stressor event. These three stages are termed alarm, resistance, and exhaustion.

THE ALARM STAGE

In the alarm stage, an event is interpreted as a stressor and bodily reactions are triggered. Alarm involves two phases, shock and countershock.

During the first phase of alarm, the shock phase, signals from the brain (the cortex and hypothalamus) initiate the activity of the adrenal glands. The adrenal medulla secretes adrenaline directly into the bloodstream. The effect of adrenaline is heightened heart rate and respiration, as well as other consequences of sympathetic nervous activity.

A "backup" response is initiated by hypothalamic stimulation of the pituitary gland, which begins a sequence of hormonal messages to the adrenal cortex. The adrenal cortex produces corticosteroids, hormones which energize striated muscle strength and endurance. Steroid effects are visible in one's ability to continue running from danger even after the initial adrenaline rush, as well as in the shakiness and weak-kneed sensation that can follow a stressful or frightening experience.

The second phase, countershock, restores and conserves physical energy through rapid response of the parasympathetic branch of the autonomic nervous system.

For example, on first seeing a threatening situation, a person in shock will gasp, experience a rapid heartrate, and react reflexively (shock). Soon thereafter she may feel faint as her body reacts to the sudden expenditure of energy (countershock).

RESISTANCE

During the second stage, resistance, physical defenses are employed in response to the threat identified in the alarm stage. The activity of the sympathetic branch of the autonomic nervous system takes the form of "fight or flight."

If the threat can be attacked ("fight"), resources will be directed to the upper body, and the individual will strike and dodge.

If the threat can be escaped ("flight"), energy and strength (in the form of increase blood supply and muscle tension) will be channeled to the lower-body muscles, and the threatened individual will run.

If the threat is more subtle, like increasing cold, one's resistance will be as subtle as piloerection (body hairs rising to create some insulation) and shivering (which keeps the body moving and circulation active).

Resistance then can take the forms of both physical reflexes and behavioral reactions.

EXHAUSTION

In most experiences of stress, resistance strategies will succeed in solving the problem. The cold person will stay alive and awake long enough to find shelter. The person who is attacked will escape or defend herself.

However, if resistance fails to reduce the stressor (if one continues to interpret events as requiring adaptation), one enters the third stage, exhaustion.

In exhaustion, the physical activity begun in the alarm stage begins again. The danger in exhaustion is that the body has fewer resources to expend in its weakened state. Continued, unrelieved sympathetic arousal results in the breakdown of the body's stress response systems. Consequences will take the form of endocrine, vascular, muscular, and gastric illness and symptoms.

SOURCES OF STRESS

The irony of human stress response is that it is an effective system for responding to basic stressors, but in response to excessive or incessant demands it can become a source of breakdown and illness.

Because the human stress response is presumed to be unchanged over much of human evolution, research attention has focused instead on changes that have occurred in the stressors, the events that humans interpret as requiring the stress response.

Fight-or-Flight

Primitive stressors could be coped with through normal resistance, the "fight-or-flight" behavior pattern.

PRIMITIVE MORTAL THREATS

The human stress response is a legacy of our primitive human ancestors. The fight-or-flight response was effective for the three basic mortal threats to primitive human life: starvation, exposure, and attack.

Primitive humans needed the energization of the stress response to gather and secure food to stave off starvation. Thus hungry people feel energized before they become too weakened by hunger to find food.

Primitive humans also needed the energy to find shelter and protection against the elements and weather extremes.

Finally, primitive humans needed a quick fight-or-flight pattern to respond expediently to the threat of attack from predators or aggressive humans.

MODERN STRESS

Modern humans living in industrial societies are seldom challenged by these three primitive "mortal threats." Modern stress research attributes excessive stress response to our tendency to interpret many events as "threatening." Once having interpreted an event as a stressor, we reflexively initiate the stress-response activity of the autonomic nervous system.

Modern Stressors

Research has identified several kinds of events and experiences to be likely candidates for interpretation as "stressors."

Modern stressors include frustration, conflict, low-level hassles and pressure, the behavior of the Type A personality, major life changes, and extreme stressors like trauma and environmental disaster.

FRUSTRATION

Frustration is the experience of having one's path or access to a goal blocked. A goal may be blocked because an obstacle has been introduced to prevent access, as when a roadblock stops a vehicle from continuing to its destination. Alternatively a goal may be inaccessible because one lacks the resources to approach it, as when the vehicle is out of gas.

Psychologists have identified three general reactions to frustration: aggression, regression, and nonaction.

Aggression. The classic reaction to frustration is aggression. Aggressive behavior intends harm, in this case originally to the source of the frustration. For example, if a rival steals one's mate, the jilted lover will make the rival the target of aggression. Aggression can be *displaced* onto a safer, less retaliatory target. A student who is frustrated by having received a low grade on a test may express anger at his roommate rather than his professor. Finally, aggression may cause damage without alleviating frustration. Feeling frustrated because a vending machine has kept one's money but not produced the ordered soft drink, one may kick the machine in anger, leaving a dent but retrieving no reward. (For a more detailed discussion of aggression, see chapter 10).

Regression. Regressive behavior reflects the immature tactics of an early age. A frustrated friend may whine childishly to get his or her way or win attention. A frustrated manager may bully his coworkers, arousing their fear but not winning their respect.

Nonaction. Finally, repeated frustration may result in nonaction, which may appear to be apathy, or a lack of concern. A more common explanation is that the frustrated individual suffers from *learned helplessness* (see Chapter 6). A wife who has been battered may fail to seek escape or help because she believes such efforts would do no good. A college student who has tried and failed to register for two closed classes may give up before attempting a third, although that one may well be open.

Learning Productive Responses. Research and therapy suggest that these unproductive responses to frustration can be modified through learning and changed reinforcement contingencies. Aggressive and regressive individuals can learn to be assertive and independent. Helpless individuals can learn to make efforts when their goals are attainable and rewards are immediate.

CONFLICT

Conflict is probably the most common stressor. Conflict is the experience of incompatible goals or demands. Two people are in conflict when one opposes what the other desires. Two nations are in conflict when they seek the same limited resource: if one acquires it, the other will not.

Gestalt psychologist Kurt Lewin (1890-1947) described conflict as involving two kinds of forces between persons and goal-objects: approach and avoidance. Approach is the attraction toward a desired goal, while avoidance is the aversion felt toward an undesirable state or event. Given that conflict involves two or more incompatible goals, approach and avoidance combine to form various forms of conflict.

Approach-Approach Conflict. In approach-approach conflict, one must choose between two mutually exclusive attractive goals. For example, a college applicant may have to choose between attending a large university in an exciting urban setting or a small high-quality school in a beautiful scenic region.

Avoidance-Avoidance Conflict. An unpleasant experience is avoidance-avoidance conflict, where one must choose which of two threatening or unpleasant possibilities can be escaped. For example, one may have a severe toothache but fear the pain involved in visiting the dentist. Coping with such conflict usually involves choosing the "lesser of two evils," as in facing brief dental treatment to prevent a worsening tooth disease.

Approach-Avoidance Conflict. The most difficult conflicts to resolve are approach-avoidance conflicts, where one is both attracted and repelled by the same goal. For example, a college student may want to marry rather than delay being with a partner, but fear the loss of freedom and the burden of responsibility involved in young marriage.

Approach-avoidance conflicts are complex and difficult to resolve, because both the attraction and the repulsion create tension, especially as the goal comes closer (e.g., a deadline for making a decision approaches). Avoidance becomes stronger than approach, however, with the result that one often panics, pulls back, becomes attracted again, and continues in a cycle of vacillation until matters are otherwise resolved.

HASSLES AND PRESSURE

Much of the stress of modern life arises from self-imposed expectations and "nonevents," like waiting, disappointments, and boredom.

Hassles. Hassles are small-scale annoyances, irritations, and frustrations. Hassles include lost keys and umbrellas, being stuck in traffic, getting a busy signal, and having minor arguments with others. While no hassle alone can trigger dangerous levels of stress response, hassles tend to accumulate and the resultant stress level builds.

Pressure. Pressure is experienced when expectations or demands for behavior increase. As a result, we feel forced to speed up our actions, hurry our decisions, or intensify our efforts. Pressures can come from internal sources, as when we worry about our own appearance, grades, or performance. They can also come from external sources, such as parents, peers, employers, and cultural norms about what is considered attractive, popular, or successful.

THE TYPE A PERSONALITY

As reviewed in Chapter 14, research has identified a sort of stress-prone personality profile, dubbed the Type A personality. The Type A personality is characterized by perfectionism, an obsession with time and punctuality, and high standards for performance. Type A's are highly competitive and often achieve success and rewards for this behavior pattern. They are often impatient, angry, and frustrated, especially when prevented from completing tasks well or on time, as when traffic delays their travel or others are not punctual.

The Type A personality was originally identified when it was found to be a behavior pattern associated with a greater risk for heart disease. Type A behavior is thus considered coronary-prone behavior. The opposite pattern has been labeled Type B, a profile that is relaxed, unhurried, and cooperative rather than competitive.

The Type A pattern is probably learned over many years, and strategies for change involve learning new behaviors. Thus Type A's might reduce their risk of heart disease and other stress-related ailments by learning to wait patiently, relax, and manage stress.

LIFE CHANGES

A common-sense approach to stress suggests that we are stressed by unpleasant experiences like threat and conflict. An illuminating area of research, however, has indicated that any kind of life change—whether it requires a major or minor alteration in subsequent behavior—acts as a stressor.

Research by Thomas Holmes and Richard Rahe in the 1950s and 1960s resulted in development of a scale of illness-producing life changes. The "top 10" life changes on the list, in descending order of magnitude, includes the following: death of a spouse; divorce; marital separation; jail term; death of close family member; personal injury or illness; marriage; loss of job; marital reconciliation; and retirement. Not all of these experiences are usually considered unpleasant, but all do initiate changed and adaptive behavior, activating the stress response system.

EXTREME STRESSORS

Laboratory research on stress necessarily involves only mild and short-term stressors. Real-life stressors are unconstrained by such ethical considerations. Naturalistic observation has identified stress response patterns in the wake of extreme stressors like natural and technological disasters, personal losses, and societal changes. We can identify five major categories of such extreme stressors: unemployment; relationship termination; bereavement; combat; and environmental disasters.

Unemployment. Increases in the rate of joblessness have been correlated with mental and physical illness and suicide. People seem to react to the loss of a job in four stages: first they are confident of reemployment; secondly they actively job-seek; thirdly they suffer from doubt and deteriorated relations with others; and finally, feeling cynical and unhealthy, they give up.

Evidence indicates that the effects of unemployment are, like other life changes, to exacerbate existing problems rather than create new ones. Similar effects are ironically observable after economic upturns, another form of life change.

Relationship Termination. Divorce and separation are major sources of stress, whether one seeks to end a relationship or is the victim of rejection or abandonment. After separation, an individual experiences separation distress, a reaction to loss of an attachment figure. Emotions become labile (suddenly, dramatically changeable) and ambivalent. Insomnia, lethargy, preoccupation, and depression are not uncommon. Loneliness is experienced because one has lost both one's intimate partner and one's social connection with the community.

Bereavement. It is not surprising that death of one's spouse tops the list of stressful life changes. Reactions to loss through death involve disruption in activity and change in identity. Grief work—behavioral and emotional strategies to cope with the death of a loved one—involves a likely sequence of numbness, despair, yearning, depression, and apathy, before achievement of acceptance. Bereavement, like responses to separation and divorce, is often characterized by the use of defense mechanisms such as denial and displacement.

Combat. After World War I, psychologists identified the syndrome of "shell shock," in which soldiers were disabled by their responses to the trauma of warfare. Common symptoms subsequently observed among veterans of other wars include low threshold for frustration, spontaneous crying or rage, sleeplessness, fear of sudden noises, and confusion. Effects have sometimes been long-term. The condition, identified among Vietnam veterans, has been labeled the *posttraumatic stress disorder*.

Environmental Disasters. Reactions to catastrophes like earthquakes, floods, hurricanes, fires, and plane crashes appear to involve at least three common stages. In the shock stage, victims appear stunned, dazed, numb, or even amnesic. In the suggestible stage, victims passively cooperate with their rescuers and therapists. In the third stage, recovery, anxiety threatens regaining emotional stability, and victims may repeat their stories in an effort to control and understand. Some research suggests the development of later stages involving guilt for having survived when others did not.

RESPONDING TO STRESS

Responding to stress generally takes one of two forms: defending or coping. Defending behaviors reduce the stress or anxiety without eliminating the source. Coping responses restore balance and remove the threat. Because coping requires resources like strength and time, most early responses to stress are defensive rather than effective in coping.

Defending

Defensive reactions to stress, conflict, and anxiety can involve either palliative treatments or defense mechanisms.

PALLIATIVE MEASURES

Palliative measures are treatments that alleviate the pain or distress without effecting a cure. Some palliatives are medicinal, such as taking a pain-relieving drug for a tension headache (instead of identifying and removing the source of tension). Others are distracting or numbing, such as drinking alcohol or taking psychoactive drugs to forget about problems or reduce anxiety.

Obviously, palliative measures can solve an immediate problem (symptomatic distress) but increase the risk of a greater problem in the long term. Like other defensive measures, palliatives may ultimately make the effects of stress even worse than before they were applied.

DEFENSE MECHANISMS

According to psychoanalytic theories of personality, a product of unconscious conflicts is *anxiety,* a feeling of dread or fear (see Chapter 14). Because the conflicts are unconscious, they cannot be recognized or addressed in a directly conscious behavioral strategy. As a result, behavior is likely to become defensive rather than to effectively cope.

The behavioral strategies or responses made to alleviate or reduce anxiety are termed defense mechanisms. Freud and other psychoanalytic theories identified a number of patterns in defense mechanisms. We examine nine of them here: repression, denial, displacement, projection, regression, reaction formation, rationalization, intellectualization, and sublimation.

Repression. Repression is the most common defense mechanism and underlies all the others. In repression, painful thoughts are excluded from conscious awareness. A student ill-prepared for work in a college course "forgets" that the examination is scheduled for today. A victim of child abuse cannot remember exactly how he was bruised.

Denial. Denial involves behaviors that reduce the severity or importance of unpleasant information. In denial one refuses to acknowledge a painful reality. A woman whose husband has left her tells her friends they have agreed to a trial separation. A man who has chest pains decides it must be indigestion (rather than a heart problem) and chooses to buy an antacid rather than consult a physician.

Displacement. In displacement one redirects emotions and motives from their original targets to substituted objects. (See discussions of displacement of aggression above and in chapter 10). After being criticized unfairly by her boss, a woman returns home and starts an argument with her husband, displacing her aggression from her employer to her spouse. Positive feelings can also be displaced. A shy young man who loves an attractive, popular woman may redirect his attentions to her less intimidating, more approachable best friend.

Projection. In projection one attributes one's own motives or feelings to someone else. A man who has cheated on his wife may feel guilty at first, and then angry, accusing his wife of having cheated on him. Participants in failed ventures may later accuse each other with "it was all your idea." Projection allows one the opportunity to relocate the problem outside of oneself.

Regression. One regresses when one's behavior takes an immature form, like whining, throwing a tantrum, or bullying. It is a common reaction to frustration (see discussion above). An older child who is jealous of her parents' attentions to a new baby may resurrect her own "cute" infantile behaviors in an effort to win their attentions again. A man who is angry at his wife's insistence on visiting her family may pout and complain until they leave.

Reaction Formation. Sometimes a person is motivated in ways that he or she knows are unacceptable to cultural or religious values. If the unacceptable goal is attractive, he or she may develop a reaction formation by excessively attacking or eliminating it. Reaction formation expresses the opposite of the individual's true feelings. A worker who is jealous of a colleague's success may exaggeratedly praise his work. A woman who feels guilty about disliking her own child may become inordinately protective and affectionate. A community leader with a secret interest in pornography may become a hostile anti-pornography, pro-censorship crusader. Exaggeration and fanaticism are the hallmarks of reaction formation.

Rationalization. Rationalization involves inventing acceptable reasons for one's behavior. An alcoholic will justify "one more drink" by arguing that it will relax him and help him gain the strength to abstain. A consumer who has paid too much for a vehicle because it is attractive justifies the purchase as a good investment with high resale value. Rationalization is also a process involved in self-justification in the wake of cognitive dissonance (see chapter 19).

Intellectualization. Sometimes emotional conflicts can be made bearable by analyzing them in an intellectual, unemotional way, a process called intellectualization. Surgeons and nurses who face life-and-death crises may discuss them in cold, clinical terms, or even make macabre jokes. A leader who advocates war may talk of "deploying a weapons system targeted at guerrilla headquarters" instead of bombing a town full of men, women, and children.

Sublimation. For Freud, all defense mechanisms involved the dangers of maladjustment and increased anxiety—except sublimation. Sublimation is a process of transforming unconscious conflict into a more socially acceptable form. An aggressive child works to become a star athlete instead of a violent criminal. A person suffering from unrequited love devotes effort to loving and caring for unwanted children. Freud believed that sublimation might be a necessary strategy for reconciling one's selfish urges to the constraints of civilized society.

Coping

Coping requires dealing with the source of stress or anxiety, not merely alleviating the symptoms. Coping involves three choices for action: confrontation, compromise, and withdrawal.

CONFRONTATION

In confrontation one faces a stressful situation honestly and forthrightly. This may involve intensifying effort, learning new skills, or enlisting others' aid.

For example, a woman who is worried about paying the bills may confront her situation by selling her car and using public transportation instead, or moving to a smaller apartment, and packing lunches instead of eating out. In contrast, defensive responses like shopping for fun and going out with friends might improve her mood in the short run but will only worsen the situation.

A key experience in many confrontations is anger, the emotional readiness to act aggressively. Anger can be experienced constructively, as a way to make a grievance known. Assertive behavior can be learned to correct injustices without becoming aggressive. Humor can also be employed to relieve tension and restore perspective.

COMPROMISE

Compromise is one of the most effective and common ways of coping with conflict. In compromise, each party in the conflict gains something and sacrifices something. A woman wants her husband to accompany her to a movie, while he wants to watch a game on television. By compromising they could agree that she will run errands while he watches television undisturbed, and after the game they will go to dinner and a movie. He agrees to go out later but gets to watch the game, and she agrees to wait but gets to go out later.

A creative variation on compromise is collaboration, in which the two parties work together on a solution to their problem. Two brothers argue over who will eat the last piece of pie. In pure compromise, each would get half a piece. But through collaboration they could decide to buy ice cream, and each enjoy a half piece a' la mode.

WITHDRAWAL

Sometimes the best response to conflict is to remove oneself or withdraw from the situation. A victim of abuse may be better off escaping the abusive household than either staying and trying vainly to change the abuser or calling on police to "teach him a lesson."

Withdrawal as a coping response should not be confused with avoidance learning or learned helplessness. Withdrawing from a severe conflict will not necessarily teach one to avoid or give up in all future conflict experiences. When faced realistically, withdrawal from hopeless conflict may be the only effective response an individual can choose.

Adjustment

One criterion for mental health is adjustment—a pattern of coping with stress and conflict across life situations. The alternative is a maladjusted pattern of behavior, a characteristic of behavioral disorders (see chapter 16).

Research on adjustment frequently begins as stress research that discovers effective coping strategies. Some important characteristics of adjustment are control, a sense of self-efficacy, and development of a stress-resistant personality.

CONTROL

An important common factor in stressful situations is loss of control. For example, sounds are not necessarily stressful but noises usually are. Noise is defined as "unwanted sound," and noise usually persists if it is beyond one's control. Research on learned helplessness has shown that subjects were more likely to keep trying to solve new problems when they had some control over their experiences.

Adjustment involves identifying ways one can establish control over stressful experiences or factors. In many cases the control may not be real, but the perception of control is sufficient to help one cope and adjust.

SELF-EFFICACY

As noted in chapter 14, social learning theorist Albert Bandura has argued for the value of self-efficacy, a sense of competence and effectiveness, to well-being. Self-efficacy is a product of experience with one's environment. Research has shown that apathy and helplessness in institutionalized individuals can be overcome by giving them manageable responsibilities, like caring for plants or pets. The experience of success in being effective with such care can generalize to greater responsibilities and an overall sense of self-efficacy.

THE STRESS-RESISTANT PERSONALITY

Recent research suggests that people who cope well with stress have some common abilities and qualities, including a feeling of control (as described above), a sense of commitment, and an acceptance of challenge.

Commitment involves pledging one's actions to a future goal, investing in long-term rather than immediate reward. Workers who have input into management decisions and care about the future of the company are better able to cope with job stress.

Challenge involves a moderate amount of change and adaptation that one expects to be able to meet. Contrary to "common sense" advice that we should avoid stress by "taking it easy," research indicates that challenge and novelty are important in meeting demands and developing a stress-resistant personality.

Stress is anything that places demands on an organism. Early work on stress indicated its role in psychosomatic illness. More recently the role of environmental stressors has increased popular interest in the topic.

Selye's research identified three stages in the general adaptation syndrome: alarm (shock and countershock), resistance, and exhaustion. This response pattern adapts to stressors that must be either fought or escaped from.

The fight-or-flight response was originally effective for primitive humans facing the mortal threats of starvation, exposure, and attack. Anything interpreted as a stressor prompts the autonomic nervous system to initiate the stress response.

Modern stressors are more varied than mortal threats. These include frustration, conflict, hassles and pressure, the concerns of the Type A personality, major life changes, and extreme stressors like personal loss, combat, and environmental disasters.

Responding to stress involves either defending or coping. Defensive reactions to stress can include palliative measures, which reduce the severity of symptoms, or defense mechanisms. Defense mechanisms reduce anxiety without eliminating its sources. These include repression, denial, displacement, projection, regression, reaction formation, rationalization, intellectualization, and sublimation.

Coping generally takes the forms of confrontation, compromise, or withdrawal from the situation. A long-term pattern of adjustment is facilitated by a sense of control, feelings of self-efficacy, and development of a stress-resistant personality, including a sense of commitment and an acceptance of challenge.

**Selected
Readings**

Avrill, J. R. *Anger and Aggression.* New York: Springer Verlag. 1982

Janis, I. L. *Stress, Attitudes, and Decisions.* New York: Praeger. 1982

Lazarus, R. S. and S. Folkman. *Stress, Appraisal, and Coping.* New York: Springer. 1984

Monat, A. and R. S. Lazarus (Eds.). *Stress and Coping.* New York: Columbia University Press. 1984

Polasky, N. *Integrated Ego Psychology.* New York: Aldine Publishing Company. 1982

Shalit, B. *The Psychology of Conflict and Combat.* New York: Praeger. 1988

Singer, J. L. (Ed.). *Repression and Dissociation: Implications for Personality Theory, Psychopathology, and Health.* Chicago: University of Chicago Press. 1990

16

Abnormal Behavior

*M*any laypersons' first associations with psychology are ideas about abnormal behavior and its treatment. Ideas of abnormality have varied over time and have affected attitudes toward disordered behavior and its treatment.

In this chapter the nature and definitions of abnormality are explored, and identifiable patterns of psychological disorders are reviewed and distinguished. In chapter 17 the major approaches to treating disordered behavior are reviewed.

ABNORMALITY

Abnormality is a derivative concept, since it depends on an understanding of normality. Moreover, normality describes norms of behavior but does not prescribe what is necessarily healthy or adaptive. Models of abnormality have changed over time, from ascribing spiritual causes to disorders, to viewing abnormality as erroneous behavior, to finally understanding abnormality as involving disorders. Abnormality can be defined and understood in statistical, cultural, and psychological terms.

Models of Abnormality

THE SPIRITUAL MODEL

Archaeological and archival evidence indicates that abnormal behavior has been identified throughout human history. Originally abnormal behavior was ascribed to spiritual sources, and its treatment was related to religious practices and concepts. Thus disorders might be labeled as demonic possession and their victims beaten, ostracized, exorcized, or executed.

It is believed that many of the men and women charged with and executed for witchcraft during the Middle Ages were suffering from various psychological disorders. The spiritual "model" of abnormal behavior provided social and legal rules but no understanding of its causes or treatments.

THE MORAL MODEL

A moral model of abnormal behavior emerged gradually from the 16th century onward in Western Europe. Physical treatments were attempted (e.g., bloodletting to release "bad humors"), but those with psychological disorders were segregated from those with physical disorders. A difference between the two was perceived, although no therapeutic models had yet been developed. Beginning with the work of French physician Philippe Pinel in the late 18th century and continued by American teacher and social activist Dorothea Dix in the 19th century, the moral model of abnormal behavior advocated the view that the mentally ill needed compassion, kindness, and pleasant surroundings.

THE MEDICAL MODEL

The medical model of abnormality was developed in the late 19th century with the growth of the medical specialty of psychiatry. In the medical model, disordered behavior and thought are the *symptoms* or observable signs of diseases that affect the function of the nervous system. Cures and treatments are applied to the *patients* to alleviate their symptoms and eliminate the illness.

In the 20th century, with the development of psychotherapies independent of medical therapies (see chapter 17), the medical model has given way to a more eclectic (varied) view of abnormality and its treatment. Nonetheless the medical model remains popular and influential today. An example of an application of the medical model can be observed when social problems like drug addiction and crime are referred to simplistically as "diseases."

PSYCHOLOGICAL MODELS

Psychological theories have led to different models of abnormal behavior, each with its own assumptions about the causes and forms of abnormality. The *psychoanalytic* model explains disordered behavior in terms of unconscious conflicts. According to the *behavioral* model, abnormal behavior is learned, just as normal behavior is, through experiences of associations, reinforcements, and punishments. More recently, the *cognitive* model has argued that internal processes like expectations, biases, errors, and illusions in conscious thought result in maladjusted and disordered behavior. Each of these models makes therapeutic recommendations on the basis of its own terms and assumptions (see chapter 17).

Defining Abnormality

"Abnormal" literally means "away from the norm." The norm is the average or typical behavior or characteristic of the population. Thus norms are different for different populations and can change with time and conditions.

Abnormal behavior has been defined four different ways by psychologists and social scientists: statistically, culturally, in terms of psychological adequacy, and in terms of categories of symptoms.

STATISTICAL ABNORMALITY

In terms of statistics (see chapter 2), abnormal behavior includes any behavior that is significantly different from the norm. In a normal distribution of characteristics or qualities, both very high scores and very low scores are considered statistically abnormal.

For example, in terms of intelligence only "average" intelligence is considered statistically normal. Significantly below-average intelligence is considered abnormal, but so is significantly above-average intelligence. Thus in the statistical sense, unusually well-adjusted behavior might be considered abnormal, just as disordered behavior would be.

CULTURAL ABNORMALITY

In cultural terms, it is normal to abide by cultural norms. Cultures have norms for every social behavior, from personal practices in sexual behavior and child-rearing, to public actions like driving a car or choosing what to wear. The cultural definition of abnormality includes any behavior that deviates from cultural norms. If an individual does not know how to dress in public, he or she will be considered abnormal. If an individual deliberately chooses to be a nonconformist in some way, he or she will be considered abnormal.

A problem with the cultural definition is its arbitrariness across time and cultures. It was normal in the 18th century for American men to wear wigs and pigtails, but not so in the mid-20th century. Judging nonconformists to be abnormal because they do not abide by a dress code will lead to erroneous identifications of abnormality.

PSYCHOLOGICAL INADEQUACY

Closer to the "true" understanding of abnormal behavior is a definition in terms of psychological adequacy. This has taken two forms, a value-based interpretation and a practical interpretation.

Adequacy as a Value. In one sense, an individual is abnormal if his or her behavior is not healthy. This view assumes common understanding about what "healthy" behavior is. Insofar as these values might vary across individuals, even across professionals, this view of abnormality has the same liabilities as the cultural definition. Most people will not achieve "ideal" mental health but will still functional adequately and should not be considered abnormal.

Practical Adequacy. One's behavior is "psychologically adequate" if he or she sets and achieves goals, is capable of independent living, and can form and sustain close relationships with others. In this view, abnormal behavior is that which is self-defeating, out of touch with reality, socially unskilled, and personally distressed. This approach to abnormality is more practical and "common-sensical" than the foregoing.

CLASSIFICATION SYSTEMS

In recent years psychologists have been less concerned with agreeing on a definition for abnormality than with identifying its common patterns. This is done by keeping records of symptoms, how often they are observed, and in what combinations they appear. Different disorders are then identified as patterns or categories of such symptom combinations.

The classification approach to abnormality can assist in treatment because, once a pattern of symptoms is recognized and the category diagnosed, recommendations for successful treatments can be identified.

The DSM System. The primary system of classification for abnormal behavior in use today is the *Diagnostic and Statistical Manual of the American Psychiatric Association, Third Edition, Revised,* abbreviated DSM-III-R or simply DSM. Because psychiatrists are medical doctors, it is not surprising that the DSM accepts the medical model of abnormality.

The DSM system lists commonly observed patterns of symptoms and assigns each a label. The practice of labeling provides convenience and prescriptive action, but it has been criticized for its judgmental assumptions. Research suggests that once a diagnostic label has been applied, professionals may look for confirmation of the label rather than signs of improvement or change.

Changes in DSM. The latest revision of DSM summarizes important changes in assumptions and terminology about abnormality.

Psychoanalysts used the term neurosis to describe a treatable disorder and psychosis to connote a severe disorder. This distinction and these terms are no longer applied. In modern revisions of DSM, most classifications of abnormal behavior are simply labeled as "disorders," varying on a continuum from less severe (less disruptive to adjustment) to more severe (more disruptive).

Another important change in the latest DSM revision is the removal of "homosexuality" from the list of disorders. Once considered a disorder in itself, homosexuality is no longer viewed as pathological (a form of illness).

DSM continues to be revised in the light both of the actual occurrences of disordered behaviors and prevailing psychological and medical theories of behavior.

PSYCHOLOGICAL DISORDERS

The DSM includes many categories and subcategories of abnormal behavior. The major ones are described and distinguished here: anxiety disorders, somatoform disorders, psychosexual disorders, dissociative disorders, affective disorders, schizophrenic disorders, and personality disorders.

Anxiety Disorders

An anxiety disorder is a condition in which severe anxiety interferes with normal adjustment and functioning. Four types are panic attacks, posttraumatic stress disorder, phobias, and obsessive-compulsive disorder.

PANIC ATTACKS

A panic attack is a sudden, unpredictable experience of intense fear. It may be accompanied by chest pains, difficulty breathing, dizziness, and a feeling that one is about to die. A panic attack typically lasts only a few minutes, but the threat of recurrence is constant.

POSTTRAUMATIC STRESS DISORDER

Research among veterans of war and victims of terrorism and environmental disasters has identified a pattern of panic attacks traceable to the original traumatic experience. This pattern comprises the posttraumatic stress disorder (see also chapter 15).

PHOBIAS

Phobias or phobic disorders are characterized by experiencing intense, irrational fear associated with a particular condition or target. Phobias are different from fears in that they usually focus on normally nonthreatening stimuli. For example, aversion to being bitten by a poisonous snake is a fear, but intense aversion to any snake, poisonous or not, or anything that resembles or depicts a snake is evidence of a phobia.

OBSESSIVE-COMPULSIVE DISORDER

Obsessions are recurring, uncontrollable, unwanted thoughts. Compulsions are repetitive, ritualistic, urgent behaviors. Obsessions and compulsions are usually linked, a pattern known as obsessive-compulsive disorder. For example, a man who is obsessively worried about cleanliness and keeping clean and healthy may feel compelled to wash and rewash his hands dozens of times every time he touches something.

Somatoform Disorders

Somatoform disorders involve serious physical symptoms that have no apparent physical causes. Three types of somatoform disorders (from the Greek *soma* or "body") are somatization disorders, conversion disorders, and hypochondriasis.

SOMATIZATION DISORDERS

In a somatization disorder, an individual experiences vague, recurring, sometimes unrelated physical pains and dysfunctions for which medical examinations can find no organic cause. Common complaints involve back pain, dizziness, partial paralysis, and abdominal pains.

CONVERSION DISORDERS

Less common somatoform complaints involve loss of sensory function (e.g., blindness), extensive paralysis, seizures, and false pregnancy. In these conversion disorders a psychological conflict is apparently "converted" into a distinct, debilitating physical symptom or handicap. Conversion disorders have been recorded for many centuries and were once thought to affect only women, hence the archaic term hysteria (from the Greek *hysteros* for "uterus," once thought to be the origin of the symptoms).

The real physical symptoms of conversion disorders are painful or debilitating, but are frequently accepted by sufferers with good humor and apparent indifference. Such acceptance is a diagnostic clue to a somatization disorder.

HYPOCHONDRIASIS

One who suffers from hypochondriasis, a hypochondriac, experiences almost the reverse of a conversion disorder. A hypochondriac has few or no symptoms of physical illness but complains of pain and other difficulties, perhaps "shopping" from one physician to the next for treatments like drugs and even unnecessary surgery.

Psychosexual Disorders

Sexual behavior is far more varied than was once believed. As a result of research on sexual behavior, many behaviors once thought "abnormal" are no longer considered to be disorders. The DSM recognizes two categories of psychosexual disorder: sexual dysfunctions and paraphilias.

SEXUAL DYSFUNCTIONS

Sexual dysfunctions involve inability to function effectively in sexual behavior. Men's inability to achieve or maintain erection is termed impotence; women's inability to achieve orgasm is termed frigidity.

Other sexual dysfunctions include inhibited sexual desire (lack of sexual interest); inhibited sexual excitement (inability to sustain sexual arousal to the point of orgasm and resolution); and inhibited orgasm (inability to achieve orgasm though able to achieve and sustain arousal up to that point).

PARAPHILIAS

The use of unconventional sex objects or situations is known as a form of paraphilia. Occasional unconventionality in practice or fantasy is normal and not disordered. However, narrow restriction of sexual interest to non-human objects or socially unacceptable circumstances is probably disordered.

Repeatedly using a nonhuman object like a shoe or belt for sexual arousal is known as fetishism. Fetishes usually involve articles of clothing associated with childhood attachment figures.

Watching others while they are undressed or having sex is known as voyeurism. The compulsion to expose one's genitals to others inappropriately is called exhibitionism. Wearing clothing of the opposite sex to achieve sexual arousal is termed transvestism. Transvestites are usually male, and usually heterosexual.

Some paraphilias are dangerous in that they may harm others. Sadomasochism involves associating sexual arousal with inflicting or experiencing physical pain. One of the most serious paraphilias is pedophilia, acts or fantasies involving sexual activity with children. Pedophiles are almost always young males, and most are heterosexual.

Dissociative Disorders

Dissociative disorders are rare conditions in which part of an individual's personality becomes dissociated from the rest, and he or she cannot reestablish the associations. Rare as these disorders are, they are a source of great popular fascination. Three patterns have been identified: amnesia, multiple personality disorder, and depersonalization disorder.

AMNESIA

Amnesia is a loss of memory that can follow physical experiences like injury or illness. When no organic cause is identified, amnesia is considered a dissociative disorder. An extremely rare form of amnesia in which an individual forgets his or her identity, and resumes a new life, is called a fugue state.

MULTIPLE PERSONALITY DISORDER

Rarer than psychogenic (psychologically caused) amnesia is multiple personality disorder, where an individual manifests several different personalities that emerge at different times. In true cases, the names, mannerisms, histories, memories, voices, and even intelligence levels are quite different across the personalities. Sometimes the separate personalities do not know about each other or that the individual body is so disordered.

DEPERSONALIZATION DISORDER

A more common and subtler dissociative disorder is depersonalization disorder, characterized by feelings that one is changed or different. Some sufferers complain that they feel like they have left their bodies, or that they are acting within a dream. One's behavior feels out of control and one's environment seems changed. Individuals with this disorder commonly are young people whose lives are changing dramatically and rapidly.

Affective Disorders

Many disorders involve disruptions in experiencing and controlling affect or emotion. These affective disorders usually involve a restricted range of emotional behavior and inflexible change within this range. The most common affective disorders involve the extremes of depression and mania.

DEPRESSION

The term "depression" commonly refers to a period of sadness and inactivity in the wake of disappointment or loss; such a reaction is normal and not considered disordered. However, when one is overwhelmed with grief or guilt, unable to resume or enjoy normal living and activities, and immobilized by lethargy or apathy, the diagnosis of a depressive disorder is likely. Depression may not be traceable to a triggering event, or it may extend dangerously beyond normal periods of grief.

MANIA

Less common than depression is a state termed mania, characterized by hyperactivity, euphoria, talkativeness, and impulsive behaviors. Manic episodes can involve aggression and hostility. They often end in self-exhaustion.

BIPOLAR DISORDER

Mania rarely appears by itself in its "pure" form. It is more usually coupled with periods of depression. When an individual's behavior alternates between cycles of manic and depressive behavior, he or she may be diagnosed as "manic-depressive" or suffering from bipolar disorder (alternating between those two "poles" or extremes of emotion).

Schizophrenic Disorders

Generally considered the most serious of psychological disorders, schizophrenia is a pattern of behavior characterized by disordered thought, perception, and judgment. Though the term "schizophrenia" is formed from Greek roots (*skhizein*, "to split" + *phren*, "mind") that suggest the "split personality" synonymous with multiple personality disorder (above), the term refers instead to symptoms of a seemingly disconnected and misfunctioning mind.

SYMPTOMS OF SCHIZOPHRENIA

Schizophrenic disorders are characterized by two distinct kinds of symptoms: hallucinations and delusions.

Hallucinations. Hallucinations are false sensory perceptions. When hallucinating one may see or hear stimuli that are not in fact present. While common impressions about hallucinations deal with "seeing things," in fact schizophrenics are more likely to experience auditory than visual hallucinations. For example, a schizophrenic may attribute her unusual ideas to the "voices" of important people who whisper advice to her.

Delusions. Delusions are false beliefs about reality with no basis in fact. For example, a schizophrenic may suffer from the delusion that others are spying on him, or that he is the victim of an international conspiracy.

TYPES OF SCHIZOPHRENIA

Different types of schizophrenic disorders have been identified, with distinct patterns of symptoms and themes. These are labeled the disorganized type, the catatonic type, the paranoid type, and the undifferentiated type.

Disorganized Type. Formerly called "hebephrenic" schizophrenia (from the Greek hebe, "youth"), disorganized schizophrenia is characterized by such childish behavior as giggling, making faces, wild gestures, and abandonment of toilet training skills.

Catatonic Type. Catatonic schizophrenia involves a distinctive pattern of motor disturbance. A common form is extreme immobility and rigidity, in which the individual seems to "freeze" in midposture. Alternatively, catatonia may involve constant movement, talking and shouting, or robot-like movement.

Paranoid Type. The paranoid pattern of schizophrenia is characterized by the delusions of grandeur and persecution. A delusion of grandeur involves imagining oneself to be important or famous, sometimes a specific individual like Jesus Christ or the president. A delusion of persecution is a belief that one is being victimized, attacked, or followed by others. Paranoid schizophrenics can be hostile if their delusions are questioned or challenged.

Undifferentiated Type. Undifferentiated schizophrenia has a mixture of symptoms from the various other types—such as delusions, hallucinations, or incoherence—but do not clearly resemble any one of them.

Personality Disorders

The most complex and hard-to-describe disorders are the so-called personality disorders. These are not all characterized by the same pattern of symptoms. Rather personality disorders reflect a failure of the personality itself to develop, adjust, and learn. If the function of personality is to help the individual adjust and adapt across situations (see chapter 15), then the disordered personality is not doing its job.

Many patterns of personality disorders have been identified and described. Following are descriptions of five types: antisocial type, paranoid type, schizoid type, narcissistic type, and borderline type.

ANTISOCIAL PERSONALITY DISORDERS

The antisocial personality disorder has been widely studied, and is commonly referred to as psychopathic or sociopathic. People with this disorder consistently violate the rights of others—they lie, cheat, steal, manipulate, and harm others—with no evidence of guilt or remorse. They often blame others—their parents or society or the school system—for forcing them to behave as they do.

PARANOID PERSONALITY DISORDERS

Just as paranoid schizophrenia is characterized by delusions of grandeur and persecution, similarly the paranoid personality disorder involves suspicion, mistrust, and hypersensitivity to any criticism or threat. Although such disordered individuals see their behavior as rational and fair, they are secretive, self-aggrandizing, and argumentative.

SCHIZOID PERSONALITY DISORDERS

An individual with schizoid personality disorder lacks the skills to form or maintain relationships with others, as well as warm or tender feelings for others. Such a person may be viewed as cold and distant, and may act distracted and withdrawn.

NARCISSISTIC PERSONALITY DISORDER

People with narcissistic personality disorder are totally self-absorbed, self-important, obsessed with fantasies of success, and demanding of others' attention and love. They are, however, incapable of loving or caring for others. For example, such an individual might establish a "commit-mentphobic" behavior pattern, serially establishing brief, superficial relationships with others and seemingly driven by the need for reassurance.

BORDERLINE PERSONALITY DISORDER

The little-understood pattern of the borderline personality disorder varies widely, but most cases share the general tendencies of unstable self-images, uncertainty about their relationships and work, impulsiveness, and self-destructiveness. Borderline individuals may behave promiscuously, abuse drugs and alcohol, and threaten or attempt suicide.

Abnormal behavior is technically any behavior that deviates from the norm. Psychologists use the term to refer to disordered behavior. Different models of abnormality—including the ancient spiritual model, the later moral model, and the recent medical and psychological models—advocate different meanings for abnormal behavior and advocate different treatments.

Abnormality can be defined statistically as any behavior significantly different from the norm, including both higher and lower than average levels of a quality. Cultural abnormality is defined as deviation or nonconformity.

The psychological inadequacy concept of abnormality involves either values of ideal health or a common-sense understanding of effective, well-adjusted behavior.

Most modern approaches to abnormality utilize the terminology of the classification system abbreviated as the DSM. The DSM is revised and updated regularly to reflect recent developments in theory and research on disordered behavior. Psychological disorders represented in the DSM include a wide variety of patterns of symptoms.

Anxiety disorders involve the disruption of adjusted life by anxiety. Anxiety disorders include panic attacks, posttraumatic stress disorder, phobias, and obsessive-compulsive disorder.

Somatoform disorders involve physical ailments without clear organic causes. Examples include somatization disorders, conversion disorders, and hypochondriasis.

Psychosexual disorders involve disrupted or problematic sexual behavior. These include sexual dysfunctions and paraphilias.

Dissociative disorders are rare disorders in which parts of cognitive function are dissociated from other parts. Major categories include amnesia, multiple personality, and depersonalization disorder.

Affective disorders are disorders of emotional experience and control. The major types are severe depression and the rarer form of mania, as well as the cyclic combination of mania and depression known as bipolar disorder.

Schizophrenic disorders, often thought to be the most severe, are disorders of thought and perception characterized by the symptoms of hallucinations and delusions. Four categories of schizophrenia are disorganized, catatonic, paranoid, and undifferentiated type.

Personality disorders are little understood but appear to involve a breakdown in the function of the personality in keeping behavior both consistent and adaptive. Five types include the antisocial, paranoid, schizoid, narcissistic, and borderline personality disorder.

Selected Readings

Andreasan, N. *The Broken Brain*. New York: Harper and Row. 1984

Carson, R. C., J. N. Butcher and J. C. Coleman. *Abnormal Psychology and Modern Life, 8th Edition*. Glenview, IL: Scott, Foresman. 1988

Gay, P. (Ed.). *The Freud Reader*. New York: W. W. Norton and Company. 1989

Hooley, J. M., J. M. Neale and G. C. Davidson. *Readings in Abnormal Psychology*. New York: John Wiley and Sons. 1989

Paykel, E. S. (Ed.). *Handbook of Affective Disorders*. New York: Guilford Press. 1982

Seidenberg, R. and K. DeCrow. *Women Who Marry Houses*. Cambridge, MA: McGraw-Hill. 1983

17

Therapy

Psychological disorders vary in form, symptoms, and severity. Most disordered behavior is not severe and does not require formal therapeutic treatment. However, therapy for psychological disorders is a major application of professional psychology.

This chapter reviews the history of treatment, the diverse structures of treatment available, and the different kinds of medical therapies and psychotherapies practiced today.

TREATING DISORDERED BEHAVIOR

Whatever the form or theoretical perspective, all forms of therapy for disordered behavior share the common goal of *changing behavior*.

The history of treatment closely parallels the history of approaches to understanding abnormal behavior. The structure of treatment today varies widely among helping professions, settings, and whether it targets individuals or groups.

History of Treatment

Although abnormal behavior has been documented throughout recorded human history, it has not always been understood. Whether individuals with behavior disorders were treated—and how they were treated—has depended on the model by which societies understood such behavior.

Four broad approaches to therapy can be identified in human history: punitive approaches; moral therapy; medical therapy; and psychotherapy.

PUNITIVE APPROACHES

Evidence suggests that ancient societies believed in spiritual causes for abnormal behavior. Through the late Middle Ages in the Western world, individuals whose behavior we might recognize today as disordered were assumed to be possessed or influenced by evil spirits or demons. Disordered individuals were likely to be imprisoned, tortured, or executed.

The assumption often made in such treatment was that behavior was not so much disordered as evil. It required discipline or destruction in order to protect the rest of the community. These punitive approaches caused abnormal behavior to be viewed with suspicion and fear, and prompted the families of such individuals to react with shame and guilt. The influences of this view are persistent today in similar concerns for how disordered behavior will reflect on one's family and community.

MORAL THERAPY

In the late 16th century Henry VIII of England declared that Bethlehem Hospital in London—a name corrupted to "Bedlam"—should house the mentally ill exclusively. Punitive attitudes gave way to social segregation. Disordered individuals were housed not in prisons but asylums, where conditions were hardly different. Crude medicinal treatments such as bloodletting and confinement in cages were practiced with predictably poor results.

In the late 18th century the French physician Philippe Pinel (1745-1826) argued for the treatment of mental patients with dignity and compassion. In the 19th century the American social activist Dorothea Dix (1802-1877) campaigned for humane treatment of the mentally ill. Though not yet supported by medical or psychological theory, the essence of this moral therapy movement was that disordered behavior could benefit from treatment with kindness, compassion, and pleasant surroundings.

Ironically the increasing public concern generated by the moral therapy movement led to legislation for the care of the mentally ill. As a consequence more people demanded treatment than facilities were available for the provision of individual care. Private asylums became state institutions, and their function again emphasized warehousing the mentally ill and separating them from their communities. The book *A Mind That Found Itself*, by former mental patient Clifford Beers (1876-1943), exposed the deterioration and inhumanity of state institutions around the turn of the century.

MEDICAL THERAPY

With the development of psychoanalytic theory and the medical specialty of psychiatry in the late 19th century, the medical model (see chapter 16) of abnormal behavior gained prominence. Psychological disorders came to be viewed as illnesses, with identifiable symptoms, causes, and courses of treatment. Those suffering from them were patients who needed the services of professional physicians. Psychiatrists moved into clinical settings like hospitals and institutions to treat their charges. Individuals who were not severely disordered could seek treatment as they might consult physicians about any physical malady.

Since psychological disorders were viewed as diseases, medical treatments were favored. These included surgical procedures (psychosurgery) and later electroconvulsive therapy (ECT). A revolution in medical therapies occurred in the first half of the 20th century, when psychoactive drugs were identified and developed to alleviate the symptoms of many severe psychological disorders. These drugs made restraints and confinement unnecessary in many cases and changed the operation of psychiatric hospitals and asylums.

PSYCHOTHERAPY

Beginning with the development of psychoanalysis, other methods of treatment besides medical approaches were developed. Psychotherapeutic techniques emphasize psychological approaches, such as dialogue and behavior change, rather than medical. Psychotherapies today include insight therapies like psychoanalysis and humanistic therapy, as well as behavior therapies like applied operant conditioning and modeling.

The Structure of Treatment

While it is common to think of psychologists and psychiatrists as the sole providers of treatment for disordered behavior, a wide variety of helping professions exist for such conditions. Clinical settings also vary, from institutions to public clinics to private practices. Therapies have been designed to address clients individually or in groups.

HELPING PROFESSIONS

Within the broad profession of psychology, counseling psychologists and clinical psychologists can work as therapeutic practitioners. Counseling psychologists work with the problems of normal adjustment rather than abnormal function, including stress management, relationship conflict, and behavior modification. Clinical psychologists work with so-called clinical populations, individuals treated on an inpatient or outpatient basis for more severe disorders, including affective, addictive, and schizophrenic disorders.

Within the medical profession, physicians who have trained in the specialty of psychiatry work as practicing therapists. Psychiatrists may utilize many of the psychotherapeutic methods that psychologists use, as well as medical therapies like drugs.

Other practitioners in the helping professions may be trained as counselors (degrees in education) or psychiatric social workers (degrees in social work). See chapter 1 for a review of the spectrum of helping professionals.

CLINICAL SETTINGS

Intitutionalization. Hospitalization has been the "treatment of choice" in the United States for the last 150 years. Mental hospitals admit almost two million people annually. Nonetheless, the majority of mental illness admissions are made to general hospitals without psychiatric units. There is more "demand" for hospital treatment of disordered behavior than there is room in such facilities.

Community Mental Health. The 1963 Community Mental Health Act legislated massive *deinstititutionalization* or releasing of mental patients back to their communities. Instead, community mental health centers were established nationwide to provide treatment on an out-patient basis or through residential centers like halfway houses.

Key missions of community health centers are public education and prevention. The investment in prevention, according to the rationalization, will result ultimately in reduced need for radical treatments and institutionalization.

Many neighborhoods are still ambivalent over housing such patients and former patients. The private and public high cost of insurance and treatment is also controversial. Consequently the quality and effectiveness of such treatment varies widely.

Private Practice. For disorders that are not severe and families that can afford it, private practice—privately chosen arrangements for therapy—is the preferred approach to treatment. Such arrangements have the advantage of allowing clients to make their own choices among practitioners. Because no institution or agency governs the arrangement, however, they have the disadvantage of some risk. Not all therapists have comparable training and credentials, and clients must become critical consumers of therapeutic information and services.

INDIVIDUAL VERSUS GROUP THERAPIES

In both private practice and institutional settings, many problems can be addressed in group contexts rather than individually. The cost of group therapies may be comparably lower. A therapy group may consist entirely of clients meeting with a facilitator, or may include other helping professionals like hospital staff members. Group therapies can be particularly useful in family and marital therapy, where the problems themselves have social implications. They can also employ techniques like role-playing and *psychodrama* (see Gestalt Therapy, below), which often rely on dialogues and group settings.

A nonprofessional extension of group therapies has been the development of support and self-help groups. Organizations such as Alcoholics Anonymous, Weight Watchers, and support groups for the families of crime victims or cancer patients have all been found to provide important benefits like sympathy, understanding, and practical advice.

MEDICAL THERAPIES

As a result of the medical model popularized in the early 20th century, many therapies were developed which emphasize medical techniques. These have included psychopharmacology, electroconvulsive therapy, and psychosurgery.

Psycho-pharmacology

The use of drugs to achieve psychological change is termed psychopharmacology. The development of psychoactive drugs to alleviate the symptoms of severe psychological disorders has been revolutionary in therapeutic practice. Drugs produce only temporary changes in affect, cognitive processes and/or behavior, and their side effects are easier to predict than surgical techniques.

There are three classes of psychoactive drugs primarily used for the treatment of psychological disorders: sedatives, antipsychotics, and antidepressants.

SEDATIVES

Sedatives include substances as varied as alcohol, barbiturates (e.g., Seconal), methaqualone (e.g., Quaalude), and *tranquilizers* like Valium and Librium. Sedatives depress central nervous system activity. In large doses they induce sleep, and in smaller doses they can relieve anxiety and reduce inhibitions. Valium is a popular treatment for anxiety, reducing anxious symptoms although not "curing" their sources. As a result, Valium is estimated to be the most widely-abused prescription drug in the United States.

ANTIPSYCHOTICS

In the early 20th century sedatives were used to calm mental patients but were not useful as therapeutic agents because they induced sleep. In the mid-20th century, however, the major tranquilizers *reserpine* and the *phenothiazines* were found to reduce psychotic (e.g., schizophrenic) symptoms as well as alleviate anxiety and aggressiveness. Thorazine and Haldol are commonly the treatments of choice for schizophrenic symptoms such as hallucinations and delusional thought. Antipsychotic drugs do not cure schizophrenia, however, and can involve numerous undesirable side effects like blurred vision and motor disturbance.

ANTIDEPRESSANTS

Antidepressant drugs work to increase the levels of certain neurotransmitters in the brain. They can have dramatic effects alleviating the symptoms of depression. However, they are not equally effective in all cases, and full recovery from affective disorders may require a combination of drug therapy with psychotherapy.

Electro-convulsive Therapy

A dramatic and controversial treatment that has proven effective in treating many cases of severe depression is so-called "shock therapy," more accurately termed electroconvulsive therapy (ECT). In ECT, a sedated, relaxed (via muscle relaxants) patient experiences a mild convulsion induced with electrical current. On awakening a few minutes later, the patient may have some memory loss and confusion, but over time (several sessions) the depressive symptoms are alleviated. Critics have argued that no one knows why or how ECT works, and that it entails unwarranted risk to cognitive function. Supporters contend that, as a last resort treatment, it has proven higly effective where other methods have failed.

Psychosurgery

Prior to the development of antipsychotic drugs, psychosurgery or neurosurgery to effect behavior change was sometimes employed to reduce a patient's violence to self and others. In a prefrontal lobotomy, the brain's frontal lobes are severed from deeper brain connections. Effects of such surgery vary widely among individuals, and such techniques are rarely practiced today.

PSYCHOTHERAPIES

While the goal of all therapies is to change behavior, the psychological techniques of the psychotherapies differ dramatically from the biological techniques of medical therapies.

Common to most psychotherapies is the establishment of a relationship between client/patient and therapist, and the use of behaviors (e.g., talking, modeling) to provide new ideas and behavior and relationship patterns.

Psychotherapies vary and overlap considerably. Most practicing therapists are *eclectic*, meaning they employ a variety of techniques from different therapeutic models. Psychotherapies can be loosely categorized into two approaches to behavior change: insight therapies and behavior therapies.

Insight Therapies

The assumption of insight therapies is that an individual's behavior is disordered because of conflicts he or she cannot understand. It is the work of therapy to help him or her gain insight into the nature and origins of this conflict. Once insight is achieved, the individual's disorder will be unnecessary and behavior will change.

Three psychotherapeutic approaches can be considered forms of insight therapy: psychoanalysis ; humanistic therapy ; and Gestalt therapy.

PSYCHOANALYSIS

Originally developed by Sigmund Freud in his work with individuals suffering from "hysteria" (the former term for conversion disorder), psychoanalysis is a therapeutic system that emphasizes identifying an individual's unconscious conflicts. Psychoanalysis follows the medical model and employs medical terminology: the client is called a patient ; the complaints are his or her symptoms.

Originally Freud employed hypnosis as a means of relaxing patients and inviting them to reveal the origins of their conflicts. He abandoned this procedure and came instead to rely on *free association*, a process in which the patient talks openly and without censoring, while the analyst listens for clues to unconscious motives and themes.

The relationship between analyst and patient is essential to the work of therapy. During psychoanalysis, which may take years, the patient may project feelings about personal or past relationships onto the analyst, a process called *transference*. The patient may also try to protect defenses from being analyzed by engaging in *resistance*, by refusing to talk, forgetting to keep appointments, or not paying the analyst's bill.

Psychoanalysis is considered effective when the patient has achieved insight into the unconscious motivations and conflicts that the disordered behavior has been defending against.

HUMANISTIC THERAPY

Just as humanistic personality theory disagrees with psychoanalytic theory about the nature of personality and conflict, so does its therapeutic approach differ from that of psychanalysis.

Unlike psychoanalysis, wherein the therapist takes the role of expert in revealing the truth about the patient's problems, humanistic therapists assume that the client —not referred to as a "patient"—is the best judge of his or her needs and goals. Thus the humanistic system developed by Carl Rogers (see chapter 14) is termed client-centered therapy.

In client-centered therapy the therapist's goal is to help the client become a fully functioning human. Client-centered or "Rogerian" therapists provide unconditional positive regard to their clients, accepting them no matter what they say or do. They also emphasize the importance of being nondirective, refusing to tell the client what to do or direct his or her actions. Instead, using techniques like active listening, client-centered therapists reflect back to the client what he or she seems to want and believe, offering this as the basis for genuine behavior change.

GESTALT THERAPY

The German word "Gestalt" means "whole pattern" (see Chapter 1), and Gestalt therapy emphasizes the importance of helping an individual to contact and understand his or her "whole" self. According to its developer, Fritz Perls (1894-1970), Gestalt therapy seeks to make the individual aware of who he or she is and what he or she is doing. The emphasis is not on the "why" insights of psychoanalysis, but rather on "how" to live and go on with life. One Gestalt technique is *psychodrama*, acting out scenes (e.g., parent-child conversations) in order to bring out their emotional significance.

Behavior Therapies

If a woman suffers from a phobia of elevators, she may have the option of using an insight therapy like psychoanalysis to find out why she irrationally fears to use elevators. However, treatment could take years of effort and expense, and there is no guarantee that her insight into her phobia will relieve her disordered avoidance of elevators. If she lives in a big city with many high-rise buildings, she may need to change her phobic behavior as soon as possible.

Behavior therapists argue that, for some disorders at least, insight is unnecessary to alleviate symptoms and change behavior. Instead, a behavior therapist might consider how to "train" the phobic woman to feel relaxed on elevators, so that her incompatible anxiety can no longer prevent her from living and traveling as she wishes.

Many behavior therapies are used in combination with each other and with other psychotherapeutic techniques. Here we consider five techniques and approaches to behavior therapy: operant conditioning; aversive conditioning; desensitization; modeling; and the cognitive behavior therapies.

OPERANT CONDITIONING

The application of operant conditioning principles in behavior therapy involves providing changes in reinforcement to bring about changes in behavior. For example, a client who wants to eat less will identify non-food rewards to be earned by sticking to a behavior-change contract. He may permit himself to buy a book or make a long-distance phone call only if he eats 1,000 fewer calories on a given day.

A common operant conditioning strategy is the *token economy*, whereby token rewards are provided for performing desired behaviors. These tokens can then be exchanged for valued items or services. For instance, a retarded child will be paid in tokens for brushing her teeth. When she earns enough tokens, she may exchange them for toys or treats.

AVERSIVE CONDITIONING

Aversive conditioning applies the principles of classical conditioning by pairing an aversive stimulus (e.g., a painful electric shock or drug-induced nausea) with a behavior one wishes to eliminate. For example, an alcoholic who takes the drug Antabuse will become nauseous and vomit if he drinks any alcohol. While on the drug, he will become conditioned to associate alcohol with nausea, and will eventually generalize this association to drinking when not taking the drug.

DESENSITIZATION

Desensitization is a behavior therapy commonly employed in the treatment of phobias (see chapter 16). Desensitization involves developing a "hierarchy of anxiety," a rank-ordered listing of phobic situations the client imagines. The therapist then teaches the client how to relax, through breathing exercises, guided imagery, muscle control, and *biofeedback* (information about physiological arousal). Finally, the client imagines each item on the anxiety list, beginning with the least frightening, while maintaining effective relaxation. Gradually the client is able to imagine and then behave in the most phobic situation while retaining controlled relaxation. In this way the phobic's anxious behavior is "replaced" with nonanxious behavior. In the course of the process, each anxious image has become less and less sensitive, or *desensitized.*

MODELING

Desensitization is sometimes augmented by modeling, teaching new behaviors by having the client observe others doing them. For example, a man with a phobia of snakes might practice desensitization and learn to imagine snakes without anxiety. By watching a model touch and handle a snake, he benefits both from clearer imagery and the behavioral model he himself may learn to copy.

COGNITIVE BEHAVIOR THERAPIES

In recent years behavior therapies have been extended to include thoughts, feelings, and reasoning as forms of "behavior." The goal in cognitive behavior therapies is to change the way the client thinks and the content of his or her thinking. Because the techniques often involve behavioral techniques like operant conditioning and modeling, these are referred to as cognitive behavior therapies.

Three broad techniques have been considered forms of cognitive be-havior therapies: cognitive and attributional therapy, stress-inoculation therapy, and rational-emotive therapy.

Cognitive Therapy. Psychologist Aaron Beck has proposed that depres-sion results from a negative *style of thinking*. For instance, a young woman who has been stood up for a date may tell herself that this would not have happened if she were attractive and worthy of love. As a result, she concludes she must be unattractive and unworthy of love. In cognitive therapy the therapist focuses on the client's unrealistic expectations and distorted as-sumptions. The therapist may point out that relationships are not controlled by only one person, and that it is unrealistic to think that all disappointments are deserved.

The client will also be encouraged to keep a "mood diary" to discover patterns of depressive thoughts and the events that seem to have triggered them.

A more specific rationale for cognitive therapy involves understanding *attributions*, which are our explanations for our own and others' behaviors (see chapter 18). Research has found that some kinds of depression can be traced to erroneous patterns of attribution, or to a "negative attributional style." The negative attributional style is characterized by three dimensions of explanation: internal versus external; global versus specific; and stable versus unstable. Internal attributions blame one's personality or skills, while external attributions blame circumstances. Global attributions generalize effects across one's experience, while specific attributions focus narrowly on individual incidents, and stable attributions expect no change while unstable attributions anticipate that change is possible.

For example, if a student has received a poor grade on a paper, an internal, global, stable attribution might be, "I did poorly because I am a poor student, I get poor grades on everything, and I'll never do any better." Not surprisingly, this negative style can lead to depression.

Alternatively, *attribution therapy* questions these negative attributions and suggests replacing them with more realistic explanations. For example, the same student could make the following external, specific, unstable attribution about receiving a poor grade: "I got a poor grade because it was a hard paper to do, but it's only one paper, and I'm sure I can do better next time."

Stress-Inoculation Therapy. A similar form of therapy involves help-ing a client to reduce the stress he or she feels in certain situations. This may be done in three stages: first by analyzing self-statements ("I hate being stuck in traffic"); second by practicing new self-statements ("When I'm stuck in traffic, I can listen to the radio and enjoy the music"); and third by rehearsing such new strategies in behavioral situations.

Rational-Emotive Therapy. Psychologist Albert Ellis has developed rational-emotive therapy (RET) to question and correct the irrational beliefs that underlie disordered feelings and behaviors. In RET, every disordered behavior is the last event in a three-stage sequence: (1) an *activating event* triggers (2) a belief (either rational or irrational), which leads to (3) a *behavioral consequence.*

For example, a young man receives a call from his girlfriend canceling their date for the next evening. This activating event could prompt him to consider either a *rational* belief ("This is disappointing; now I will have to change my plans for tomorrow evening"), or an *irrational* belief ("This is terrible! She never wants to see me again, and I will never find true love"). As a result, the emotional and behavioral consequences will be either rational ("Even though it won't be as special, I'll call a friend and go to a movie"), or irrational ("I may as well sit at home and get used to living the rest of my life alone").

In RET, the beliefs underlying one's behaviors and feelings are analyzed, and irrational ones are questioned and discarded in favor of more rational ones. RET is considered effective for normal individuals who are behaving in self-defeating ways and wish to change.

Approaches to treatment of disordered behavior closely parallel the models of its causes. Historically disordered behavior was punished or segregated. The development of moral therapy advocated humane treatment of the mentally ill. In the 20th century the rise of the medical and psychological therapies have broadened the possibilities of treatment.

Many professionals are trained to provide treatment of disordered behavior. These professionals include psychologists, psychiatrists, and counselors. Treatment may be provided in various clinical settings, such as hospitals and institutions, community mental health centers and residential centers, and private practice settings. Most therapies involve individual treatment, but many group therapies are also available and appropriate for certain applications.

Medical therapies employ biological techniques to effect behavior change. These include psychopharmacology, electroconvulsive therapy, and psychosurgery. Psychoactive drugs useful in medical treatment of disordered behavior include sedatives, antipsychotics, and antidepressants.

Psychotherapies can be categorized as advocating either insight therapy or behavior change. The insight therapies include psychoanalysis, humanistic therapy, and Gestalt therapy. Behavior therapies apply the principles of learning theory to change behavior. Representative therapies are operant conditioning, aversive conditioning, desensitization, modeling, and cognitive behavior therapies. Cognitive behavior therapies include cognitive and attributional therapy, stress-inoculation therapy, and rational-emotive therapy.

Selected Readings

Endler, N. S. *Holiday of Darkness: A Psychologist's Personal Journey Out of His Depression*. New York: Wiley. 1982

Franks, C. M. and Wilson, T. G. (Annual). *Annual Review of Behavior Therapy: Theory and Practice*. New York: Brunner/Mazel.

Garfield, S. C. and A. E. Bergin (Eds.). *Handbook of Psychotherapy and Behavior Change, 3rd Edition*. New York: Wiley. 1986

Goleman, D. and K. R. Speeth (Eds.). *The Essential Psychotherapies*. New York: New American Library. 1982

Gurman, A. S. and D. P. Kniskern (Eds.). *Handbook of Family Therapy*. New York: Brunner/Mazel. 1981

Karasu, T. *The Psychiatric Therapies*. Washington, D.C.: American Psychiatric Press. 1984

Sheehan, S. *Is There No Place on Earth for Me?* New York: Vintage Books. 1982

Spiegler, M. D. *Contemporary Behavior Therapy*. Palo Alto, CA: Mayfield Publishing. 1983

Torrey, E. F. *Surviving Schizophrenia*. New York: Harper and Row. 1983

Valenstein, E. S. *Great and Desperate Cures*. New York: Basic Books. 1986

Wolpe, J. *The Practice of Behavior Therapy*. New York: Pergamon. 1986

18

Social Perception and Cognition

*S*ocial psychology is the field of psychology that studies the social influences
on the individual. It has common interests with both sociology, which studies
groups, and personality psychology, which studies individual differences.

   This chapter and chapters 19 and 20 examine the major topical areas
comprising social psychology. The present chapter examines the major
aspects of social cognition, cognitive processes like perception and thought
that concern social experiences. Chapter 19 examines attitudes, a major area
of research within social psychology. Chapter 20 looks at social influences
and interactions, including interpersonal relationships and group processes.
Social perception and cognition provide a good introduction to psychology
because these processes apply much of what has already been reviewed in
other areas of psychology to the unique concerns of social psychology. Like
other fields of psychology, social psychology studies individual thought and
behavior. However, other fields study these phenomena by examining internal
structures or processes (e.g., the nervous system, learning, perception) or
individual characteristics and developmental experiences (e.g., personality
theory, developmental processes). In contrast with these internal or personal
perspectives on behavior, social psychology adopts the situational perspective
on behavior and thought. In other words, whereas other fields are more likely
to ask "What is going on inside the person?", social psychologists ask "What
is going on around the person?"

ATTRIBUTION

One of the most basic questions people (including psychologists) ask about behavior is "Why?" Research on motivation essentially endeavors to answer that question about human behavior. Social psychologists refer to this explanation process as *causal attribution*, attributing behavior and events to appropriate causes.

Nonpsychologists ask attributional questions about others' behavior all the time. Often the reasons for others' behaviors are obvious. Why did she stop at the red light? She stopped because she knew the law required her to do so. Why did he eat all the cake? He ate it all because he wanted to and no one objected.

At other times the reasons for others' behavior are not so obvious: Why did my supervisor give me such a low rating? Why was that student so late for class? Why is my spouse so distant lately? When the behaviors in question are important to us, surprising, or have negative consequences, we are especially likely to ask attributional questions.

Theories of Attribution

Social psychologists have identified patterns in the ways people make attributions about their own and others' behavior. Hypotheses about these patterns include Fritz Heider's "naive psychology"; the theory of correspondent inferences; and Harold Kelley's "common-sense analysis" of behavior.

INTERNAL VERSUS EXTERNAL ATTRIBUTIONS

Gestalt psychologist Fritz Heider criticized "depth psychologies" like psychoanalysis for assuming that so much of everyday life has obscure unconscious motivation. Instead, Heider argued for a "naive psychology of everyday life." Most of the time, he argued, the explanations for behavior are either obvious or easy to hypothesize.

In trying to explain someone's (the "actor's") behavior, we generally consider two categories of reasons: internal factors such as the actor's disposition or personality, and external factors, such as the immediate demands of the actor's situation. Although behavior is usually a product of both sets of influences, people tend to make either internal attributions or external attributions about a given actions.

For example, why did the car in front of you veer into your lane of traffic, forcing you to brake suddenly and almost causing a collision? An internal attribution about the driver's action might be, "That driver is unskilled and not paying attention, and began to change lanes without noticing my presence." Such an attribution would be grounds for anger and blame toward the "bad driver." Alternatively, an external attribution might be, "Traffic up ahead is very congested, and the weather is bad. The driver is having difficulty being careful because conditions are poor." This kind of attribution would provide grounds for caution but probably not anger at the driver ahead.

CORRESPONDENT INFERENCES

Another theory about how people assign attributions suggests that we are simplistic in understanding causality. We assume that the outcomes of people's behaviors are intended, and that their motives must be deliberate. In this view, called the theory of correspondent inferences, we first observe others' behavior and its effects; we then infer corresponding motives.

For example, if you see a couple you know talking quietly at a party and notice that the man is speaking in a sharp tone while the woman is crying, you may infer that he is "angry" and is deliberately "making her cry" by frightening or threatening her.

This pattern of making correspondent inferences is simplistic because it ignores alternative explanations, such as the influence of external factors. It unfairly conceptualizes all behavior as intentional and planned. When we consider how many of our own actions are in fact unintentional or have consequences we ourselves would like to prevent, we recognize the limitations of our own correspondent inferences of others' behavior.

COMMON-SENSE ANALYSIS

Social psychologist Harold Kelley has proposed that, in making careful attributions about others' behavior, we analyze that behavior, separately considering its possible causes and forms. According to Kelley, we should specifically consider three qualities in analyzing behavior: its *consistency* across situations, the *distinctiveness* of its occurrence, and the *consensus* of others about its conditions.

For example, consider an attributional analysis about why your professor has criticized you for arriving five minutes late to class. Is the professor's behavior consistent: Does she usually criticize you for arriving late? Is the professor's criticism distinctive: Does she criticize other latecomers, or only you? Finally, what is the consensus about the professor's criticisms: Do other professors criticize you for being late?

Depending on the answers to these questions, we make common-sense attributions about the specific reasons for another's actions. This can be important, for example, in deciding whether a professor is being fair or unfair, whether one's own lateness must be corrected, and so on. The results of our causal analyses have implications for our future behavior.

The Fundamental Attribution Error

Researchers have found that when explaining "negative" or unpleasant behaviors, we reveal a bias in our causal attributions. Specifically, when we have done something with unpleasant consequences, we make an external or situational attribution about our own behavior. But when another person has done the unfortunate thing, we more readily make internal or dispositional attributions about his or her behavior.

IDENTIFYING THE FUNDAMENTAL ATTRIBUTION ERROR

This tendency to underestimate situational influences and overestimate dispositional influences in explaining behavior is termed the fundamental *attribution error* (FAE). We are more likely to commit the FAE when explaining others' behavior than our own. We seem to give ourselves the benefit of the doubt and blame uncontrollable circumstances when our own actions have been wrong or unsuccessful. In contrast, we are quicker to blame others for intending the harm or deserving the failure that results from similar actions.

For example, if a driver veers into your lane of traffic and forces you to brake suddenly, you might become angry because he or she is such a "terrible driver." But if you veer into someone's lane and he or she angrily blares the horn at you, you might reassure yourself that "I had no choice, the weather is so bad, I couldn't see the other car, and it shouldn't have been moving so fast anyway." Thus you attribute another's driving to his or her disposition ("bad driver") but your own to your situation ("bad weather, low visibility"). This is the FAE in action. It is called "fundamental" because it can affect our attitudes and actions, such as how stressed we become in traffic and how aggressive or considerate we are to other drivers.

EXPLAINING THE FUNDAMENTAL ATTRIBUTION ERROR

The fundamental attribution error has been itself attributed to several factors that influence causal analysis. These include the actor and observer's divergent perspectives; one's degree of self-awareness; and the attributional effects of cultural values.

Divergent Perspectives. In the typical attributional scenario, there are two characters: the actor whose behavior is being analyzed and the observer who is analyzing it. The actor's perspective on his or her own behavior is different or divergent from the observer's view of the action. The actor is likely to be focusing on the surrounding situation and its demands and details. In contrast, the observer is focusing primarily on the actor him- or herself. Not surprisingly, the actor's explanation for his or her own behavior tends to blame "the situation," while the observer's explanation blames "the actor." Their different explanations are due to their divergent perspectives, a result of focusing their attention in different directions.

Self-Awareness. Can the actor recognize that there might be different perspectives on his or her own behavior? Research says that this is difficult when we are involved in what we are doing. We are not aware that we are being observed, and so we fail to consider how our actions might look to others.

However, if our self-awareness is increased, we are more likely to see our actions as due to internal rather than external factors. Self-awareness, a self-conscious state of focusing our attention on ourselves, can be increased by a variety of conditions. Research has shown that hearing one's own voice (e.g., on a tape recording), seeing oneself in a mirror or on a video screen, or hearing one's name repeated can all result in an increase of self-awareness. Increased self-awareness focuses our attention inward—making us self-conscious instead of situation-conscious. As a result, we make internal rather than external attributions for our own behavior and are less likely to commit the FAE.

Cultural Values. So-called Western societies (like Europe, the United States and Canada) traditionally favor seeing people rather than circumstances as the cause of events. Rationalist and religious values have emphasized the idea of people as doers who freely choose their actions and deserve the consequences. Thus in Western cultures we would expect more internal attributions and trait-ascriptions in explaining behavior, such as blaming minorities for being discriminated against or looking for someone to blame or sue when a disaster occurs.

Non-Western cultures, on the other hand, may be less individualistic and more accepting of ideas like fate or uncontrollable circumstances. The FAE is less likely to occur where this nonblaming attitude prevails.

SELF-PERCEPTION

Early psychological research focused on the experience of consciousness. It took for granted people's abilities to introspect and reflect honestly and accurately. More recently social psychologists have observed that we are not "experts on ourselves" at all. On the contrary, we know as little about our true selves as we do about other people, and we must learn about ourselves as we do about others, through trial-and-error, information processing, and hypothesis testing.

Self-Perception Theory

According to social psychologist Daryl Bem, people come to understand themselves by making inferences based on observations of their own behavior. This is the reverse of the common-sense notion that we know ourselves and then act in such a way as to be "true to ourselves."

An example of the self-perception process would be figuring out how to answer a question about your own political values. If you have not already formulated an answer to the question, you will have to consider what your position is on several issues, and then draw a conclusion about what your basic position—e.g., political liberal or conservative— must be. In a sense, you "observe" your own behavior by reviewing your positions and remembering how you have voted. Then you make an inference about the connective causes of your behaviors. You thereby arrive at a perception of yourself.

Self-perception theory has important implications for attitude formation and change, as shall be reviewed in chapter 19. It also explains why people's behavior is not always consistent or predictable. We may not always "know ourselves" well enough to act in ways that fit in with past behaviors.

Self-Serving Biases

Although we may not know ourselves very well without time and effort, we are apparently predisposed to like ourselves and (as in the FAE above) give ourselves the benefit of the doubt.

One demonstration of this tendency is the application of *self-serving biases*, tendencies to perceive and judge our own actions in ways that preserve our self-esteem. Research has identified several examples of self-serving biases: patterns in self-attributions ; unrealistic optimism ; illusions of invulnerability ; and false comparison effects in judging the normality of our actions.

SELF-ATTRIBUTIONS

Numerous studies indicate that we explain and judge the causes of our behaviors in positive ways while making negative attributions about others' actions.

As the FAE predicts, we attribute our own failures or crimes to "bad luck" or "terrible circumstances" while blaming others' on criminal intentions or negligence.

In explaining positive behaviors, moreover, we make internal attributions about our own actions ("I gave money to that charity because I am generous") but external attributions about others' similar behaviors ("She made a large donation just to impress the boss").

Winners at games of chance credit their skill, while losers cite "bad luck." Relationship partners each claim that they do the majority of household work, while their spouses make minimal contributions.

Self-serving biases in attribution can help preserve a sense of self-esteem, but they can also hinder good interpersonal relations and make it hard to sympathize with or respect others' points of view.

UNREALISTIC OPTIMISM

To some extent self-serving biases require distorting reality. Real life involves unfairness and disaster. Healthy functioning may require one to be optimistic in spite of the evidence. It has been found that some depressed individuals are not pessimistic about life situations, but are rather realistic. In contrast, non-depressed persons are not realistic, but they are unrealistically optimistic about their ability to overcome obstacles to success and happiness.

For example, in judging one's likelihood of suffering from major illness or divorce, respondents say they have a lower probability of such negative life experiences than others. Alternatively, they claim they are more likely to experience such successes as home ownership, wealth, and career success.

Unrealistic optimism can strengthen people's resolve in dealing with adverse circumstances and can enhance mood. However, it can also lead one to be unprepared for realistic risks.

ILLUSIONS OF INVULNERABILITY

One consequence of unrealistic optimism is to develop illusions of invulnerability, false perceptions that one is immune to error, pain, or failure. For example, believing oneself to be "safer" than others, one may take greater and unnecessary risks, such as driving without wearing a seatbelt, smoking cigarettes, or not using contraception. Individuals who maintain such illusory ideas have been found consequently to be at great risk for injury, illness, or unwanted pregnancy. Our self-protective illusions can have self-destructive consequences. Illusions of invulnerability have also been found to contaminate group problem solving efforts and make irresponsible decisions more likely (see Groupthink, chapter 20).

FALSE COMPARISON EFFECTS

Believing ourselves to be more moral than average, better than average, safer than average, we may wrongly judge how our actions compare with those of others.

One example of this is the *false uniqueness* effect. We see our positive actions, skills, and abilities to be relatively unusual, misjudging the likelihood that others are also good or talented.

Alternatively, when we acknowledge the selfishness or failures we have experienced, we may suffer from the *false consensus effect*. We overestimate how common our negative behaviors and prejudices are, justifying cheating on our taxes by arguing that "everyone does it," and excusing an angry outburst by claiming "it's normal for people to lose their temper once in a while."

Self-Handicapping

An ironic extension of self-serving tendencies is our search for self-serving attributions about expected failures or losses. For example, the coach of a team who fears they may lose an upcoming match may warn, "Because of players' illnesses and injuries, we may have a hard time beating our rivals." This having been said, the team's loss can be rationalized as due to unavoidable difficulties rather than incompetence.

Such self-disparagement in quest of more acceptable reasons for failure is known as self-handicapping. For example, a student who worries that she will do poorly on an upcoming examination must decide whether to spend the previous evening studying or partying. If she studies and then fails, she will be forced to conclude that her best efforts were still incompetent—an unacceptable self-attribution. Alternatively, if she parties and then fails, she may conclude that her failure was due to negligence rather than incompetence—a more acceptable self-attribution.

Self-handicapping can involve engaging in somewhat self-defeating or self-destructive behavior, in the cause of establishing relatively acceptable reasons for failure. A shy man invites a woman to an unpleasant bar on a date; later he explains her rejection of him as due to bad atmosphere rather than his own unattractiveness. An intimidated job applicant oversleeps and fails to shower, groom, or prepare prior to the hiring interview; later she blames not being hired on her "stupid alarm clock" rather than her own lack of skills or confidence.

The danger of self-handicapping obviously is that in manufacturing a "more acceptable" excuse for failure, we may guarantee a failure that may otherwise have been unlikely.

PERCEIVING OTHERS

In self-perception we have the luxury of time with ourselves and a broad perspective on our actions over many situations. In perceiving others, however, we are usually granted only limitied time and circumstances. Nonetheless we may have to make important decisions about others with lasting consequences. Faced with important decisions and insufficient opportunity to collect information, we resort to various strategies and heuristics (informal guidelines) to draw conclusions about others. These patterns of social cognition influence our experiences and actions in three broad areas: impression formation; interpersonal attraction; and social prejudice.

Impression Formation

According to Heider's "naive psychology," we look for reasonable explanations of others' behavior rather than assuming that people are inscrutable and impossible to understand. Other researchers have pointed out that, in everyday life, we often behave like "naive scientists" in forming impressions of others. Specifically, when we meet someone, we collect information by various means (e.g., asking others about him or her, making observations of his or her likes and dislikes, and direct "interview" of the target person). After collecting the information (data), we speculate about the connections among the person's characteristics (form hypotheses) and test these in real life.

We rely on numerous strategies for combining and interpreting information about others. Some of these strategies include reliance on stereotypes and central traits, and being influenced by primacy and recency effects.

STEREOTYPES

A stereotype is a generalization about a group of people that distinguishes them from others. Thinking of the British as conservative, the French as romantic, blacks as more athletic than whites, and men as more politically sophisticated than women are all forms of stereotypes. A stereotype is not necessarily inaccurate, but by generalizing about all members within a group and ignoring their individual differences, it is more likely to be inaccurate than otherwise.

Stereotypes can be triggered by any clue to an individual's group membership: physical appearance, accent, language, or context. Stereotypes are a common factor in prejudice, an unjustifiable negative attitude toward all members of a group (see Social Prejudice, below).

CENTRAL TRAITS

In classic research, social psychologist Solomon Asch asked students to form an impression of individuals whose traits had been listed for them. Half of the students read a list including the trait "warm," while the other half read an otherwise identical list which included the trait "cold." The trait dimension "warm-cold" was found to be central to impressions formed of the other traits. For example, someone who is "warm and intelligent" seems to be a different kind of intelligent than someone who is "cold and intelligent." Central traits are traits influential in modifying the total impression formed as well as the way each trait in the impression is interpreted.

Central traits may vary among people. If kindness is important in someone's life, the impression he forms of others may be centrally influenced by whether those others appear to be kind or not.

PRIMACY AND RECENCY EFFECTS

In further work Asch gave subjects lists of traits to form impressions about. Half received a list of several positive traits followed by several negative traits. The other half received the same list in reverse order. The impressions subjects formed were influenced more by the first traits on each list. This first-impressions influence is termed the primacy effect. Its wisdom is common-sensical. Most of us behave as though we believe that our first contacts with others will set the tone for all later interactions.

In some cases it has been found that the last information available has swayed the impression being formed, the so-called recency effect. However, the recency effect seems to occur only under special circumstances, as when we are caused to doubt the truth of first impressions or warned against the dangers of hasty social judgments. In those conditions, when the latest information contradicts the first, last impressions count stronger.

Interpersonal Attraction

An important focus of social perception research in recent decades is interpersonal attraction, or the processes involved in forming preferences for specific others. While most people like being with their own kind (affiliation; see chapter 10), attraction involves moving beyond mere affiliation to being with specific others.

Several factors have been found to influence interpersonal attraction, including the three reviewed here: proximity and familiarity; physical attractiveness; and similarity.

PROXIMITY AND FAMILIARITY

What is the first determinant of whether or not we like someone else? Classic research by the late Leon Festinger and his colleagues examined the best friend selections among older college students and their spouses. In analyzing the various factors that seemed to link students with those they liked most, only one emerged as a common denominator: *proximity*. Students who came to like each other lived closer to each other than those who did not.

The *proximity effect* —the influence of physical nearness in increasing interpersonal attraction—has since been extended to many environments and situations. Social popularity is also influenced by proximity; people who have more contact with others—e.g., by living on the ground floor of a high-rise building, near an exit, or near a common facility like a laundry room—are more popular than those who have less contact with others.

Research by social psychologist Robert Zajonc has identified the key variable in the proximity effect as the power of "mere exposure" or *familiarity*. The familiarity effect works with inanimate objects as well as humans. People can become fond of a landmark they once considered an ugly eyesore, simply through a process of getting used to it over time. As things and people become familiar, less novel, they become more predictable, and our uncertainty about them is reduced. In general, familiar people are attractive people.

PHYSICAL ATTRACTIVENESS

When people are described as "attractive," most of us assume that means "good-looking," although attraction is a process that can involve many kinds of appeal.

Research on interpersonal attraction has consistently concluded that we are attracted to good-looking, or physically attractive, people.

In one study, students attended a matchmaking dance and were paired with assigned dates for the evening. At several intervals, the assigned dates were separated and asked to rate their partners on a number of characteristics, including physical attractiveness. At the end of the evening, dates were asked to indicate whether they would like to date their partners again. When results were analyzed, only one of the many factors recorded predicted the preferences for a second date: physical attractiveness. Good-looking people were generally afforded a "second chance" while physically unattractive people were not.

One reason for the physical attractiveness effect is the *physical attractiveness stereotype*. Physically attractive people as a cognitive "group" are considered to be attractive in other ways, such as in talent, friendliness, intelligence, and conversational skills. In essence, most of us seem to believe that "what is beautiful is good." While good looks can help someone to succeed or make favorable impressions, follow-up research on some physically attractive people indicates that their only difference from average-looking people is that they may be more likely eventually to marry. Beautiful people do not appear more likely to be successful in other ways than the rest of us.

SIMILARITY

By far the most consistent finding in analyzing interpersonal attraction is that we like others who are similar to ourselves. This similarity can be a quality of our intelligence levels, physical appearances (a trend known as "matching"), or especially our attitudes. Research on long-term relationships indicates that, the more alike two people are at the beginning of their relationship, the more likely their relationship will last.

Social Prejudice

Because we frequently must make decisions about future interactions based on inadequate information, we often make hasty and automatic judgments about others. For example, we like the way someone looks, so we decide to ask him or her out, or to hire him or her. Alternatively of course, we may decide we dislike something about another person: a trait we judge to be negative, an unattractive appearance, or an abrasive style of interacting.

Often the source of quick dislike is a *prejudice,* a negative attitude we have formed, unjustifiably, about all members of a particular social group. Prejudice may involve stereotyping, but the terms are not synonymous. For example, if we meet someone who has a Southern accent, we may think, "A typical Southerner." That is a stereotype. But if we think, "A typical stupid Southerner that I don't want to get to know," that is a prejudice. Prejudice involves more than stereotyping; it involves an unfair and negative pre-judgment.

Research on prejudice and discrimination (treating people in unfairly different ways because of their perceived group membership) has identified three major sources of social prejudice: social influences, emotional factors, and cognitive factors.

SOCIAL ORIGINS

Rationalizing Social Injustice. Prejudice against certain social groups rationalizes inequalities in groups' rights and status. Arguing, for example, that women cannot be effective in combat roles serves to justify denying women in the military the same combat-related advancement opportunities as men. Similarly, early American advocates of slavery might have argued that blacks were incapable of caring for themselves without help, an opinion that justified the "protection" offered by enslaving blacks but not whites.

Religious Attitudes. Certain sets of religious ideas have also been found to correlate highly with racial and gender prejudice. Organized religions have often produced rationalizations for prejudice, as when fundamentalist Christians cite Biblical justifications for denying the civil rights of homosexuals, or Moslem leaders in Saudi Arabia forbid women to drive cars.

Ingroup-Outgroup Bias. Merely separating people into social groups appears to facilitate prejudice. When schoolchildren are assigned to play games on different teams, they quickly agree that their own teams are "better" in various ways and that the other teams are "worse." This is an example of ingroup bias, the belief that the members of one's own social group (the ingroup) are superior to nonmembers (the outgroup). Even when such groups are formed on no criterion, purely arbitrarily, members seek and invent arguments to support such ingroup bias. Classic research by Muzafer Sherif concluded that ingroup bias and intergroup competition were the only ingredients necessary to develop intergroup conflict.

EMOTIONAL INFLUENCES

Scapegoats. A common theory of aggression (see chapters 10 and 15) is that it is triggered by the experience of frustration. When the source of frustration is difficult to identify or might retaliate, an aggressor will often displace hostility onto a scapegoat, an alternative target blamed and victimized. The persecution of Jews in Germany by the Nazis in the 1930s and 1940s, after a wartime defeat and an economic depression, illustrates prejudice against a scapegoat.

The Authoritarian Personality. In the 1950s studies of antisemitism (anti-Jewish prejudice) in the United States, a distinct personality profile was identified as being particularly prone to prejudiced attitudes like racism and antisemitism. This pattern, called the authoritarian personality, was found to include such tendencies as superstition, anti-intellectualism, a tendency to stereotype, exaggerated respect for conventional authority, and ethnocentrism, a bias in favor of one's own and against others' ethnic groups. Research on the authoritarian personality provided some intriguing clues to the emotional origins of prejudice. Many authoritarians in an early sample were found to have been raised in harshly disciplinarian homes by punitive fathers and weak, submissive mothers. Self-esteem among such individuals may have depended on displacing such harsh judgment onto others.

COGNITIVE FACTORS

Categorizing. Human information processing has a limited capacity. Inabilities to handle overloads of information result in simplifying information. When forming impressions of others, we may simplify our cognitive chores by categorizing people in various ways. Once having categorized people, we tend to see those within categories as more like each other and as more different from people outside those categories. This strategy for simplifying thought is a powerful factor in prejudice. It is common to assume that all Southerners are alike or all Japanese are workaholics, that "if you've seen one, you've seen them all" whether referring to races, age groups, or the other gender. The sexist sentiment that "All men/women are alike" illustrates this oversimplification effect of categorization.

Salience. Within an otherwise all white group, one black member is more distinctive. Within an otherwise all-male group, a lone female member draws more attention. We pay more attention to salient or distinctive cases, and we remember them better. Thus a minority group member may get more than his or her "fair share" of attention and scrutiny.

When an individual feels he or she is receiving undue amounts of attention from others—whether true or not—he or she feels more self-conscious. Since such self-consciousness can heighten arousal, it can interfere with the performance of complex tasks (see chapter 10). If the majority already believes that a minority group member is less competent because of his or her group membership, that individual's salience can create a self-fulfilling prophecy in inferior performance.

The Vividness Heuristic. We remember things better if they are vivid at the time of encoding. This is known as the vividness heuristic. Remembering a restaurant where you had a terrible meal more easily than one where you had an acceptable meal is an example of the vividness heuristic at work.

Ironically, events and people are more likely to be vivid if they are unusual or atypical. Over time, the memorability of vivid cases leads to confusion about whether these cases are typical or not. For example, if newspaper headlines repeatedly describe an offender as a "homosexual child molester," the vividness of the information may create the erroneous impression that most "child molesters" are also "homosexual" (although heterosexuals make up the significant majority of convicted child molesters). The *illusory correlation* —false impression of a connection—caused by the vividness heuristic can be another source of prejudice.

One way to correct illusory correlations is to remind ourselves that commonplace or typical cases and conditions are not newsworthy and do not make headlines. "News" is more likely to reflect the exception than the rule. Vividness makes information more memorable, but it does not equate with typicality.

Social psychology studies the social and situation influences on individual behavior, thought, and feeling. An important area of research in social psychology is social perception and cognition. These processes include causal attribution, self-perception processes, and perceiving others.

Attribution is the process of analyzing the causes of behavior. Heider's "naive psychology" theory of attribution argues that attributions are either internal or external. The theory of correspondent inferences argues that we explain others' actions by inferring dispositions that correspond with the behaviors observed. Kelley's common-sense analysis proposes that causal attributions are determined by an assessment of a behavior's consistency, distinctiveness, and consensus.

We commit the fundamental attribution error by making dispositional attributions about others' negative behaviors. This error has been explained in terms of divergent perspectives, reduced self-awareness, and cultural values favoring the blame of people rather than situations.

Self-perception is theorized to be no more automatic than the perception of others. Self-perception theory suggests that in understanding ourselves, we observe our own behavior and make inferences about its meaning. Our objectivity is hampered by self-serving biases, including our tendency to make favorable self-attributions, maintain unrealistic optimism, harbor illusions of invulnerability, and judge our behavior falsely in comparison with others. One ironic self-serving tendency is self-handicapping, the creation of handicaps to provide acceptable excuses for failure.

If self-perception is limited, the perception of others is difficult and challenging. We develop and rely on guidelines and strategies to collect and interpret information about others. One application of these strategies can be seen in impression formation. Our impressions of others are often influenced by stereotypes, the weight of central traits, and primacy and recency effects in information collected over time.

Interpersonal attraction is another application of person perception strategies. Our liking for others is influenced by their proximity to us and our resultant familiarity with them. Liking is also greater for those who are perceived to be physically attractive and similar to ourselves.

Social prejudices can also result from the process applied to perceiving others. The social origins of prejudice include rationalizations of social injustice, some religious attitudes, and ingroup-outgroup bias. Emotional factors in prejudice include the tendency to displace aggression against scapegoats, and to see prejudice as part of an authoritarian world-view. Finally, cognitive factors in prejudice include categorizing others, the salience of minority group members, and reliance on the vividness heuristic in forming memories and perceiving correlations.

Selected Readings

Aronson, E. *The Social Animal, 5th Edition*. New York: W. H. Freeman and Company. 1988

Dane, F. C. *The Common and Uncommon Sense of Social Psychology*. Pacific Grove, CA: Wadsworth. 1988

Dovidio, J. F. and S. L. Gaertner. *Prejudice, Discrimination, and Racism*. Orlando, FL: Academic Press. 1986

Frisk, S. T. *Social Cognition*. Boston, MA: Addison-Wesley. 1984

Harvey, J. H. and G. Weary. *Perspectives on Attributional Processes*. Dubuque, IA: Wm. C. Brown. 1981

Hatfield, E. and S. Sprecher. *Mirror, Mirror: The Importance of Looks in Everyday Life*. Albany, NY: State University of New York Press. 1986

Katz, P. A. and D. A. Taylor . *Eliminating Racism: Profiles in Controversy*. New York: Plenum. 1988

Myers, D. G. *Social Psychology, 3rd Edition*. New York: McGraw-Hill. 1990

Pogrebin, L. C. *Among Friends: Who We Like, Why We Like Them, and What We Do With Them*. New York: McGraw-Hill. 1986

19

Attitudes

An interest in understanding, predicting, and controlling the effects of human behavior is central to psychology. Social psychology in particular applies this sequence of interests to social behavior and experience. Social perception and cognition, as examined in chapter 18, focuses on understanding social behavior. In the present chapter we focus on an important approach to predicting human social behavior: understanding attitudes and their relation to behavior.

THE NATURE OF ATTITUDES

Defining Attitudes

An attitude is an evaluative reaction to a person, object, or event. A dislike of broccoli is an attitude, as is a preference for liberal Democratic candidates. A neutral "attitude" is a contradiction in terms: to be "neutral" about something—neither positive nor negative—is equivalent to having no attitude about it.

ATTITUDES, VALUES, AND OPINIONS

An attitude is more specific than a value. One might value freedom in general but have a positive attitude about the Bill of Rights. Values are more general and abstract than attitudes, which tend to be more focused and concrete.

Many researchers use the term "attitude" interchangeably with "opinion." Social psychologists use the more precise term attitude to connote the several components attitudes involve.

COMPONENTS OF ATTITUDES

Attitudes are comprised of three components: beliefs, emotions, and behaviors.

Beliefs. Beliefs make up the cognitive component of an attitude. For example, an unfavorable attitude about eating meat might include beliefs that eating meat causes health problems, and that most meat is processed and packaged in unhygienic ways.

Emotions. Emotions make up the affective component of an attitude. In the example of an unfavorable attitude about eating meat, related emotions might include feeling nauseated by the sight of raw meat, and reacting with anger to meat industry advertising campaigns.

Behaviors. Behaviors comprise the responsive or active component of an attitude. If one has an unfavorable attitude about eating meat, one will probably refuse meat at meals, and this attitude may generalize to other forms of behavior, such as criticizing others for eating meat or boycotting stores and restaurants that sell meat.

Attitude Acquisition

Attitudes are acquired rather than inborn, although many attitudes appear to "run in families" and are obviously acquired through such contact from childhood.

Attitudes are thought to be acquired through the three major forms of learning: classical conditioning, operant conditioning, and observational learning.

CLASSICAL CONDITIONING

Some attitudes may be developed from emotional or sensory associations. An individual may associate a particular sensory experience with an emotional reaction: the US-UR connection (see chapter 6). Later the US may be associated with a new association, the attitude object. After repeated pairings of the US with this new CS, the attitude object alone will elicit the emotional reaction: the CS-CR connection.

For example, a person you care for treats you badly. You then associate bad feelings with this person, the US-UR association. He or she also wears a particular cologne all the time. Because encounters with him or her (an unpleasant experience) always involve perceiving the fragrance of the cologne (originally a neutral experience), over time you associate bad feelings with the smell of the cologne by itself, whether the other person is in the vicinity or not. Thus a negative attitude toward the cologne has been classically conditioned through associations from another experience.

OPERANT CONDITIONING

While classical conditioning may explain quick, gut-level responses like emotions, it cannot explain more complex attitude formation. More complex attitudes are probably formed through operant conditioning, as an individual is reinforced for holding and voicing certain attitudes.

For example, a child whose parents are politically conservative may find that voicing liberal opinions is met with argument or rejection, while voicing conservative opinions is followed by praise and attention. After a time, the conservative opinions are voiced more than the liberal ones, and the child "learns" that conservative attitudes "pay off" in this particular environment.

One's social environment will include a variety of people and opinions. Some groups will shape our attitudes, as in the example above. Over time we will also choose and shape our groups—called *reference groups*, the social networks we consult for information and with whom we compare ourselves—in line with our developing attitudes. Disagreement within a reference group is rare, but when it occurs it has powerful effects on both belief systems and group structure (see discussions of social comparison in chapter 20).

OBSERVATIONAL LEARNING

Especially when we consult reference groups, we may come to rely on other kinds of learning besides operant conditioning. Your reference group may include people like celebrities whom you admire but whom you do not personally know. Nonetheless, you may observe these people's actions and learn attitudes from them.

The attitudinal influence of observational learning is the basis for an important factor in the process of persuasion (see discussion below). For this reason, opinion leaders like celebrities, athletes, and entertainers are often requested to endorse products being advertised or candidates running for office.

Attitudes and Behavior

Given the desire we have to predict others' behavior, the behavioral component of attitudes is of great interest to most people. The traditional assumption has been that attitudes can predict behaviors. If we know someone's attitude toward a product or political candidate, we can predict what he or she will buy or how he or she will vote.

USING ATTITUDES TO PREDICT BEHAVIOR

Advertisers and political advisors conduct "opinion polls" and "consumer surveys" in order to learn people's attitudes about certain products and people. They hope that the results of such surveys will help predict behavior like buying and voting. The common-sense notion that attitudes predict behavior has been challenged in recent years. Some researchers argue that little if any of one's behavior is an expression of one's pure attitudes. Other influences such as social pressure and self-awareness may intervene and cause us to behave in ways that differ from our original attitudes.

As a result of the poor prediction power of many attitude measures, researchers have examined another direction underlying the attitude-behavior connection.

EFFECTS OF BEHAVIOR ON ATTITUDES

While traditional theories argued that attitudes predict behaviors, modern research suggests that the reverse direction is more accurate: behavior shapes attitudes.

Several examples of this relationship have been studied, including the foot-in-the-door phenomenon, role-playing, and social movements.

The Foot-in-the-Door Phenomenon. A popular technique among old-fashioned door-to-door salesmen was to knock, get the homeowner to open the door slightly, and then wedge one's foot in the door in order to have a captive audience for at least the first appeal of the sales pitch. The rationale was that if you could get a "foot in the door," you could get a sale.

Recent research suggests that this technique works psychologically for a variety of persuasive efforts. Specifically, if you want someone to grant you a favor, first make a smaller, related request. When the other person agrees, he or she will form an attitude in favor of granting you favors in general. Later, when you request your original favor, although the behavior may require more effort, he or she will be more likely to grant it than if you had asked for it "cold" or without any preparation. In a sense, your first, smaller request got your "foot in the door," and the later request was more assured.

The foot-in-the-door phenomenon is thought to involve a sequence in which a behavior (the first favor) creates an attitude (willingness to grant favors) that leads to future behavior (granting bigger favors).

Role-Playing. When actors play roles they take on a character's characteristics and motives. In the course of role-playing, they become sympathetic to the attitudes that underlie the character's actions.

Research has shown that subjects who played the part of lung-cancer patients were later more likely to quit smoking than those who had not played such roles. Apparently the behavior that involved formation of an attitude stuck with the actors even when their roles were finished.

Social Movements. Civil rights legislation in the United States required employers and political leaders to treat minority groups fairly and without segregation or discrimination before these behaviors were supported by popular attitudes. Over time, it was theorized, treating people fairly would lead to an unprejudiced attitude. Thus social movements are thought to guide behaviors which themselves develop attitudes to further those movements.

A simple example of using social action to inculcate attitudes is having children recite prayers or the Pledge of Allegiance in school. Most young children do not understand the words of the memorized prose they are reciting. But the ritual behavior, practiced faithfully (whether coerced or not), leads to attitudes that favor such behavior in other situations and contexts.

THEORIES OF BEHAVIOR-ATTITUDE INFLUENCE

Several theories have been offered to explain how and why one's behavior can, seemingly retroactively, influence one's attitudes. These include self-presentation theory, self-perception theory, and self-justification theory.

Self-Presentation. One of the simplest explanations for why our attitudes match our behavior is self-presentation theory. We present ourselves to others and are concerned with their impressions of us. We know that others' opinions of us will affect our lives, including career opportunities (e.g., whether we will be hired) and social involvements (e.g., whether another person will find us attractive).

One quality we know is valued in our society is consistency. People like people who behave in a consistent, reliable, predictable manner. Once we have acted a particular way, then, it is desirable to insist that we have done so on purpose. Thus it is socially desirable to form attitudes that reflect our behaviors.

Self-Perception. As described in chapter 18, self-perception involves observing our own behavior and making inferences about our true underlying motivations. This explains how behavior might influence attitudes: once we have done something, we consider our action and infer that we must have an attitude in favor of that action. For example, why did you purchase a particular brand of shampoo? By inference, you must conclude that you prefer that brand to others, and will make the same kind of purchase again.

Self-Justification. Attitude-behavior consistency is not only socially desirable, it is also psychologically comfortable. *Consistency theories* (see below) argue that cognitive elements like behaviors and attitudes must be in harmony for people to feel comfortable with themselves. Disharmony—e.g., a mismatch between a behavior and one's attitude—results in discomfort, and motivates one to restore harmony to relieve the tension.

When one has done something that does not match a previously stated attitude, one experiences disharmony and desires to restore consistency again. Since the behavior itself is already done and cannot be changed, an obvious option for restoring harmony is to change one's old attitude to match the new behavior. This is the process of self-justification.

For example, a woman has always been outspoken about the need for gun control and the dangers of handgun ownership. One day a house in her neighborhood is burglarized, and the next day she herself purchases a handgun "for self-protection." When her friends challenge her about this apparent inconsistency, she justifies her behavior by changing her attitude.

She now insists that she still favors keeping guns out of criminals' hands, but not out of everyone's hands. She has changed her attitude to realign it with her most recent behavior, in order to justify her behavior to herself and others.

CHANGING ATTITUDES

As is apparent from the previous section, attitudes are not rigid and inflexible. People may change their attitudes in order to justify recent behaviors, understand themselves better, or present themselves to others as consistent.

Theories of Attitude Change

On the other hand, in an effort to simplify our social thinking, we resist changing our attitudes unless it is necessary to do so. Thus there are patterns in the ways attitudes are changed. Two important theories of attitude change include social-judgment theory and consistency theories.

SOCIAL-JUDGMENT THEORY

Social-judgment theory argues that attitude change is affected by factors like the original attitude—the attitude being changed or replaced—and the difference between it and the new or replacement attitude. For example, the attitude "No one but the police and the military should have guns," is extremely different from the attitude "Everyone should have the right to own guns," but not too different from the attitude "Only qualified people should be allowed to own guns." According to social-judgment theory, the first attitude will be more easily changed to a similar attitude than to a different attitude.

According to this theory, attitudes about related issues are judged along a continuum, like the degrees of a thermometer, rather than as completely separate categories like an "on-off" switch. Thus there is no sharp line between liberal and conservative. Instead, there are extremely liberal, moderately liberal, slightly liberal, slightly conservative, moderately conservative, and extremely conservative attitudes. It is easier to change attitudes from one position to an adjacent position than to a position at the opposite end of the continuum.

Attitude change professionals, like advertisers and campaign managers, use social-judgment theory when they portray their product or candidate as similar to those already favored by the audience. If the audience accepts this similarity, it will be easier to change their attitude than if they believe their preexisting attitudes are in opposition to the new product or candidate.

CONSISTENCY THEORIES

Consistency theories argue that people need to keep their own thoughts and actions consistent with each other. When such cognitive elements are inconsistent, an uncomfortable tension results from the disharmony. Efforts to reduce this tension will result in attitude change.

Two types of consistency theories are reviewed here: balance theory and cognitive dissonance theory.

Balance Theory. According to balance theory, people assign positive or negative values to the people and objects they think about and the relationships between them. For example, a Person (P) likes his parents (the Object or O). This liking relationship (+) is symbolized as P + O. The Person also likes his girlfriend X (symbolized as P + X). If his parents also like his girlfriend, then O + X. In this situation, all relationships are balanced: P + O, P + X, and O + X.

If, however, his parents dislike his girlfriend (P - X), this introduces a single negative relationship into the three relationships: P + O, P + X, but O - X. This set of relationships is said to be imbalanced.

Because of the problem created by the imbalance, one or more of the relationships will have to be corrected to restore a sense of balance. For example, the person could break up with his girlfriend (P - X). When P + O, O - X and P - X, relationships are once more balanced: P still likes O, but now both P and O dislike X.

Balance theory explains that attitudes are changed when they are incompatible with other attitudes. Suppose you have always liked a particular actor but disliked a particular politician. The actor has just publicly supported that politician. You will now have to change either your attitude toward the actor (to dislike) or your attitude toward the politician (to liking). After this change in attitude, your relationships will once more be balanced.

Cognitive Dissonance Theory. According to self-justification (above), we sometimes form attitudes to justify our own recent behavior. Cognitive dissonance theory, developed by the social psychologist Leon Festinger, asserts that self-justification is necessary because a mismatch between attitudes and behavior creates disharmony (*dissonance*), which produces psychological tension. This tension works like a drive that we are motivated to reduce. Tension reduction is achieved when we change our attitudes so they are harmonious with our recent behavior.

For example, a person has always purchased Brand A cereal which she likes very much. One day she notices that a similar cereal, Brand B, is ten cents cheaper than Brand A, so she buys B instead. The next time she goes shopping, Brand B is marked with its usual, slightly higher price. She asks herself which brand she should buy, A or B. If she decides to buy A, she must conclude that she switched to B only because of that one-time ten-cent difference. If she feels that a ten-cent savings is not enough justification for the switch, she may conclude that she "must have" switched to B because she likes B better. To justify having bought B last time, she changes her attitude to be pro-B and buys B again. To reduce dissonance ("I always liked A but I bought B"), she changes her attitude ("I must really like B better").

Persuasion

Persuasion is a form of social influence that involves application of the principles of attitude change. Persuasion occurs when individuals change others' attitudes. A popular approach to understanding persuasion involves studying the components of the persuasion process. Once these components are understood, it is also possible to learn how to resist persuasion.

COMPONENTS OF PERSUASION

A group of social psychologists at Yale University have developed a communication model of persuasion that identifies the following major components: the source; the message itself; the context of the message; and the audience.

The Source. The source of a persuasive message is the communicator who is presenting it. A source is more persuasive if he or she is seen as *credible* (believable) and *attractive*. There are two ways to be credible: claiming to be an expert, and appearing to be trustworthy. When a tennis star endorses a particular brand of athletic shoe, she is persuasive because she is an expert. When an actor who always plays heroes endorses a product, he is persuasive because his career as a "good guy" makes him appear trustworthy.

There are also two ways for a source to be attractive: physical appeal and similarity to the audience. When automobile commercials feature beautiful men and women at the wheel, advertisers hope that the models' physical appeal will make the commercial persuasive. When a beer commercial portrays a group of blue-collar men enjoying a particular brand of beer, the commercial is persuasive to audience members who consider themselves similar to the characters depicted.

The Message. Persuasive messages can involve emotional appeals or rational arguments. When time is limited, short emotional appeals may be more effective than rational arguments. For example, anti-smoking campaigns with slogans like "Smokers Stink!" may be more persuasive than lists of recent statistical findings about the health of smokers versus nonsmokers.

Should a message be one-sided or should it present both sides of an issue? Research shows that when the audience is highly involved and already sympathetic, a one-sided message is more persuasive. In contrast, when an audience is undecided or uninvolved, a two-sided message seems more fair and persuasive. There is also evidence that more intelligent audiences are persuaded better by two-sided messages, probably because they more readily recognize that there are two sides to the issue.

The Context. Advertisers often have difficulty overcoming the internal arguments that compete with their persuasive messages. When we listen to or read a persuasive message, we are usually free to limit our attention or silently *counterargue* with its arguments. For this reason, many salespeople will try to prevent internal counterarguing by distracting a customer. For example, if a customer is urged to "try out" a new appliance while the salesperson talks about its features, the customer will already be paying attention to two things—using the appliance and listening to the salesperson—and will have difficulty rehearsing counterarguments. Laboratory research has shown that when subjects are distracted, they are more likely to accept a persuasive message than when they have been allowed to concentrate on their counterarguments.

The Audience. Numerous research efforts have focused on the recipients of persuasive messages, the audience, to discover when some people are more persuadable than others. Many audience characteristics interact with message variables, like involvement or intelligence, as mentioned above. Intelligent recipients are more persuaded by complex messages, while unintelligent recipients are more persuaded by simple emotional messages.

Other audience research has identified characteristics like age or lifestyle as relevant to persuasiveness. For example, young people may be more likely to accept a message that promised popularity, while older people would find security or health a more appealing promise.

RESISTANCE TO PERSUASION

There are numerous ways to resist persuasion if one understands the components and strategies involved in most messages. These techniques include counterargument, forewarning, and reactance.

Counterargument. As described above, when not distracted, we tend to counterargue silently while we listen to a persuasive message. We can resist others' persuasive efforts by concentrating on our own counterarguments, resisting distractions, and taking more time between hearing the message and making the decision (e.g., what to buy, how to vote).

Forewarning. When people know they are going to hear a persuasive message, this forewarning tends to make them less persuadable. We can apply this strategy by reminding ourselves that a television commercial is a form of advertisement, not entertainment. Forewarning ourselves and others about the messages we are about to hear can increase our resistance to persuasion.

Reactance. People dislike having their freedom and choice limited. When messages dictate restrictions or policies, we often respond with reactance, a preference for the forbidden or restricted action. For example, a sign that says "Keep Off the Grass" may result in the reactant behavior of stomping deliberately on the grass, whereas one that appeals "Please Walk on the Sidewalk" is subtler and more willingly obeyed.

To resist persuasion, we can stimulate our own reactant tendencies by asking ourselves "Who says?", and reminding ourselves that "No one tells me what to do!"

Attitudes are evaluative reactions toward persons, things, or events. They are more focused than general values and may be synonymous with opinions. An attitude has three sets of components: beliefs, emotions, and behaviors. Attitudes are probably acquired through learning, including classical conditioning, operant conditioning, and observational learning.

The relationship between attitudes and behavior has long been of interest. Traditional theories that attitudes predict behavior have given way recently to arguments that behaviors generate and influence attitudes. Explanations for this behavior-attitude connection include self-presentation theory, self-perception theory, and self-justification theory.

Although attitudes are important, they are not rigid and can be changed. Two theories of attitude change include social-judgment theory and consistency theory. Social-judgment theory suggests that new attitudes are compared with old ones. Similar positions are easier to accept than extremely different ones. Consistency theories claim that the maintenance of consistency among cognitive elements motivates us to change attitudes to restore harmony. Balance theory explains this process in terms of a balance among attitude relationships. Cognitive dissonance theory argues that, to reduce dissonance caused by attitude-behavior mismatch, we are more likely to change the attitude than the behavior.

Persuasion involves applying principles of attitude change. Components of persuasion involve the source, the message, the context, and the audience. Resistance to persuasion involves processes like counterargument, forewarning, and reactance.

Selected Readings

Aopostle, R. A., C. Y. Glock, T. Piazza and M. Suelzle. *The Anatomy of Racial Attitudes.* Los Angeles: University of California Press. 1983

Cialdini, R. B. *Influence: Science and Practice.* Glenview, IL: Scott, Foresman. 1988

Cushman, D. P. and R. D. McPhee (Eds.). *Message-Attitude-Behavior Relationships: Theory, Methodology, and Application.* New York: Academic Press. 1980

Jamieson, G. H. *Communication and Persuasion.* Dover, NH: Croom Helm. 1985

Petty, R. E. and J. T. Cacioppo. *Communication and Persuasion: Central and Peripheral Routes to Attitude Change*. New York: Springer-Verlag. 1986

Petty, R. E., T. M. Ostrom and T. C. Brock (Eds.). *Cognitive Responses in Persuasion*. Hillsdale, NJ: Erlbaum. 1981

Zimbardo, P. G. and M. R. Leippe . *The Psychology of Attitude Change and Social Influence*. New York: McGraw-Hill. 1991

20

Social Influence and Interaction

The majority of work in social psychology focuses on people's social actions and the ways that behaviors are influenced by social considerations and processes. This chapter reviews major work on two spheres of social behavior: social influence and social interaction.

THEORIES OF SOCIAL INFLUENCE

The previous chapter briefly reviewed research on persuasion, one form of social influence. Unquestionably our ideas, feelings, and actions are influenced by the people around us. In some cases, like persuasion and obedience, that influence is intentional. In others—conformity, for example—influence is effective although not consciously intended.

How does social influence work? Two general approaches are reviewed that address this question: social comparison theory, and the distinction between normative and informational influence.

Social Comparison

According to social psychologist Leon Festinger, social influence is a by-product of our quest for meaning. According to Festinger's theory of social comparison, we compare ourselves with others socially, using others' opinions and actions as a standard for judging our own. In brief, people seek information and compare their judgments with those of other people in an effort to verify that information.

Four premises explain the social comparison process:

(1) Everyone has beliefs (e.g., "It is raining," "Ronald Reagan was the worst president in American history").

(2) It is important that our beliefs be correct. For example, if we are wrong about whether it is raining, we may plan outdoor activities and end up getting drenched by a downpour.

(3) Some beliefs are easier to verify than others. To test an objective belief like whether it is raining, we need only consult a standard (e.g., by putting our hand out a window to see if it gets wet). It is harder to test a subjective belief like "Ronald Reagan was the worst American president." There is no objective standard to test a subjective belief. Instead of consulting an encyclopedia, we rely on other people to agree with us, a process called *consensual validation*. If people agree (provide us with a consensus), the belief is verified (validated).

(4) When there is disagreement about a subjective belief, people will communicate until agreement is restored. Sometimes the deviant minority will convince the majority to agree. More likely the majority will persuade the deviators to give in. If all else fails, the majority may exclude the deviators from the group so that there is once more agreement among those who remain.

Social comparison theory explains why communication is important, and why we so often turn to others and consult their opinions before making our own decisions.

Normative versus Informational Influence

Another approach to social influence suggests that there are two kinds of influence we seek from others: normative influence and informational influence.

Normative influence occurs when an individual agrees with the norm or central view of a group. This is the type of influence that affects decisions of taste and opinion rather than fact.

Informational influence occurs when an individual is persuaded by the informational content others provide. This occurs when a group discussion provides new, persuasive information.

Conformity

One of the most interesting forms of social influence is conformity. Conformity occurs when an individual changes his or her behavior as a result of real or imagined group pressure. It is interesting because the pressure to conform can be imaginary or unspoken. An example would be arriving at a party to find people lined up at the door, and joining the waiting line instead of going past them through the door.

NORM FORMATION

Classic research by Muzafer Sherif in the late 1930s studied the power of conformity in forming norms or standards for behavior.

In his study, Sherif had a group of subjects watch a small pinpoint of light in a dark room, and take turns calling out their estimates of how far the light had moved. In fact, the light was not moving at all; its apparent movement was the result of a well-known illusion. Sherif found that, although there was no "real" movement, subjects called out answers. Further, over time their answers influenced each other, and a norm for the light's movement distance emerged for each group of subjects.

Sherif's work illustrated the power of social influence in conforming to imaginary norms. Subjects in his study relied on each other's answers to provide a standard of comparison for their own. Once a norm was established, it was seldom deviated from.

PRESSURE TO CONFORM

The most famous experiment on conformity was a study of group pressure originally conducted by Solomon Asch in the late 1940s. Asch was interested in whether judgments of fact would be less susceptible to conformity pressures than judgments of opinion.

For example, imagine a teacher asking her students how many of them would like to cancel that day's class. This is a question of opinion rather than fact. Some students will probably want to hold class because they have prepared for it or traveled some distance. But if the majority votes for canceling, the minority will probably conform with majority opinion, raising their hands along with the rest. It is only an opinion, after all. It is not that difficult to give in to pressure when the question is a matter of taste, not fact. Asch's experimental situation presented subjects with decisions about matters of fact, in which the majority disagreed with the obvious facts.

In Asch's experimental situation, a subject was grouped with several confederates in a line-length judgment task. Each person called out his judgment of the length of a vertical line presented to the group. Unbeknownst to the subject, on predetermined trials, the rest of the group unanimously called out obviously false judgments. Results indicated that, although these judgments were obviously false, subjects conformed and called out the same wrong answers on 37% of the trials.

Some subjects never conformed; Asch termed these the "independents." Others always conformed, a group Asch called "yielders." Most subjects conformed at least once. Asch concluded that eye contact and glaring were important aspects of the "pressure" the confederates put on the subjects. However, later research indicated that subjects often conformed with false group judgments even when the other members of the group were not physically present. Apparently group judgments are an important source of influence, whether normative or informational.

Obedience

Critics might argue that the price of conformity is small, and that group pressure easily outweighs any personal preference for accuracy. What if the behavior being encouraged seems morally wrong or distasteful to the subject? Would he or she resist even direct pressure under such circumstances?

MILGRAM'S RESEARCH

This was the question asked by the late Stanley Milgram (1933-1984) in a classic series of studies he commenced in the early 1960s. After World War II, much propaganda and public opinion maintained that the horrors of Nazi Germany were impossible in the United States, since Americans value independence and would never accept orders to harm others. Milgram wondered if such tendencies to obey authority would indeed vary across cultures, so he designed an experiment to test this comparison.

In Milgram's famous experiment, subjects were asked to act as "teachers" reciting word-pairs for a "learner" to memorize. If, in being tested, the learner made a mistake, the teacher was to punish him by administering an electric shock. With each mistake, the voltage level of the shock would be increased. (Milgram in fact assured that no pain would actually be involved, by having an actor play the part of the learner. The teacher, unbeknownst to himself, was the only subject in this experiment). An experimenter would urge the teacher to obey the rules of the experiment but would not threaten or harm him. How far would the teacher go before refusing to obey the experimenter's orders?

Social experts Milgram consulted insisted that only a small percentage of subjects would obey such orders, especially if the learner protested. Much to everyone's surprise, although the learner moaned and shouted throughout the "painful" experience, 63% of the subjects in Milgram's first experiment went all the way to the upper limit of voltage ("450 volts") without disobeying. In a second series, Milgram had the learner complain of a heart condition and refuse to answer after 300 volts. In this series, 65% of the subjects nonetheless obeyed all the way to the upper limit of voltage.

INFLUENCES ON OBEDIENCE

Milgram concluded that the situational factors in his experiment were too powerful for most individuals to overcome. In subsequent experiments he varied several factors in the situation to learn their importance in obedience to authority.

Subject-Victim Distance. Subjects (teachers) were more likely to obey if their victims were physically distant. Obedience dropped (subjects increased their tendency to disobey by ceasing to deliver shocks) as victims were brought closer to them. Obedience was lowest in a condition where subjects had to make physical contact with victims in order to shock them.

One conclusion of this is that obedience and aggression are easier when they are impersonal. When one's victim is distant or "not human," it is much easier to rationalize harming him or her.

Subject-Authority Distance. Subjects were more likely to obey if the authority figure (the experimenter) was physically near. Obedience dropped when the authority figure left the room or the building. Obedience was lowest when the authority figure had never been personally met, but only delivered orders by tape recording.

Nature of Authority. Subjects were obedient only when they considered the authority figure respectable and legitimate. When the experiment was conducted in a non-university location, the obedience level was lower. When intruders "illegitimately" took over the experiment and gave orders, subjects refused to obey them. For orders to be obeyed, one's authority must be perceived to be legitimate and credible.

SOCIAL INTERACTION

Humans are social creatures and tend to seek out the company of others. Much social psychological research in recent years has focused on the ways in which we interact and form various kinds of relationships. In this section we review three kinds of social interaction: interpersonal relationships; group processes; and prosocial behavior.

Interpersonal Relationships

Interpersonal relationships include friendships, coworker relationships, and intimate relationships like love and marriage. Social psychologists have studied the processes involved in three kinds of interpersonal relationships: affiliation; friendship; and intimate relationships.

AFFILIATION

People like to be with other people. This tendency to be with others of one's own kind is termed affiliation (see chapter 10). Research suggests a number of reasons for affiliating. Two reasons for affiliating with others include social comparison and fear-reduction.

Social Comparison. As described above, social comparison occurs when we want to validate our own behaviors or beliefs by comparing them to others'. For example, if you want to know when during a lecture you should be taking notes, you can observe the behavior of those around you and start writing when most of your classmates do so.

Fear Reduction. As reviewed in chapter 10, affiliation may be a response to fear. When we feel threatened, we may prefer to be with other people because of the comfort they provide. This "misery loves company" effect was demonstrated by Stanley Schachter's study of university women who believed they were about to receive painful electric shocks.

Further research suggests that "misery loves miserable company." People who expected to be painfully shocked, when offered a choice, expressed a preference to wait with others who also expected to be shocked, rather than with other non-shock subjects.

Affiliation may reduce fear because of social comparison. When one is afraid and in the company of others who are also afraid, one can observe the reactions of others to confirm the "right" way to feel and act.

FRIENDSHIP

Interpersonal Attraction. Work on friendship has involved research on the factors in interpersonal attraction (see chapter 18) as well as the study of how relationships are maintained over time. As reviewed in chapter 18, friendship is initially affected by such variables as proximity, familiarity, physical attractiveness, and attitude similarity.

Exchange versus Communality. Further work on relationship maintenance suggests that friendship involves different interpersonal processes than mere social contact. In casual interactions and in the early stages of friendship, relations are conducted on principles of *social exchange*. According to the rules of social exchange, relationships are maintained as long as they are mutually rewarding. For example, if an acquaintance does you a favor, you are obligated to return the favor or pay her back. In a sense, an exchange relationship involves a sense of "keeping score" to make sure that both parties are being treated fairly.

As relationships progress, however, returns become long-term rather than short-term. They begin to think of themselves as "we" and do things that are good for the relationship rather than good for themselves. The basis of the relationship is no longer exchange but *communality*. Both parties contribute to their common interests. They stop "keeping score." For example, if you do a favor for your best friend, you do not expect to be repaid, either immediately or perhaps ever. Doing each other favors is a natural part of friendship, part of your common investment in your relationship.

A shift from an exchange basis to a communal basis can be a signal that a relationship has deepened. Likewise, a shift from communal to exchange interactions can signal a deterioration in relations. If you do your best friend a favor, and he or she pays you back right away "because I owed you," you may interpret that as a sign that you are not as close as you thought.

INTIMATE RELATIONSHIPS

Hard as it is to study intimate relationships objectively, social psychologists have been able to learn much about the more intimate processes of love and intimate communication. Significant work includes theories of love, communication processes, and the importance of equity in close relationships.

Theories of Love. An early theory of love sought to distinguish it from "mere" liking. This *liking versus loving* approach studied the ratings people gave their best friends and their lovers on a variety of qualities. Results of this work suggested that liking and loving are both attitudes that involve different dimensions. Liking consists of feelings of affection and respect, and perceptions that the other person is trustworthy and similar to oneself. Loving consists of attachment, intimacy, and caring. Most of the time these attitudes are intermeshed: we like the people we love, and we somewhat love the people we like. An important finding was that the future of a relationship depends more on liking than loving. People who love each other but do not like each other are not likely to stay together. This suggests that friendship is the most solid foundation for any more intimate relationship.

Another theory of love distinguishes between *companionate love* and *passionate love*. Companionate love is the love of deep friendship, while passionate love is the intense, emotional, labile experience we associate with "falling" in love. Researchers suggest that passionate love is doomed to be temporary; it may be an elaborate form of "stress response" which lessens as lovers get used to each other. While companionate love does not seem as romantic as passionate love, it tends to endure and satisfy partners over more time and in more ways.

Finally, an interesting theory of love is Robert Sternberg's *triarchic theory of love* (see chapter 8 for Sternberg's triarchic theory of intelligence). In Sternberg's theory, the three dimensions of love are passion, intimacy, and commitment. Different combinations of these three dimensions make up different kinds of love, like empty love, infatuation, and consummate love.

Communication. Research repeatedly points to the critical role of communication in establishing and maintaining intimate relationships. Inadequate communication may leave individuals feeling unknown and lonely. Distorted or one-sided communication can lead to serious relationship conflict. And failures in communication can cause relationships to be terminated.

A critical process in communication is *self-disclosure*. In communicating with each other, verbally and nonverbally, two people disclose information about themselves to each other. As people get to know each other better, it is important that they disclose more and more personal and relevant information. For example, if a couple have been dating for 18 months but still converse about only "safe" subjects like sports and the weather, their relationship is not intimate and it is not progressing. It is also important that self-disclosure be reciprocated. That is, both partners must communicate on levels of similar depth. For example, if one partner wants to confide feelings of insecurity, the other partner must respond sensitively instead of changing the subject and talking about something superficial.

Equity. One of the most important findings in relationships research has been the value of equity or fairness. When partners are both contributing to a relationship (e.g., money, sex, housekeeping), they should both reap the benefits (e.g., security, comfort, pleasure). If one partner is contributing more than his or her share, but they get the same benefits, the overdoer will see the relationship as inequitable. Some theorists have argued that all relationship breakups can ultimately be traced to inequity.

Group Processes

A group consists of three or more people who interact with and influence each other. Group influences can be categorized as either deriving from the presence of others or group dynamics.

THE PRESENCE OF OTHERS

By definition, groups put people in each other's presence. However, one can be in the presence of others without belonging to a group. For example, when you attend a movie, you sit in the dark and watch a film with many others around you. You will probably behave differently—laugh louder, refrain from talking or burping—than you would alone in front of your television set. However, you are not participating in a group. You do not even notice who the other audience members are.

The mere presence of others can be very influential. Two such influences are social facilitation and deindividuation.

Social Facilitation. Early research found that when people perform simple tasks like riding bicycles they work better and faster in the presence of others than when alone. An example of this is the tendency of athletes to work out harder or play better when their teammates are around or when an audience is watching.

In other circumstances, it seems that the presence of others is distracting. For example, if someone is watching you work or solve a difficult problem you may complain that your performance is worse when you are being watched. Why does others' presence sometimes enhance, but sometimes hinder, human action?

This paradoxical effect has been dubbed social facilitation because it involves facilitating either doing well or doing poorly as a result of the mere presence of others. The explanation for social facilitation is that the presence of others is arousing. As reviewed in chapter 10, arousal will enhance performance of simple tasks but hinder performance of complex tasks. The interesting discovery of social facilitation research is that the presence of others has an arousing effect in the first place.

Deindividuation. When we are immersed in group or crowd situations, we may lose some self-awareness and become less inhibited. This is more pronounced when we feel anonymous, either because the crowd is so large or some other reason (e.g., the room is very dark). The combined effects of social immersion and anonymity result in deindividuation, a state of reduced self-awareness that results in uninhibited, irresponsible behavior.

An example of deindividuation is what happens when a group of people panics and becomes a violent mob. Research indicates that each member of such a mob feels less like an individual self (" *de*-individuated"), and so less accountable for his or her actions.

Research on deindividuation suggests that its destructive potential can be reduced by increasing self-awareness and reinforcing individual identity. For example, calling people by name, turning up the lights, or watching people individually can all work as reminders to group members that they are individually accountable for their actions.

GROUP DYNAMICS

Interests in group problem-solving and management have stimulated the study of group dynamics, the ways in which group members work together. Findings have yielded new insights into such processes as group polarization, groupthink, and minority influence.

Group Polarization. When group members talk together, their opinions provide a sense of the group norm. Research has shown that such discussion enhances a group's preexisting opinions, an effect known as group polarization. For example, if most people on a jury are already feeling somewhat pro-conviction before they begin deliberations, their discussion will probably polarize their opinions more extremely in favor of conviction. Knowing this tendency, it is sometimes useful to have group members consider their opinions more carefully before group discussion, to avoid becoming caught up in group momentum.

Groupthink. Groupthink is the term given to the tendency of group members to give higher priority to a sense of cohesiveness than to the quality of their work. If a group is assembled to work on a task or solve a problem, they will first develop a sense of group membership and purpose. If they become very cohesive, they may fear the disruption that would be caused by disagreeing about how to solve the problem. As a result they may distort their true opinions, pressure each other to conform, and nurture illusions about their abilities in an effort to stay friendly. When this effort becomes more important than the task at hand, a group is capable of making extremely confident but very bad decisions.

Prescriptions for avoiding groupthink include the following: agreeing to take turns chairing the meeting so a single leader does not emerge; appointing some members to officially question every group recommendation; breaking the group into smaller subgroups that work in parallel; and encouraging members to make their opinions known anonymously so that no one feels "on the spot" about saying something unpopular.

Minority Influence. Given the pressures of conformity, authority, norms, and groupthink, can a majority ever be persuaded by a minority? Democratic systems are based on the assumption that minorities will at least influence the rest of the group, even though they may not win a debate.

Research on the role of minorities in group discussions (i.e., individuals who disagree with majority opinion) suggests that three characteristics can make a minority both effective and influential. First, a minority must be *confident*. This demonstrates to the majority that other points of view deserve respect. Secondly, a minority must be *consistent*. By not wavering, a minority will not invite inroads or persuasive criticism. Finally, a minority should try to win *defections from the majority*. Because a defector cannot gain popularity by joining the minority, the implication is that he or she is motivated by the truth and rightness of the minority position.

Prosocial Behavior

Societies depend on prosocial behavior for survival. It is natural to help our family members and friends; helping is a part of our close relationships. It may be less natural to give help to strangers. Yet we measure civilization in terms of how willing people are to help each other when they have nothing to gain and no personal interest. Helping others with no apparent expectation of personal benefit is known as prosocial behavior.

Social psychologists have studied several aspects of prosocial behavior, including norms for prosocial behavior, the bystander effect, and ways to promote prosocial behavior.

NORMS FOR PROSOCIAL BEHAVIOR

Norms are prescriptions for behavior, suggesting how we "ought" to behave. Two norms can be identified for prosocial behavior: the reciprocity norm and the social responsibility norm.

Reciprocity. Reciprocity involves responding in kind. The reciprocity norm says that if people help us, we should help them in return. One example of the reciprocity norm in action is shown when charities soliciting donations first offer small tokens like pencils or flowers, asking for "just a donation." To reciprocate, we should make a contribution for the token we have accepted.

Social Responsibility. The social responsibility norm argues that we should help people who need help, whether or not they can or will ever repay our help. The social responsibility norm is illustrated by the New Testament parable of the Good Samaritan, who helped a crime victim he did not know and never expected to have to face again.

We may judge need in terms of deservingness or responsibility. For example, you would probably feel more socially responsible for lending your class notes to a classmate whose notebook had been stolen than to one who had "left it in a bar last night." The former classmate is an "innocent" victim who "deserves" help, while the latter is responsible for his or her own dilemma and therefore less "deserving."

THE BYSTANDER EFFECT

A central focus of much research on prosocial behavior is the bystander effect, the tendency of an individual to be less helpful if other witnesses are present at the emergency. One series of studies concluded that responding in a crisis, such as helping a stranded motorist or running to the aid of a stranger who is being attacked, depends on how we answer a series of questions: (1) Is something happening? (2) Is it an emergency? and (3) Should I take responsibility for helping?

Research has shown that the presence of others at any one point inhibits bystander intervention. When others are also present, a witness is less likely to notice that something is happening, is less likely to interpret it as an emergency, and is less likely to take personal responsibility for intervening.

PROMOTING SOCIAL BEHAVIOR

Studies of the bystander effect and other inhibitions to prosocial behavior have identified several factors that can influence people's willingness to help others. These include reducing ambiguity; increasing personal responsibility; inducing guilt; and modeling helping behavior.

Reducing Ambiguity. One reason bystanders may fail to help is that they have failed to notice or correctly interpret the signs of an emergency. If you hear someone scream, you may be unsure whether it is a cry for help or a peal of laughter. If you hear people arguing, you may be unsure whether you should call the police or stay out of their domestic affairs.

People who want help can reduce ambiguity by using specific signals whenever possible. A white handkerchief attached to a car aerial or window is a signal of distress. A cry of "Call the police, I'm being attacked!" is less ambiguous than the cry, "Somebody help!"

Increasing Personal Responsibility. A part of reducing ambiguity is indicating which of the bystanders should help and what he or she should do. Crying to a crowd, "Somebody help me," is ambiguous because no one thinks of him- or herself as "somebody." Instead, it is more effective to point or to say, "You in the green shirt, call the police!" or "You in the glasses, get the fire extinguisher near the elevator!" Such specific indications increase would-be helpers' self-awareness, and consequently increase personal responsibility.

Inducing Guilt. Sometimes the help we seek is not a response to a sudden crisis but a form of ongoing support like a donation to charity or obedience of a rule. Research indicates that people are more helpful when they first feel guilty, and then are shown that helping will reduce those guilt feelings.

For example, if a sign at a zoo says "Do Not Feed The Animals," it may make people feel reactant (stubborn and unwilling to take direction) so they will feed them anyway. But if the sign is worded, "Please remember that feeding people-food to the animals can make them sick," it can make tempted visitors feel guilty, so they will be more likely to obey.

Similarly, when asking for a donation, reminding would-be donors that "Even a penny will help!" may make them feel guilty about being completely ungenerous, so that they make an even larger donation than one cent.

Modeling Helping Behavior. One of the most effective ways to prompt prosocial behavior is to model it. By doing the helpful thing, one demonstrates to others both how it is done and what its rewards are.

Many children's programs employ examples of prosocial modeling by having celebrities, puppets, or cartoon characters demonstrate acts of kindness for viewers to emulate. Heartening research also suggests that the effects are just as powerful for adults and the media they watch.

*M*uch *of social psychology focuses on social behavior, such as forms of social influence and social interactions. Theories of social influence include social comparison theory and a distinction between the value of normative influence and informational influence.*

Research on conformity has shown that individuals may unintentionally attend to and abide by emerging group norms. Studies of group pressure show that subjects will conform in matters of fact as well as of opinion.

Classic research on obedience revealed a much higher rate of obedience to authority than experts had anticipated. It is possible that situations involving obedience to authority have more power than individuals expect or can easily overcome. Variables that can influence obedience include the distance between the subject and the intended victim, the distance between the subject and the authority figure, and the legitimacy and respectability of the authority figure.

The study of social interactions has explained basic processes in interpersonal relationships, group processes, and prosocial behavior.

Research on interpersonal relationships has examined affiliation, friendship, and intimate relationships. Affiliation may be motivated by social comparison or by a desire to reduce fear. Friendship may begin with processes of interpersonal attraction, but it continues with a shift from an exchange basis to valuing communality of interaction and investment.

Studies of intimate relationships have resulted in the development of several theories of love, including liking-versus-loving theory, companionate versus passionate love, and the triarchic theory of love. Intimate relationships depend critically on the quality of communication, particularly on the quality and pacing of self-disclosure. Finally, research suggests that equity is an essential quality of lasting relationships, and that inequitable relationships are likely to experience conflict and deterioration.

Group processes involve three or more people who interact and influence each other. Some group processes are a function of the mere presence of others, while others are particular to problem-solving groups. "Mere presence" effects include social facilitation and deindividuation. Specific group dynamics include group polarization, groupthink, and minority influence.

People's willingness to help each other, or prosocial behavior, has been the subject of much research in recent decades. Prosocial norms such as reciprocity and social responsibility encourage helping behavior, while inhibitions like the bystander effect discourage it. Prosocial behavior can be increased through the use of such strategies as reducing ambiguity, increasing personal responsiblity, inducing guilt, and modeling helping behavior.

Selected Readings

Brehm, S. S. *Intimate Relationships.* New York: Random House. 1985

Duck, S. *Friends, for Life.* New York: St. Martin's Press. 1983

Greenberg, J. *Equity and Justice in Social Behavior.* New York: Academic Press. 1982

Janis, I. L. *Groupthink.* Boston: Houghton Mifflin. 1982

Kelley, H. H., E. Berscheid, A. Christensen, J. H. Harvey, T. L. Huston, G. Levinger, E. McClintock, L. A. Peplau and D. R. Peterson. *Close Relationships.* New York: W. H. Freeman and Company. 1983

Latane, B. and J. M. Darley. *The Unresponsive Bystander: Why Doesn't He Help?* New York: Appleton-Century-Crofts. 1970

Marsh, P. (Ed.). *Eye to Eye: How People Interact.* Topsfield, MA: Salem House Publishers. 1988

Milgram, S. *Obedience to Authority.* New York: Harper and Row. 1974

Perlman, D. S. and S. Duck (Eds.). *Intimate Relationships: Development, Dynamics, and Deterioration.* Newbury Park, CA: Sage Publications. 1986

Shaw, M. E. *Group Dynamics: The Psychology of Small Group Behavior.* New York: McGraw-Hill. 1981

Sternberg, R. J. and M. L. Barnes (Eds.). *The Psychology of Love.* New Haven, CT: Yale University Press. 1988

Glossary

abnormal	Literally, "away from the norm"; used by psychologists to refer to disordered behavior
absolute threshold	Minimum energy necessary to activate a sensory system
accommodation	A process in which new information is integrated into existing knowledge and new responses are acquired
achievement tests	Tests that measure what a person has learned
achievement motivation	One's need to achieve, excel and overcome obstacles
acquisition	In learning, the attaining of a response that becomes part of the behavioral repertoire of the organism
ACTH	Adrenocorticotropic hormone, which stimulates activity of adrenal cortex
adaptation	A process of formulating new rules and structures to organize knowledge, to reason and to solve problems
adjustment	A pattern of coping with stress and conflict across life situations
adolescence	The life stage, beginning with puberty, between childhood and adulthood
adrenal gland	Endocrine gland involved in autonomic nervous system function; consisting of an adrenal medulla and an adrenal cortex
adrenaline	Epinephrine
afferent nerves	Nerves which carry impulses from the senses to the brain
affective disorder	Condition involving disruptions in experiencing and controlling affect or emotion
affiliation	Desire to be physically close to others of one's own species
aggression	Any behavior intending harm to another
aggressive type	An individual who attacks others

alarm stage (of the stress response)   First stage: an event is interpreted as a stressor; includes shock and counter-shock

algorithm   A procedure or formula guaranteed to produce a solution

alternate-form reliability   A measure of the equivalency between forms of a test

Alzheimer's disease   A neurological memory disorder

ambiguous stimulus   A visual pattern, like an inkblot, which can be interpreted in different ways; used in projective tests

amnesia   Loss of memory; when no organic cause (such as a head injury) is identified, amnesia is considered a dissociative disorder

amniotic sac   Structure that encloses the embryo in amnion

anal stage   Psychosexual stage of development when pleasure is associated with the elimination functions

analogical reasoning   Forming a concept about something new based on its similarity to something familiar

analogue   A likeness in form or proportion

analogy   An inference that two things or ideas that are similar in some ways also share other qualities

analysis of variance (ANOVA)   A statistical analysis which indicates whether the differences among two or more treatment conditions are significant

anima   Jungian concept of female persona in males

animus   Jungian concept of male persona in females

anorexia   Eating disorder characterized by fasting and self-starvation

antecedent conditions   Causes, stimuli

anterograde amnesia   The loss of newly forming memories

antidepressants   Drugs that alleviate the symptoms of depression

antipsychotics   Drugs that reduce schizophrenic (psychotic) symptoms

antisocial personality disorder   A disorder in which the individual consistently violates the rights of others with no evidence of guilt or remorse

anvil   Tiny, vibration-sensitive bone in the middle ear; also termed (Latin) *incus*

anxiety   An overwhelming feeling of dread similar to fear

anxiety disorder A condition in which severe anxiety interferes with normal adjustment and functioning

apathy Lack of concern

applied psychology Psychological theories and research used to solve practical problems

approach The attraction toward a desired goal

approach-approach conflict Having to choose between two mutually exclusive attractive goals

approach-avoidance conflict A complex situation in which one is both attracted and repelled by the same goal

aptitude tests Tests designed to predict future behavior

archetypes Ideas and memories that people have had in common from primitive human origins

artificial intelligence Computer programs that mimic the intelligent behavior of humans

assimilation The process by which new information is incorporated into existing knowledge and is dealt with through existing behaviors

associative play Playing with the same materials as others but using them in different ways

asymptote In a learning curve, the point at which the performance has approached near maximum and begins to level off

Atkinson-Shiffrin model A model of memory which contains three stages: sensory storage, short-term memory, and long-term memory

attachment Need for the contact and presence of a significant other

attitude Evaluative reaction toward a person, event, or object; involving beliefs, emotions, and behaviors

attribution The process of explaining behavior

audition Hearing

auditory nerve Nerve transmitting sound impulses to the brain

authoritarian personality Personality pattern characterized by antisemitic and other prejudices, ethnocentrism, and exaggerated submission to conventional authority

autonomic nervous system Branch of the peripheral nervous system involved in maintaining homeostasis and survival functions

aversive conditioning Pairing an aversive stimulus with a behavior one wishes to eliminate

avoidance Preemptive behavior motivated by aversion

avoidance-avoidance conflict   Having to choose which of two threatening or unpleasant possibilities can be escaped

axon   The single long fiber extending from the cell body of a neuron; carries the signal to the synapse

balance theory   Consistency theory arguing that one assigns positive or negative values to attitude objects and relationships among them

basic psychology   Psychological theories and research used to better understand behavior and mental processes

basilar membrane   Vibration-sensitive tissue in the cochlea

behavior therapy   Therapeutic technique applying the principles of learning

behavioral model (of abnormal behavior)   States that disordered behavior is learned through experiences of associations, reinforcements, and punishments

behavioral contagion   Process in which activities are copied by others who observe them

behaviorism   A psychological approach which stresses the study of observable action, the importance of the environment, and the primary role of learning

Binet-Simon scale   Early educational placement test

binocular cues   Depth perception clues perceivable only by both eyes working together

binocular disparity   Difference in images provided to both eyes

biofeedback   Information about physiological arousal

bipolar disorder   Manic-depression; disorder in which an individual alternates between cycles of mania and depression

birth order   Position in the family's sequence of children

borderline personality disorder   Disorder characterized by an unstable self-image, uncertainty about relationships and work, impulsiveness, and self-destructiveness

bottom-up model   In cognitive psychology, the idea that information travels up from the senses to the brain where it is interpreted

bystander effect   Tendency of an individual to be less helpful if other witnesses are present

Cannon-Bard theory   Theory of emotion according to which an emotional stimulus simultaneously triggers both bodily changes and conscious awareness of the experienced emotion

cardinal traits   Attributes so central to one's personality that they influence virtually all behavior

case study	Intensive investigation of a single situation, incidence, or person
catatonic type (of schizophrenia)	Characterized by a distinctive pattern of motor disturbance
catharsis	Vicarious release of emotion
central gray	Dark core of neural tissue in the spinal cord
central nervous system	The brain and spinal cord
central tendency	Major trend in a group of data
central trait	Trait so influential in impression formation that it modifies the total impression formed as well as interpretation of other traits individually
central traits	Attributes that are often but not always detectable in behavior
cephalocaudal	"Head to toe" development of a fetus
cerebellum	Part of the brain primarily responsible for major motor functioning
cerebral cortex	Thin, expansive, infolded layer of neurons forming the outermost tissue of the brain, involved in higher-order cognitive functions
cerebral hemispheres	Two large half-spheres of the brain which control the more sophisticated mental processes
cerebrotonic	Cerebral, introverted, and self-conscious
child psychology	The study of changes in physical, cognitive, social, and personality functions from birth through adolescence
chronological age	One's physical age (years since birth)
chunk	To package several units of meaningful information together; a package of such information
cilia	Pl. of *cilium*; hairs or hair-like extensions of cells
circadian rhythm	Daily rhythm of the body
circular reactions	Seemingly meaningless repetitions of chance events that catch an infant's eye
classical conditioning	A basic form of learning in which an originally neutral stimulus, when paired with another stimulus capable of eliciting a reflexive response, comes to elicit that response through association
client-centered therapy	Approach to therapy which emphasizes acceptance of the client and unconditional positive regard
clinical psychology	A field of psychology involved in the diagnosis and treatment of severe problems in clinical populations

closure	In perception, the "completing" of an incomplete stimulus or piece of information
cochlea	Fluid-filled cartilaginous structure of the inner ear
cognitive and attributional therapy	Treatment that focuses on the client's unrealistic expectations and distorted assumptions, and erroneous patterns of attribution
cognitive behavior therapies	Therapies that emphasize changing how a client thinks and the content of his or her thinking
cognitive dissonance theory	Consistency theory which argues disharmony among cognitive elements produces tension which motivates attitude change
cognitive processes	The various mental processes responsible for how we know, including perceiving, thinking, and remembering
cognitive theory of emotion	Schachter and Singer's theory that emotional experience requires both a state of physiological arousal and a cognitive interpretation or labeling of that state as an emotion
cognitive model (of abnormal behavior)	States that internal processes like expectations, biases, errors and illusions in conscious thought result in abnormal behavior
cognitive psychology	A field of psychology that studies memory and cognition
cognitive-developmental view	Developmental perspective that focuses on the way thoughts and behaviors are organized
collaboration	A conflict resolution strategy in which the parties work together on a creative solution to their problem
collective unconscious	Level of consciousness containing memories and behavior patterns inherited from one's ancestors
combined motives	Explanations for human behavior that involve both physiological and acquired influences
communality	Quality of sharing investments in intimate relationships with no expectation of short-term gain
companionate love	Love characterized by affection, respect, and friendship
comparative psychology	The study of behavioral similarities and differences among animal species
compensation	Efforts to overcome real or imagined personal deficiencies
compliant type	An individual who submits to others to gain approval

componential intelligence	The ability to learn, acquire new knowledge, and use it effectively
compromise	A coping strategy in which each party in a conflict gains something and sacrifices something
compulsion	A ritualized behavior one feels driven to repeat
concept	A mental representation of categories of experiences according to common features
conception	Fertilization of an ovum by a sperm
concrete operational stage	According to Piaget, the third stage of cognitive development (ages 7-11), characterized by an understanding of conservation
conditional positive self-regard	Positive self-concept that is dependent on others' approval of certain behaviors
conditioned stimulus (CS)	In classical conditioning, the stimulus that was originally neutral and comes to be response-producing
conditioned response (CR)	In classical conditioning, the response elicited by the CS; usually similar to the UCR
cones	Visual receptors that function primarily in lighted conditions and operate for color vision
conflict	Experiencing incompatible goals or demands
conformity	A change in behavior as a result of real or imagined social pressure
confounded	Blended; confused; affecting same variables
confrontation	As a coping strategy, facing a stressful situation honestly and forthrightly
conjunctive concepts	Categories of things or ideas that share two or more common features simultaneously
conscience	The understanding that some acts are wrong
consciousness	A stable pattern of psychological awareness
consensual validation	Verification of a subject belief by confirming the support and agreement of one's reference group
consequences	Outcome behaviors
conservation	According to Piaget, the principle that if nothing is added or taken away from an amount, it remains the same
consistency theory	Attitude change model which argues that harmony among cognitive elements must be maintained
constitutional theory of personality	Theory relating personality to physique

construct	Process which cannot be directly observed or studied; characteristics that cannot be objectively defined
construct validity	A test's ability to measure a theoretical quality
contextual intelligence	The ability to wisely select, adjust, or adapt to one's environment
control condition	In an experiment, the group of subjects not exposed to the independent variable
control	In an experiment, the process of ensuring that the only difference between groups is the experimental treatment
conventional level of moral development	Kohlberg's second stage of moral development, in which moral actions are judged in terms of social rules or expectations
convergent thinking	Focused, deliberate thinking, directed toward a task or problem
conversion disorder	A condition in which psychological conflict is converted into a physical symptom or handicap
cooperative play	Shared play which requires coordinated actions and interactive experience
coping responses	Behaviors that restore balance by removing threat
cornea	On the eye, the clear layer of outer tissue which refracts light as it enters
coronary-prone behavior	Behavior pattern associated with greater heart disease risk
corpus callosum	The large band of fibers that connect the cerebral hemispheres
correlation coefficient	Descriptive statistic indexing the degree to which two variables change together
correlational investigation	A study that ascertains the degree of relationship between two variables without determining causality
correspondent inference	Assumption that behavior reflects one's disposition or intentions
cortex	Shell or outer structure of an organ; in the brain, the cerebral cortex; in the adrenal gland, the adrenal cortex
corticosteroids	Hormones secreted by adrenal cortex, associated with endurance and strength
counseling psychology	A field of psychology that provides guidance and therapy to normal individuals with adjustment problems
counterargue	Articulate (usually silently) one's objections to a persuasive message
countershock	The second phase in the alarm stage of the stress response
cranial nerve	One of several paired nerves originating in the brain

creativity	The ability to produce novel and unique ideas
criterion validity	Test's ability to predict appropriate performance
CR	Conditioned response (q.v.)
CS	Conditioned stimulus (q.v.)
d′	d-prime: in signal detection theory, an index of a subject's ability to detect a given signal
data	Recorded measurements of observations
decay theory	The idea that if information is not used it is gradually lost
decibel	Unit of measurement of sound loudness; abbrev. dB
declarative memory	Information that can be spoken or written
deductive reasoning	The process of reasoning from the general principle to specific cases
defense mechanisms	Behavior patterns that reduce the symptoms of anxiety but do not eliminate the sources of conflict
deindividuation	Reduced self-awareness as a result of anonymity and immersion in a group or activity
deinstitution- alization	Releasing mental patients back to their communities
delusion	False beliefs about reality with no basis in fact
delusion of persecution	A belief that one is being victimized, attacked or followed by others
delusions of grandeur	Belief that one is important or famous
dendrites	The branched fibers that serve as the signal-receiving portion of a neuron
denial	Refusal to acknowledge a painful reality
deoxyribonucleic acid (DNA)	Chemical substance in genes that contains codes which define our genetic inheritance
dependent variable	In an experiment, the factor measured by the researcher (in psychology, usually a behavior)
depersonalization disorder	Disorder characterized by feelings that one is changed and somehow different
depression	Affective disorder characterized by extreme sadness and guilt, immobility due to lethargy or apathy, and inability to enjoy normal living and activities
descriptive statistics	Numbers that summarize large amounts of data so they can be readily comprehended

detached type   An individual who withdraws from others

determinism   The philosophical assumption that all behaviors and observable events have causes

developmental psychology   The field of psychology which studies the physical and psychological changes that take place throughout the lifespan

difference threshold   Minimum recognizable stimulus change

diffusion   An incomplete sense of identity

discrimination   In learning, responding to the original stimulus, but not to other similar stimuli

disequilibrium   Imbalance

disjunctive concepts   Categories of things or ideas that share either one or the other of two specified features

disorganized type (of schizophrenia)   Characterized by childish behavior; also termed hebephrenic

dispersion   In descriptive statistics, the spread or variablilty of scores

displacement   Redirecting emotions and motives from their original targets to substituted objects

dissociative disorders   Rare conditions in which part of an individual's personality becomes dissociated from the rest

divergent thinking   Undirected thinking with different directions and conclusions

dopamine   Neurotransmitter associated with cognitive and motor functions

double-blind experiment   An experiment in which neither the subjects nor the observers know to which experimental condition the subjects are assigned

drive   A motivational force that energizes goal-directed behavior

DSM-III-R   *Diagnostic and Statistical Manual of the American Psychiatric Association, Third Edition, Revised*

dualism   Belief that human beings have rational minds and material bodies, thus governed by two systems of nature

echoic memory   The auditory sensory register

eclectic   Varied, diverse

ECT   Electroconvulsive therapy (q.v.)

ectomorph   A body type characterized by a tall, thin, fragile frame with a large head

educational psychology   A field of psychology that studies the processes of teaching and learning

effectance motives	Needs of an individual to function within and have an effect on his or her environment
efferent nerves	Nerves which carry impulses from the brain to muscles and glands
ego	In Freud's theory of personality, the problem solving part of personality; governed by the reality principle
ego ideal	Idealized self; concept of one's best performance
egocentric	Using one's own experiences and point of view to interpret the world
elaborative rehearsal	Giving extended attention to information so as to store it in long-term memory
electroconvulsive therapy (ECT)	Biological therapy in which a sedated patient experiences a mild convulsion induced with electrical current
embryonic stage	Second stage of prenatal development
emotion	The subjective experience of motivation; the feeling that accompanies motivation
empiricism	System of acquiring knowledge through sensory experience
encoding	The process by which information is put into memory
encoding specificity principle	Recall is best in the presence of the cues that were originally present
endomorph	A soft, rounded, overweight body type
engineering psychology	A field of psychology studying the interrelationship of humans and machines or equipment
engram	Memory trace (q.v.)
enteric nervous system	Branch of the peripheral nervous system that controls the viscera
epinephrine	Hormone secreted by adrenal medulla, which activates the body during sympathetic arousal
episodic memory	Memory for experienced events
equilibrium	State of balance
equity	Distributive justice; fairness of outcomes in proportion to inputs
ergonomics	Engineering psychology; study of work
erogenous zones	Parts of the body that give pleasure through stimulation
erotic	Sexually arousing
ethnocentrism	Bias in favor of one's own and against others' ethnic groups
Eustachian tube	Canal releasing pressurized air from the middle ear into the throat
exchange	Mutual short-term reinforcement

exhaustion stage (of the stress response)   Last stage, in which physical alarm resumes in a weakened state

exhibitionism   Sexual disorder involving compulsion to expose one's genitals to others

expansion   In speech, repeating a child's telegraphic speech in its complete grammatical form

experiential intelligence   The ability to adjust to new tasks, use new information, and respond effectively to new situations

experimental condition   In an experiment, the group of subjects exposed to the independent variable

experimental psychology   The branch of psychology that uses the scientific method to explore fundamental questions of human and animal behavior and mental processes

experiment   Method of research in which certain events are manipulated and their effects are measured

experimenter bias   Intentional or unintentional bias on the part of a researcher conducting an experiment

exploratory aggression   Harm that occurs incidentally due to exploration

extinction   In classical conditioning, the process by which a CS stops eliciting the CR, because the CS is no longer paired with the US; in operant conditioning, the process by which the frequency of a response decreases because it is no longer followed by a reinforcer

extroverts   Persons who are outgoing, interested in participation in external events and involvement with others

facial affect   The facial expression of emotion

factor analysis   A statistical procedure for detecting patterns among several trends of data

false comparison effects   Illusions about the normality or abnormality of one's behavior compared to others'

false consensus effect   Overestimation of how common one's negative behaviors are

false uniqueness effect   Underestimation of how common one's positive behaviors are

familiarity effect   Tendency for interpersonal attraction to increase with mere exposure to others

fetal stage   Third stage of prenatal development, begins when a basic form of each structure is present

fetishism   Sexual disorder involving repeated use of a nonhuman object for sexual arousal

fictional finalism   The values one believes in and pursues, whether they are attainable or not

field study	Research conducted in variables' natural setting
field	Natural setting of behavior being studied
figure-ground relationship	Organization of perception in terms of a coherent object (the figure) within a context (the ground)
five-factor theory	Theory that all personality traits can be summarized in five basic factors
foot-in-the-door phenomenon	Effect in which one's willingness to make a large commitment is increased after having made a smaller, related commitment
forebrain	Region of the brain, foremost in the embryonic brain, including the cerebral cortex, thalamus, hypothalamus, and limbic system
formal operational stage	According to Piaget, the fourth stage of cognitive development (ages eleven through adult), characterized by the ability to think abstractly and hypothetically
fovea	In the eye, the small region on the retina where most light is focused
frame	In decision-making, a biased or persuasive comparison used to convey an impression
fraternal twins (dizygotic)	Siblings conceived simultaneously by fertilization of two separate ova; nonidentical twins
free association	Psychoanalytic process in which patient talks openly without censoring, while analyst identifies clues to unconscious motives and themes
free will	Concept that human action is freely decided, not compelled by forces
frigidity	Sexual disorder in women involving inability to achieve orgasm
frontal lobe	Front-most lobe of cerebral cortex, containing higher associative areas and motor cortex
frustration-aggression theory	Theory that frustration always results in the impulse to aggress, and aggression can always be traced to frustration
fugue state	Rare form of amnesia involving loss and replacement of one's identity
fully-functioning	Capable of self-direction, independence, respect for others, and openness to experience
functional fixedness	Perception that elements of a problem have inflexible functions and cannot be combined in new ways
functional invariants	Processes characteristic of and operating similarly in all humans
functionalism	An approach to psychology which emphasizes the function of thought: how one's mental abilities aid adaptation to the environment
function words	Words like prepositions, articles, and modifiers that serve to make sentences grammatically correct
fundamental attribution error	Tendency to overestimate dispositional and underestimate situational factors when explaining behavior

gametes	Mature reproductive cells
gender role	The set of behavioral norms a culture considers appropriate for individuals of a given gender
general adaptation syndrome (stress response)	A physiological and psychological pattern of symptoms in the wake of a stressor event
generalization (of research findings)	The degree to which the findings from a given study apply to general population
generalization	In learning, making the same response to stimuli similar to the originally associated stimulus; in classical conditioning, making the CR to a new stimulus similar to the CS; in operant conditioning, behaving in a new situation as one did in an old situation because the discriminative stimuli in the two settings are similar
generation gap	The perceived divergence between adolescents' values and those of their parents
generativity	A sense of lasting accomplishment
genital stage	Developmental stage in which genital pleasure is associated with relating to a chosen other rather than pleasing oneself
genotype	The genetic pattern of an individual's chromosomes
germinal stage	Beginning stage of life, from conception through implantation of zygote
gerontology	The study of older adults
Gestalt psychology	The psychological approach which suggests that behavior is motivated by interest in meaning and pattern; from German *Gestalt*, "form" or "pattern"
glial cells	Cells that support, nourish, or connect other cells
glucose	A simple sugar
goal-derived concepts	Categories of objects grouped by common purpose
gonads	Reproductive gland; in women, the ovaries; in men, the testes
graded potential	Electrochemical signals, ranging in magnitude, carried within and between neurons
gray matter	The neural tissue of the cerebral cortex
grouping principles	In Gestalt psychology, principles regarding the way the eye groups visual stimuli
group polarization	Exaggeration of average group member's preliminary opinion after group discussion

groupthink	Reduction in quality of task performance as a result of giving group cohesion a higher priority
gustation	Chemical sense of taste
habit strength	Organism's practice or past experience with, or ability to perform, a behavior
hair cell	Receptor that translates vibration energy into sound
hallucinations	False sensory perceptions
hammer	Tiny, vibrating bone in the middle ear; also termed (Latin) *malleus*
hassles	Small-scale annoyances, irritations, and frustrations
health psychology	The field of psychology concerned with psychological processes involved in wellness and illness
heritability factor	Degree to which a quality is inherited
heuristic	A general solution strategy which often applies
hierarchical classification	Ranked organization
hierarchy of motives	Maslow's ordering of needs that must be satisfied in human behavior
hierarchy of needs	Hierarchy of motives (q.v.)
hill-climbing	In decision-making, reevaluating a situation after taking each step closer to the goal
hindbrain	Region of the brain, hindmost in the embryonic brain, which include the cerebellum, pons, and medulla
hippocampus	Structure in the brain's limbic system important in memory functions
holistic	Related to the whole or totality
holophrase	Single word used to convey a whole thought
holophrastic speech	Children's speech characterized by holophrases (q.v.)
homeostasis	Bodily balance essential to healthy function
hostile aggression	Aggression which intends harm as its sole purpose
human factors psychology	Engineering psychology (q.v.)
humanistic psychology	A school of psychology emphasizing that people are inherently good and motivated toward growth
humanistic therapy	Treatment based on humanistic theory
humors	Bodily fluids

hyperopic   Far-sighted

hypnosis   Altered state of consciousness characterized by increased suggestibility

hypochondriasis   A condition in which an individual has few or no symptoms of physical illness, but complains of pain or other difficulties

hypothalamus   Structure of the brain that controls drive states such as hunger, thirst, and sex

hypothesis   Guess or possible explanation

hysteria   Conversion disorder (q.v.)

iconic memory   The visual sensory register

id   In Freud's theory of personality, the most primitive or instinctive part of personality, operating according to the pleasure principle

idealism   A philosophy which states that reality exists only in the mind

identical twins (monozygotic)   Two siblings developed from one fertilized egg

identity crisis   A period during which one reevaluates oneself

illusion of invulnerability   False perception of one's immunity to error, pain, or failure

illusory correlation   False perception of an association between two variables or events

image   A mental representation of a sensory experience

immediacy   The tendency or wish to be physically close to others

impotence   Sexual disorder in men, involving inability to achieve or maintain an erection

impression formation   Processes of judging others based on perceptions of them

imprinting   Attachment and restriction of social behaviors to a significant object, formed during critical period

incentive   Value of the external stimulus that reduces a need

independent variable   In an experiment, the factor manipulated by the researcher

individual differences   Differences among persons in various traits and behaviors

inductive reasoning   The process of arriving at general principles from specific cases or facts

industrial psychology   Field of psychology that studies the person-job interface

inferential statistics   Statistics that allow conclusions beyond the immediate results of a particular study, specifically, whether or not results arose simply due to chance

inferiority complex	A paralyzing fixation on one's inadequacies
information processing	The sequence of cognitive operations whereby sensory experiences are meaningfully interpreted and acted upon
informational influence	Affect on individual behavior resulting from new knowledge or data
ingroup	Group of which one is a member
ingroup bias	Belief that members of one's own group are superior to nonmembers; also *ingroup-outgroup bias*
inhibited sexual excitement	Inability to sustain sexual arousal to the point of orgasm and resolution
inhibited orgasm	Inability to achieve orgasm though able to achieve and sustain arousal up to that point
inhibited sexual desire	Lack of sexual interest
inner ear	Fluid-filled structure bounded by the oval window and including the cochlea, tectorial and basilar membranes, and hair cells, which transmit sound energy to the brain
insight	The perception of a problem in a new way
insight therapies	Therapies based on assumption that insight will change behavior
instincts	Innate, goal-directed sequences of behavior
instrumental aggression	Aggression applied toward another goal besides harm
intellectualization	Analyzing emotional issues in an intellectual, unemotional manner
intelligence	A quality of the ability to acquire and use knowledge
Intelligence Quotient (I.Q.)	The ratio of one's mental age to one's chronological age, multiplied by 100
intelligence tests	Tests that measure verbal and/or nonverbal skills related to academic success
interactive models	Theories that factors interact to produce effects
interest inventories	Tests used to help individuals make effective career choices
interference theory	The idea that memories are inhibited (interfered with) by other memories
internal consistency	A measure of reliability within a test
intertrial interval (ITI)	Waiting period between learning trials in classical conditioning sequence

intervening variables	Changes in processes within the organism which cannot be observed but can be used to explain stimulus-response patterns
introspection	Analysis of the contents of thought by precisely reporting one's mental experiences
introverts	Persons who are less social, more withdrawn, and concerned with their private worlds
intuitive phase	A substage of Piaget's preoperational stage in which thinking begins to be more logical and objective
iris	In the eye, the pigmented, ringed muscle which controls the size of the pupil
irrational	In violation of reason; illogical
James-Lange theory	Theory of emotion arguing that an emotional stimulus causes physiological reactions which are consciously experienced as emotion
jnd	Just noticeable difference (q.v.)
just noticeable difference	Difference threshold
laboratory	Controlled environment for scientific research
LAD	Language acquisition device (q.v.)
language acquisition device (LAD)	Genetic ability to learn any human language
latency period	Developmental stage during which the child focuses more on activity than pleasure and discipline
latent learning	Learning which is not demonstrated until performance is reinforced
lateral hypothalamus (LH)	Side(s) of the hypothalamus (q.v.)
law of effect	Thorndike's theory that a response followed by the presence of a satisfying stimulus or the termination of an annoying stimulus will become conditioned
learned helplessness	Nonresponse pattern as a result of failure to control or change events
learned motives	Motives which are acquired through classical or operant conditioning
learning	A change in behavior due to experience, when the behavior change cannot be explained by instinct, maturation, or temporary states of the organism
learning theories of personality	Models applying the principles of operant conditioning and observational learning to personality development
lens	In the eye, a clear structure which refracts light and focuses light onto the fovea

LH	Lateral hypothalamus (q.v.)
life change	A stressful experience that requires an alteration in one's subsequent behavior
life cycle	The period of constant change between conception and death
limbic system	Set of forebrain structures involved with drive states, motivation, emotion, and memory
lipostat	A brain center that measures the nutrient level of the bloodstream and establishes the setpoint
lobe	One of four major regions of the cerebral cortex
localize	Identify physical origins
logic	A system of rules for making correct inferences
long-term memory (LTM)	Permanent memory store
longitudinal studies	Research strategies that study a set of individuals over a period of time
loudness	Perceived amplitude (size) of sound energy
maintenance rehearsal	Repeating information to keep it in short-term memory only until needed
mania	Condition characterized by hyperactivity, euphoria, talkativeness, and impulsive behaviors
manipulation	In research: controlled changing of independent variable; in motivation: touching and grasping behavior
material self	One's physical body and material possessions
materialism	A philosophy which states that the single nature of reality is matter
maturation	Growth due to aging
mean	The average score in a distribution of scores; calculated by summing all the scores and dividing that sum by the number of scores
means-end analysis	A process of repeatedly comparing the present situation with the desired goal and reducing the difference between the two
measure of central tendency	Descriptive statistic that summarizes primary trend of a set of data
measure of dispersion	Descriptive statistic that summarizes the variability of a set of data
mechanism	Philosophical position that all which exists is governed by the laws of matter
median	In descriptive statistics, the score that appears in the middle of a rank-ordered distribution of scores
meditation	Techniques used to focus attention

medulla	Core structure: in the brain, the medulla oblongata, the structure adjacent to the spinal cord; in the adrenal gland, the adrenal medulla, a central body of glandular tissue
meiosis	Reproductive cell division and formation
memory	The process of saving or storing information for use when needed
memory trace (engram)	A brain substrate of a memory
menarche	First menstrual cycle
menopause	A dramatic decrease in the production of female hormones, "change of life"
mental age	Age of most individuals who display a particular level of performance
mentalism	A psychological approach which stresses the study of mental events and processes
mesomorph	A muscular, athletic, thick-necked body
midbrain	Small region of the brain, central in embryonic development, including the reticular formation
middle ear	Ear cavity bounded by the eardrum, containing the small, vibrating bones and the Eustachian tube
Minnesota Multiphasic Personality Inventory (MMPI)	An objective personality measure consisting of 550 true-false items, whose response pattern reveals the respondent's scores on various personality traits
mitosis	Cell division
MMPI	Minnesota Multiphasic Personality Inventory (q.v.)
mnemonics	Strategies for memory
mode	In descriptive statistics, the most frequently occurring single score in a distribution
modeling	Teaching new behaviors by having the client observe others doing them
monism	An early system of philosophy advocating that all reality has but a single nature
monocular cues	Depth perception clues perceivable by one eye
moral development	The process by which children acquire knowledge of right and wrong
moral model (of therapy)	Advocated compassion, kindness, and pleasant surroundings as treatment for the mentally ill
moral realism	Having awareness of morality but lacking an understanding of it

moral relativism	Understanding the existence of rules to be a cooperative effort in creating a useful system for behavior regulation
motivation	The process of energizing and directing goal-oriented behavior
motor nerves	Efferent nerves
multiple personality disorder	Condition in which an individual manifests several different personalities that emerge at different times
myelin sheath	A layer of glial cells coating the axon of certain kinds of neuron
Myers-Briggs Type Indicator	A four-dimension personality inventory based on Jungian theory
myopic	Near-sighted
narcissistic personality disorder	A condition in which the individual is totally self-absorbed, self-important, obsessed with fantasies of success, and demanding of others' attention
naturalistic observation	A study that focuses on behavior naturally occurring in its natural setting, rather than manipulated or in a controlled laboratory environment
negative reinforcement	The process by which the removal of a stimulus increases the frequency of some behavior that it follows
neo-Freudian	Involving innovation on the work of Freud
neobehaviorism	Approach advocating expansion of behaviorism with the study of intervening variables whose effects can be inferred from observable conditions and responses
neonatal	Newborn
neuron	Nerve cell
neurosis	A term formerly used to describe a treatable disorder
neurotic trends	Patterns that work as defenses only at the cost of independence
nondirective	Therapeutic approach that refuses to tell the client what to do or direct his or her actions
normative influence	Affect on one's behavior resulting from awareness of group norms
norm-referenced tests	Tests designed to compare individual performance to the performance of others in a group
norms	In society, accepted and expected ways of behaving; in testing, patterns of test scores characteristic of particular subgroups
NREM sleep	Non-Rapid Eye Movement sleep; non-dream sleep
obesity	A condition of weighing at least 20% above ideal body weight for one's height and build

object permanence	The recognition a child develops that things continue to exist even when they are not readily apparent
objective personality test	Test that uses specific questions answered by selecting one of several alternatives
objective	Free from bias, prejudice or subject evaluation
objectivity	Condition of being objective (q.v.)
observational learning	Learning by observing the behavior of others; vicarious learning or modeling
obsession	A recurring, unwanted thought
obsessive-compulsive disorder	Anxiety disorder characterized by obsessions and compulsions (q.v.)
occipital lobe	Dorsal lobe of cerebral cortex, containing visual cortex
olfaction	Sense of smell
ontogeny recapitulates philogeny	The development of the individual reflects the evolutionary development of the species
operant	A voluntary behavior emitted in response to the environment
operant conditioning	Form of learning in which a response is associated with its consequences; the response becomes more likely in the future if followed by a reinforcer and less likely if followed by a punisher
operant conditioning chamber	B. F. Skinner's term for the Skinner box (q.v.)
operations	According to Piaget, rules or structures that organize thought and behavior
opponent-process theory	Theory arguing that biological or psychological processes involve opposing extremes or goals
oral stage	Developmental stage during which pleasure is associated with the mouth
organizational psychology	Field of psychology studying the structure and dynamics of work groups and organizations
outer ear	The auricle (pinna) and auditory canal
outgroup	Group of which one is not a member
oval window	Inner ear, vibration-sensitive tissue connecting the cochlea with the middle ear
palliative treatments	Measures which alleviate pain or stress without effecting a cure

panic attack	A sudden, unpredictable experience of intense fear accompanied by physical symptoms
paradigm	Perspective or world view
parallel play	Play alongside others but engaging in different activities
paranoid type (of schizophrenia)	Characterized by delusions of grandeur and persecution
paranoid personality disorder	Disorder characterized by suspicious, mistrustful, secretive, argumentative, self-aggrandizing, and hypersensitive behavior
paraphilia	Sexual disorder involving narrow restriction of sexual interest to nonhuman objects or socially unacceptable circumstances
parasympathetic nervous system	The part of the autonomic nervous system primarily involved in recuperative functions
parietal lobe	Topmost region of cerebral cortex, containing sensory cortex
Parkinson's Disease	Disease affecting motor and cognitive functions caused by a deficiency of dopamine
passionate love	Love characterized by intense, labile, emotional experiences and sexual attraction
peak experiences	Feelings of ineffable happiness and peace in the course of one's life activities
pedophilia	Sexual disorder involving acts or fantasies of sexual activity with children
perception	Organized, meaningful experience of sensation
performance standards	Behavioral goals and expectations
personal unconscious	One's own repressed thoughts, forgotten experiences, and undeveloped ideas
personality	An individual's characteristic pattern of behavior, thought, and emotion
personality disorder	A failure of the personality itself to develop, adjust, and learn
personality psychology	The study of individual differences
personality tests	Tests that measure stable personality patterns and personal qualities
phallic stage	Developmental stage in which a child associates pleasure with genital self-stimulation
phenotype	Apparent characteristics in an individual, produced by one's genotype in combination with the environment
phenylketonuria (PKU)	A condition in which afflicted individuals lack the enzyme to metabolize a basic amino acid (phenylpyruvic acid), resulting in mental retardation

pheromones	In animals, scented glandular substances which may externally influence sexual response in the opposite sex
phi phenomenon	An illusion of apparent movement
philosophy	The study of knowledge and reason
phobia	Anxiety disorder characterized by intense irrational fear of a specific target
phonemes	The basic units of a spoken language
phrenology	Erroneous system inferring character from bodily appearance, especially the shape of the skull and face
physical attractiveness stereotype	Generalization that physically attractive people have other positive characteristics
physiognomic theory	Theory that a person's character can be read in his or her physiognomy (q.v.)
physiognomy	A person's physical features
physiological dependence	A physical need for a substance
physiological motives	Motives driven by biological needs and internal bodily states
physiological psychology	The study of biological bases of behavior, concentrating on the nervous system and biochemical processes
pitch	Perceived frequency of a sound
pituitary gland	Endocrine gland and brain structure that controls hormonal and behavioral functions
placebo	A chemically inert material disguised as an active drug; allows testing expectations of subjects who believe they are actually taking a drug
placebo effect	Any situation in which subjects believe they are experiencing a manipulation by the experimenter when they are not
place principle	Physical process by which the brain analyzes pitch by detecting the location of neural activity on the basilar membrane
placenta	The protective organ that surrounds the embryo and facilitates nourishment and waste elimination
polygraphy	Records of physiological arousal, used in attempts at lie detection
pons	Upper structure in the hindbrain
positive reinforcement	The process by which the presentation of a stimulus increases the frequency of some behavior that it follows
postconventional level of moral development	Kohlberg's third and last stage of moral development, in which the adult applies personal, abstract standards for right and wrong

posttraumatic stress disorder   Anxiety disorder characterized by the reexperiencing of a traumatic or stressful event

preconceptual phase   A substage of Piaget's preoperational stage in which children are capable of symbolic schemata

preconscious   Level of consciousness containing information, like memories, just below conscious awareness

preconventional level of moral development   Kohlberg's first stage of moral development, in which a child uses only rewards and punishments to judge right and wrong

prefrontal lobotomy   Psychosurgical technique in which fibers connecting frontal lobes to deeper brain tissue are severed

prejudice   Unjustified negative attitude toward all members of a social group

premoral   Lacking awareness of rules for regulating behavior

preoperational stage   According to Piaget, the second stage of cognitive development (ages 2-7), in which a child learns to represent things by symbolic activities

pressure   Increasing expectations for or demands on behavior

primacy effect   Tendency of first impressions to more strongly influence total impression than later information

primary mental abilities   Thurstone's seven abilities for high-level test performance: spatial ability; perceptual speed; numerical ability; verbal meaning; memory; word fluency; and reasoning

proactive interference   Type of forgetting in which earlier learning interferes with later learning

procedural memory   Learning behaviors that are acted out

productive thinking   Problem solving based on new organization of a problem's elements

projection   Attributing one's own motives or feelings to another person; perceiving one's own motives or feelings in an outside stimulus

projective technique   Test that presents ambiguous stimuli onto which subjects project their own motives and feelings

proprioception   Sense of body position

prosocial behavior   Helping behavior with nonobvious benefits for the behaver

proximity effect   Influence of physical nearness in increasing interpersonal attraction

psychiatric social worker   Professional counselor qualified by degree in social work and clinical training

psychiatry	A medical specialty focusing on the diagnosis and treatment of disordered behavior
psychoactive drug	Any of a number of drugs that cause changes in behavior and/or cognitive processes
psychoanalysis	An approach to therapy, human nature, and personality theory introduced by Freud, emphasizing the role of unconscious motivation in conscious behavior
psychoanalytic model (of abnormal behavior)	Model that explains disordered behavior in terms of unconscious conflicts
psychodrama	Therapeutic technique in which clients act out scenes in order to bring out their emotional significance
psychogenic	Originating in the mind; e.g., psychogenic symptoms
psychological assessment	A process designed to identify or measure characteristics of individuals or groups
psychology	The science of behavior and mental processes
psychometrics	The measurement of psychological characteristics
psychopharma-cology	The use of drugs to achieve psychological change
psychophysics	Scientific field concerned with the relationship between physical stimuli and sensory processes they trigger
psycho-physiology	Scientific field concerned with the relationship between physiological and psychological processes
psychosexual development	According to Freud, developmental stages in which a child's instinctive needs are satisfied through stimulation of different parts of the body
psychosexual stages	Phases of psychosexual development (q.v.)
psychosis	(Archaic) a very severe disorder characterized by thought and behavior that is separated from reality; schizophrenia
psychosocial stages	According to Erikson, distinct crises of personal and social conflict which must be resolved to grow and adjust
psychosomatic disorders	Physical illnesses partially caused by psychological factors
psychosurgery (neurosurgery)	Surgery (such as prefrontal lobotomy) used to reduce violence and aggressiveness prior to the development of antipsychotic drugs
psychotherapy	Use of psychological methods to try to treat abnormal or disordered behavior
puberty	Physical period of sexual maturation

puberty rites	Cultural rituals marking passage from childhood to adulthood
punishment	Any operation which decreases the rate of response
pupil	In the eye, the aperture in the center of the iris through which light passes as it enters
qualitative (discontinuous) change	Developmental change that occurs in a series of stages
quantitative (continuous) change	Developmental change that occurs gradually
random assignment	The process of assigning research subjects to different groups on a random basis, so that each subject has an equal chance of receiving any condition
random sampling	In correlational techniques, choosing subjects in a way that ensures that each member of a population has an equal chance of being selected for the sample
range	A measure of dispersion: the highest score minus the lowest score in a distribution
Rapid Eye Movement (REM) sleep	Sleep characterized by rapid movement of eyes in spite of resistance to arousal
rational	Of a person: able to reason; of a belief: reasonable
rational-emotive therapy (RET)	Treatment that analyzes the rationality or irrationality of beliefs underlying one's behaviors and feelings
rationalization	Inventing acceptable reasons for one's behavior
reacquisition	Learning of behavior after extinction
reactance	Reassertion of freedom of choice by violating a rule or proscription
reaction formation	Acting in a way completely opposite one's unconscious feelings in order to deny true motivation
reaction time	The interval between a stimulus and a response
recall	Measure of memory when information is spontaneously produced
recency effect	Tendency for latest information to more strongly influence total impression
receptor	A sensory neuron
reciprocal determinism	A process in which situations shape persons' behavior patterns, which in turn influence future situations
reciprocity norm	Social rule requiring responding in kind
recognition	Identifying a match between perception and memory

recovery stage	The third stage of reaction to environmental disasters, in which anxiety threatens regaining emotional stability
reference group	Social network one consults for social comparison
reflex	Inborn, coordinated motor behavior triggered by specific stimuli
regression	Immature behavior in response to frustration or anxiety
rehearsal	Repeating information to keep it in memory
reinforcement	Any operation which increases the rate of a response it follows
reinforcer	A specific form of reinforcement (q.v.)
reliability	In psychological assessment, quality of a test that produces consistent results over time or administrations
REM	Rapid Eye Movement sleep (q.v.)
reorganization	Gestalt principle by which the solution to a problem depends on perceiving new relationships among its elements
replication	Repetition of findings in similar studies
repression	Pushing unwanted thoughts, feelings, or memories into the unconscious
reproductive thinking	Gestalt principle in which past solutions are applied to new problems
resistance	In psychoanalysis, protecting defenses from being analyzed by refusing to cooperate
resistance stage (of the stress response)	Second stage; physical defenses are employed to respond to the threat
RET	Rational-emotive therapy (q.v.)
reticular formation	Brain structure which controls degree of arousal and wakefulness
retina	The light-sensitive inner surface of the eye
retroactive interference	Type of forgetting in which later learning interferes with previous learning
retrograde amnesia	The loss of memory for events just prior to any event that disrupts ongoing neural activity
rods	Visual receptors that function primarily in low illumination and provide value (light/dark) information
rooting reflex	Automatic movement of head toward the source of tactile stimulation
Rorschach test	Projective technique using inkblots as ambiguous stimuli
rubella	German measles
S-R psychology	Stimulus-response psychology (q.v.)

stimulus-response psychology	Behaviorist perspective emphasizing only the observable associations between these observable stimuli and responses
sadomasochism	Sexual disorder associating arousal with inflicting or experiencing physical pain
salient	Perceptually distinctive
sample	Subset of a population chosen for nonexperimental study
satiety	A level of adequate glucose concentration; satisfaction
scapegoat	Alternative target on whom aggression is displaced
schedules of reinforcement	Temporal arrangements of partial reinforcement in operant conditioning
schema	Pattern by which information and knowledge can be organized; plural *schemata* or *schemas*
schizoid personality disorder	A condition in which the individual lacks the skills to form or maintain relationships with others
schizophrenia	A serious psychological disorder, characterized by disordered thought, perception, and judgment
school psychology	Field of psychology that provides advice and guidance in school settings, concentrating on the needs of students within the educational environment
scientific method	A way of acquiring knowledge based on empirical observation and hypothesis testing
sclera	The thick tissue layer surrounding the eye
secondary traits	Attributes that come into use in particular situations but not general behavior
sedatives	Drugs that depress central nervous system activity
self-actualization	Fully realizing one's individual human potential; highest level in Maslow's hierarchy of motives
self-awareness	Self-conscious state of focusing attention on oneself
self-concept	Self-image including assessment of abilities, attributes, and values
self-disclosure	In communication, revelation of personal information to one's partner
self-efficacy	Feelings of competence and self-control
self-handicapping	Creating an acceptable excuse for failure
self-serving bias	Tendency to perceive and judge one's own actions in ways that preserve self-esteem
semantic memory	Memory for general information or facts
sensation	Stimulation of receptors by physical changes

sensation-seeking   A readiness to take risks and try new behaviors

sensorimotor stage   According to Piaget, the first stage of cognitive development; from birth to about age two

sensory nerves   Afferent nerves

sensory register (storage)   Holds direct impressions of sensory events for short periods of time

separation distress   Reaction to loss of an attachment figure

separation-individuation   A process of distancing oneself from parents and establishing a sense of individuality

set   Perceptual expectation

set effect   The tendency to solve new problems by using past habits rather than creating new techniques

setpoint   Ideal balance of the nutrient level in the bloodstream

sex roles   Behavior patterns considered gender-appropriate

sexual dysfunctions   Sexual disorders characterized by inability to function effectively in sexual behavior

shaping   Reinforcing through successive approximations of goal behavior

shock phase   The first phase in the alarm stage of the stress response

shock stage   The first stage of reaction to environmental disasters, in which victims appear dazed, stunned, or numb

short-term memory   Brief memory store with limited capacity

signal detection theory   Theory of sensation which assumes that people distinguish stimuli from noise through a decision-making process

skin senses   Senses of touch, texture, pressure, heat, cold, and pain

Skinner box   An experimental chamber for the study of operant conditioning in animals like rats and pigeons; the chamber includes a lever the animal can press as a measurable response, metal floor rods to deliver painful shocks, and a food cup where edible rewards can be presented

social cognition   Cognitive processes concerned with social experiences

social comparison   Process by which one evaluates one's behavior in terms of the standard set by others

social comparison theory   Theory which proposes that subjective beliefs are verified by consensual validation

social exchange   Theory that relationships are based on reciprocal reward

social facilitation   Enhancement of the dominant response through the mere presence of others; for simple tasks the dominant response is performing well, while for complex tasks the dominant response is performing poorly

social learning theories   Theories which assume that much human motivation and behavior is the result of what is learned through experiential reinforcement

social motives   Motives for behavior that concern relationships with others

social psychology   Field of psychology that studies the social effects on the individual

social responsibility norm   Social rule requiring help for those who need or deserve it

social self   How one is viewed by others

sociology   The study of group structure and behavior

somatic nervous system   Branch of the peripheral nervous system which controls motor and sensory functions

somatization disorder   A somatoform disorder in which an individual experiences vague, recurring, sometimes unrelated physical pains and dysfunctions for which medical examinations can find no organic cause

somatoform disorders   Conditions which involve serious physical symptoms with no apparent physical causes

somatotonic   Active, risk-oriented, and adventuresome

somatotype   Body type

spiritual self   One's psychological faculties, including reasoning and feeling

spontaneous recovery   A phenomenon in which, after a period of rest following extinction, the CR reappears when the CS is presented alone

standard deviation   A measure of variability based on the differences of each score from the mean

standardization   Administering tests to large, representative samples of people to determine norms and patterns of responses

Stanford-Binet intelligence scale   Terman's revision of the Binet-Simon intelligence scale (at Stanford University)

status   Social rank

stereotype   Generalization about a group of people that distinguishes them from others

stimulus   Any environmental event that produces a response in an organism

stimulus needs   Needs for sensory stimulation

stirrup   One of the small bones in the middle ear, connected to the oval window; also termed (Latin) *stapes*

stratified sampling	A technique for selecting subjects in such a way that significant subgroups within the population are accurately reflected in the composition of the sample
stream of consciousness	Ongoing awareness
stress	Any demand or set of demands requiring adaptation
stress-inoculation therapy	Treatment that focuses on helping the client reduce stress in different situations
stressors	Events interpreted as requiring the stress response
structuralism	The psychological approach that emphasizes the study of consciousness through introspective analysis
subgoals	Tasks progressing to a goal
subjective	Influenced by bias, prejudice, or subjective evaluation
subjects	Participants in scientific research
sublimation	A process of transforming unconscious conflict into a more socially acceptable form of behavior
sucking reflex	In newborns, the ability to suck for nourishment
suggestible stage	The second stage of reaction to environmental disasters, when victims passively cooperate with helpers
superego	In Freudian theory, the part of the personality that sets standards for unacceptable and ideal behavior
survey	Observational or correlational study that measures reactions of respondents in a random sample; questionnaire
symbolic function	Representational activities such as language and thought
sympathetic nervous system	Branch of the autonomic nervous system that acts during arousal
symptoms	Observable signs of diseases
synapse	The gap between one neuron's axonal terminal and another's dendrite
syntax	The rules for combining words into meaningful sentences
systematic desensitization	Behavior modification technique that pairs relaxation with a feared object or situation, thus reducing anxiety
tabula rasa	Latin for "clean slate," Locke's concept of the mind at birth, on which experience can inscribe knowledge
taste bud	In the mouth, chemical-sensitive structure composed of many taste cells and microvilli
TAT	Thematic Apperception Test (q.v.)

tectonic membrane	Vibration-sensitive tissue in the cochlea
telegraphic speech	Speech containing only the minimum number of words needed to express the idea
temperament	Stable pattern of reaction to objects and events
temporal lobe	Lateral lobe of cerebral cortex, containing centers for speech and audition
test-retest reliability	A test's consistency across testing sessions
testosterone	The hormone that influences sexual behavior
thalamus	An area of the brain that processes sensory information
Thematic Apperception Test (TAT)	A personality test in which individuals construct stories to describe each of a series of pictures
theory	Model or broad explanation of cause-and-effect connections among sets of events
three-dimensional model of intellect	Guilford's three categories of intelligence test items: content, operation, and product
threshold	The level of stimulation necessary for sensory reception to occur
thyroid gland	Endocrine gland, located in the neck, involved in regulating metabolism
token economy	Operant conditioning strategy in which symbolic rewards are used to reinforce desired behaviors
top-down model	In cognitive psychology, the idea that the brain incorporates pertinent information with the sensory activity as information is collected
transference	In psychoanalysis, a process in which the patient projects feelings about personal or past relationships onto the analyst
transitions	Periods of change and adjustment
transvestism	Sexual disorder characterized by wearing clothing of the opposite sex to achieve sexual arousal
triarchic theory of intelligence	Sternberg's model of three kinds of intelligence: componential, experiential, and contextual
triarchic theory of love	Sternberg's model of three dimensions of love: passion, intimacy, and commitment
twin studies	Research done on identical twins who have been separated at birth
tympanic membrane	Eardrum
type theory	Personality theory based on categories of personality descriptions

Type A personality	A behavior pattern characterized by impatience, concern with time and punctuality, anger and perfectionism; linked to higher risk of cardiovascular disease
Type B personality	A profile that is relaxed, unhurried, and cooperative
typical examples	Examples of a concept which summarize the features and qualities of the concept category well
umbilical cord	Structure that carries nutrients to and removes waste from the developing embryo
unconditional positive self-regard	A positive estimation of self that is not dependent on any specific behaviors
unconditional positive regard	In client-centered therapy, the therapist's acceptance and positive estimation of the client independent of any client behaviors
unconditioned response (UR)	In classical conditioning, the response elicited by the US
unconditioned stimulus (US)	In classical conditioning, the stimulus that naturally elicits the response
unconscious	Level of consciousness including thoughts and feelings of which we cannot become aware
undifferentiated type (of schizophrenia)	A mixture of symptoms from various other types
unrealistic optimism	Unfounded belief in one's own probable good fortune in events to come
UR	Unconditioned response (q.v.)
US	Unconditioned stimulus (q.v.)
validity	Accuracy; in psychological assessment, a test is valid if it measures what it is designed to measure
variable	Any aspect of the experiment that can be quantified or measured
ventromedial hypothalamus (VMH)	The front, central region of the hypothalamus
vicarious learning	Learning by observing the consequences (e.g.,, reinforcements or punishments) of others' behavior
viscerotonic	Sociable, fond of food, people, and comfort
visual acuity	Accuracy of visual focus
visual cliff	Transparent bridge over a drop in a floor, used to study depth perception in infants

visual cortex   In the occipital lobe, region where information from the eyes is organized and interpreted

vitalism   The belief that all living beings were animated by a "life force" which was ultimately impossible to analyze

vividness heuristic   Guideline by which one judges the most memorable cases to be typical

VMH   Ventromedial hypothalamus (q.v.)

voyeurism   Sexual disorder involving watching others while they are undressed or having sex

Weber's Law   A mathematical summary of how changes in sensory qualities are perceived

Wechsler intelligence test   Individual intelligence test consisting of a verbal scale and a performance scale

white matter   The myelinated neural tissue beneath the cerebral cortex

white region   Layer of sensory and motor axons surrounding the core of the spinal cord

withdrawal   A coping strategy in which one removes oneself from the situation

Yerkes-Dodson Law   Principle that every task involves an optimal level of arousal; in general, an increase in one's arousal leads to improved performance on simple tasks but reduced performance on complex tasks

Zeigarnik effect   Finding in research by Bluma Zeigarnik that subjects have better recall for unfinished than finished tasks

zygote   Fertilized egg

Index

OTHER BOOKS IN THE HARPERCOLLINS COLLEGE OUTLINE SERIES

Available at your local bookstore or directly from HarperCollins at 1-800-331-3761.